T0127282

TOUCHED BY GRACE

TOUCHED BY GRACE
MY TIME WITH JEFF BUCKLEY

Gary Lucas

TOUCHED BY GRACE
MY TIME WITH JEFF BUCKLEY
by Gary Lucas

A Jawbone Book
First Edition 2013
Published in the UK and the USA by Jawbone Press
2a Union Court,
20–22 Union Road,
London SW4 6JP,
England
www.jawbonepress.com

ISBN 978-1-908279-45-3

Volume copyright © 2013 Outline Press Ltd. Text copyright © Gary Lucas.
All rights reserved. No part of this book covered by the copyrights hereon may
be reproduced or copied in any manner whatsoever without written permission,
except in the case of brief quotations embodied in articles or reviews where the
source should be made clear. For more information contact the publishers.

EDITOR Tom Seabrook
DESIGN Paul Cooper

Printed by Regent Publishing Services Limited, China

1 2 3 4 5 17 16 15 14 13

CONTENTS

THIS PAGE: Gary Lucas and Don Van Vliet, aka Captain Beefheart; playing the final chord of Beefheart's 'Flavor Bud Living' at the Venue, London, November 1980.
OPPOSITE: Studio portrait of Gary, 1988.

GARY LUCAS

solo guitar electric and acoustic NEW MUSIC SEMINAR 1988 SHOWCASE
Saturday July 16th 8:30 PM The Knitting Factory
47 East Houston Street

GARY LUCAS

solo guitar electric and acoustic
Sunday October 16th 1988
9 and 11 pm
The Knitting Factory 47 East Houston Street

THIS PAGE: A pair of flyers for solo shows by Gary at the Knitting Factory, New York, in July and October 1988.
OPPOSITE: Paul Now, Gary, Tony 'Thunder' Smith, Jared Nickerson perform as Gods and Monsters at the New Music Seminar at the Knitting Factory, July 1989.

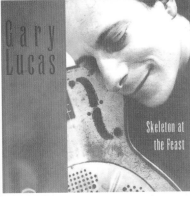

THIS PAGE: Gary, Jeff Buckley, and Julia Heyward onstage at the *Greetings From Tim Buckley* show at St Ann's, April 1991; Gary performs at a WMFU benefit at Tramps, November 1991; *Skeleton At The Feast*, Gary's debut live album. **OPPOSITE:** Studio portrait of Jeff and Gary, February 1992.

garylucasgodsandmonsters

THIS PAGE: video stills of Gary and Jeff
onstage together St Ann's, Roulette, and
CBGB's, March and April 1992; Gary's
studio debut, *Gods and Monsters*.
OPPOSITE: in the courtyard of St Luke's,
New York, August 1993; at home, 1992.

THIS PAGE: Jeff Buckley onstage at the Roseland Ballroom, New York, June 1995; *Songs To No One*, the album of Buckley–Lucas songs released by Knitting Factory Records in 2002; Gary and Portuguese singer Diana Silveira perform 'Mojo Pin' at a Jeff Buckley tribute event at the Knitting Factory, March 2010. OPPOSITE: Gary and Cuban star Haydée Milanés perform 'Grace' at the same show.

SONGS TO NO ONE
1991-1992

JEFF BUCKLEY   GARY LUCAS

Gary and Alessio Franchini at a Jeff Buckley tribute in Rimini, Italy, November 2010; playing 'Rise Up To Be' outside the Shakespeare and Company bookstore in Paris, May 2013.

Prologue

The phone rang on the afternoon of Friday May 30 1997. The caller was my friend Michael Shore, a writer who worked for MTV News.

"Gary, have you heard the news? Jeff Buckley's been missing down in Memphis since yesterday."

What? Jeff, missing? Was I hearing correctly?

"Apparently he jumped fully clothed into the Mississippi River yesterday for a swim, right before he was due to meet his band flying in from New York to start his new album ... and he's disappeared. They think he's probably drowned. But they haven't found a body yet."

I listened closely, asked a few questions, and hung up a few minutes later in a state of shock. Tears welled in my eyes, and then I erupted with a teeth-gnashing *noooooooooooooo* ...

It seemed unreal. Unreal, but not so unbelievable.

I'd just seen Jeff a couple of months earlier, playing a solo show at the tenth anniversary party for the famous Knitting Factory club. He had invited me onstage, and we'd played our song 'Grace'—the title track on his one and only studio album for Sony. I'd given him the music for this song in 1991, back when he agreed to be my lead singer in my band, Gods and Monsters.

He hadn't looked very well at the Knit. Haunted and puffy-faced, his formerly lithe, muscular body gone slack, he spoke with me briefly before the show, and in a subdued voice, weary with sadness and despair, he told me about all the problems that were consuming him, expressing profound unhappiness with his group, his management, and his label.

"You have no idea how horribly *fucked* everything is for me right now," he said, cataloguing the many miseries in his life and career at that moment.

As he walked up the stairs to his dressing room, he turned and shot me a look of pure, helpless grief—a pitiable look, a cry for help. My heart went out to him, my former partner, my greatest collaborator, my lost friend.

But then I hardened my heart. I'd seen that look before. Jeff could be both genuine and manipulative at any given time, and sometimes both aspects were present simultaneously.

I had to stay wary. He'd burned me before. And now here was that imploring look again, but etched much deeper in the haunted lines of his face, much graver—and much more to be taken seriously. It was a look that screamed, "I'm in trouble! For God's sakes, please help me!"

But really, what could I do at that point? Jeff wasn't a kid any more. He was a 31-year-old internationally adored pop star who made young girls swoon and men and women fall in love. A Golden Boy.

His landmark album, *Grace*, had been praised to the skies when it was released in 1994. He was a favorite of critics and musicians such as Bono and Jimmy Page, and he was even named one of the 50 Most Beautiful People in the World by *People* magazine. But he was approaching a watershed moment in his career—and he didn't have a kid's in-built excuses for fucking up.

He'd been given opportunities any artist would kill for, with the world's biggest record company catering to his every whim; given a gargantuan budget with seemingly no cap on it, and all the resources available to make *Grace* a worldwide hit. And yet it hadn't quite worked out for him. The record hadn't done the numbers needed for the giant corporation to even begin to recoup its considerable investment in his talent.

The pressure was on, and plagued by doubts, insecurities, writer's block, drugs, and whatever other demons were driving him, Jeff was now a ghost of his former self. It was crunch time, with all the attendant stress now of having to create the big follow-up album, the hit record that would redeem him with the big multinational label once and for all—the album he'd been unsuccessfully trying to write for the three years that had passed since *Grace* was released.

That night, I saw flashes of rage, confusion, and sorrow wash over him—and also total ecstasy when he invited me onstage to play 'Grace' with him in the middle of his set. He began soaring, singing his heart out, and for a fleeting few moments we were rocking in rhythm, back to the white-hot creation that had first brought us together.

But everything was disintegrating around him. This was clear to me. The Knitting Factory performance offered a brief respite, but not redemption.

That night, after talking to my wife about what I had seen and felt from my friend, we agreed that the best course of action was for me to stay cool and let Jeff reach out directly to me if he really required my assistance—musical or otherwise. When he did, I'd be there to help. That was always the way it had worked in the past.

Five months later, the phone rang.

But it wasn't Jeff.

Introduction

There is a backstory, of course, that leads up to that grim and alarming telephone call. Many readers will no doubt have more than a passing familiarity with Jeff Buckley's music, and also some details of his tragically short life. And many readers will also have some familiarity with my name and music.

The world at large probably knows me best for having played originally with Don Van Vliet, aka Captain Beefheart, and later for collaborating with Jeff. This despite my having released over 20 acclaimed albums in various genres in my own right, collaborating with some of the biggest names in music, scoring myriad films and documentaries, and touring constantly all over the world, in over 40 countries to date, over the past 25 years.

I've been called "one of the best and most original guitarists in America" by *Rolling Stone*, "the thinking man's guitar hero" by *The New Yorker*, a "legendary leftfield guitarist" by *The Guardian*, an "almighty guitar magician" by Dutch national newspaper *De Volkskrant*, and one of the world's "100 greatest living guitarists" by *Classic Rock* magazine.

Despite all of this, however, I fear that my tombstone might well end up reading

RIP GARY LUCAS—ex-Captain Beefheart and Jeff Buckley guitarist.

This book, however, is neither a biography of Jeff nor a book about me. It focuses instead on the story of how I originally came to know and work with Jeff—and how we created the world-shaking masterpieces 'Grace' and 'Mojo Pin' together. It's a story told from the inside.

There have been several biographies and documentaries about Jeff to date, all riddled with errors concerning my relationship with him, and I aim to set the record straight here once and for all with a loving but unvarnished account of how we first joined together, ripped asunder, and came together again in one last bittersweet encounter.

Along the way, I will provide an intimate glimpse into how we created those enduring anthems—what exactly went into the making of these songs, and what makes them tick—in a manner unlike anything written about Jeff and me previously. No one knows this story better than I do.

Along the way, I will fill in missing details, correct some misapprehensions about our working together, and pay tribute to my amazing former partner and collaborator—who, in my estimation, was one of the finest and most gifted musicians I have ever had the honor to know and collaborate with.

□

The beauty of working with Jeff was the total trust we had in one another creatively. I never ever questioned where Jeff was going with his melodies or lyrics. They were sacred to him, and thus to me; totally personal, and yet so universal, as time has proven.

Jeff's performance on 'Grace' especially—an anthem for dispossessed souls and star-crossed lovers everywhere—makes me want to cry every time I hear it. When we finished working on this song on that summer afternoon in 1991, I was speechless. There was nothing really to say.

I was left that afternoon with a warm glow inside that never went away. I was buzzing with the elegance of our new song—it felt like we'd brought something fresh and astonishing into the world. Its potential to move people was almost palpable. It was spellbinding—musically, vocally, and lyrically.

In the narrative of Jeff's lyrics, I felt I was purchasing a deep glimpse into his ultra-sensitive soul. I think Jeff was acutely aware of his own mortality, given what had happened to Tim Buckley—and was able to put all his fears and joys into his lyrics.

As far as our music goes, Jeff had the gift of being able to create sinuous melodic lines and place them in the tangled skein of my guitar instrumentals, perfectly and unerringly. Which is why our songs sound so organic. Two sensibilities fused into one.

I wrote Jeff a letter once about this, and I said that as strong as we both were individually as artists, we created something much bigger than the both of us when we came together to collaborate—something greater than anything we might have come up with on our own.

I can't fully explain why this is, beyond the obvious fact of shared tastes in music and philosophical outlook. There is also the X-factor of mysterious attraction to one another that bonded us inextricably, despite all the music biz bullshit that put us on the outs for a few years.

The chemistry between us was undeniable, borne of mutual love and respect. We shared a desire to channel the spiritual and the otherworldly and transmit this to the world through our songs, which is why our first run-through of 'Grace' in my apartment back in 1991 was so magical and so transcendental.

We were both believers, tied to this mast by the King's Chain, joined at the hip by the Holy Spirit that presides over all. We burned with the ambition to tear down the walls of music and change the notion of what a pop song could be.

Our age difference was never an issue in the creation of these anthems. We weren't bound by fashion or by any temporal ideal. We were driven to communicate the gift of 'Grace' to the world. Two wild horses, galloping together—if only for a moment. Racing with a shared dream: to create sacred music, to go for the Godhead.

I felt this so strongly when Jeff and I first wrote and played together, but never more so than on the day we first played 'Grace' together. I feel it still. The love that burned so brightly then is forever in my heart.

People from all over the world have told me for years how deeply our songs touched them; how these songs changed their lives. I am humbled every time I hear this. It is the highest honor any artist could possibly receive. It makes the whole struggle worthwhile.

Gary Lucas
New York City

Chapter One

Like many origin stories, this one begins in the spring.

One blooming spring day in late March 1991, I received a call that was to change the course of my life. Hal Willner, the music producer, impresario, and all-around professional hipster, was an old friend of mine from Manhattan, where I'd made my home for some 13 years. He was a frizzy-haired creative hustler with a Jewish showbiz sensibility updated and polished to a post-modernist sheen. A guy who knew everyone who was anyone in the avant-pop music world we inhabited.

Hal had a job at *Saturday Night Live*, where he came up with the background music for the comedy sketches, and through this he forged strong connections with many of the musical acts that had appeared on the show. He also had pioneered the multi-artist tribute, producing several acclaimed albums and concerts whereby various contemporary artists paid homage to the music of such diverse musicians as Fellini film soundtrack composer Nino Rota and jazz legend Thelonious Monk.

Now he was calling to invite me to participate in a tribute concert devoted to the music of the late great Tim Buckley. Hal was going to title it *Greetings From Tim Buckley*, as in: a message from beyond the grave.

"It's going to feature you, Gary, with the rest of the cream of the downtown scene ... going to be covering Tim Buckley songs from his entire career, in your own styles," he explained. "You do like Tim Buckley, don't you? I figured you would know his music."

As it happened, the curly-haired, soaring-voiced adonis was a particular passion of mine, a 60s singer-songwriter of immense poetic and musical gifts who had sadly never received the recognition he deserved during his short life. At the time, the world at large probably knew Tim best probably through a cover version of his song 'Morning Glory' that appeared on the first Blood Sweat & Tears album, although since his death he had become a massive cult-artist, particularly in the UK.

And there was so much more to be discovered. I had always loved Tim's music, right back to my high school days, when his second Elektra album, *Goodbye & Hello*—a heady suite of jazz/rock/folk songs with sophisticated arrangements to rival those on The Beatles' *Sgt Pepper*—touched me deeply, especially when I listened late at night in my suburban bedroom in Syracuse, New York, as I lay dreaming of the big world beyond.

When I was at college in the early 70s, at Yale, I frequently broke the house rules of my own radio show, *The Sounds From England*, by spinning tracks by both Tim Buckley and Captain Beefheart, two titans of American music whose epochal influences were to affect my own subsequent musical career indelibly. Tim's delirious 'Gypsy Woman,' an ecstatic, frenzied chant d'amour, was a particular favorite of mine, not only for its impassioned beauty but also for its side-long length. Clearly, the man took chances, and was not afraid to experiment.

Tim had distinguished himself not only with great songs but with his high, keening voice—a voice of such astonishing power and fragility that it literally gave me chills as it swooped and bayed through the swirling tides of his mysterious musical flow. His albums, originally grounded in the LA folk-rock tradition, grew increasingly complex, ornate, and just plain out-there as his career progressed.

Beautiful, experimental sound-tapestries like *Lorca* and *Star Sailor* broke new musical ground but also left a large part of his listening audience behind in the process. Tim eventually returned to his R&B roots for his final albums, which—while having their shining

25

moments—never quite hit the heights of his early recorded genius. After several years of diminishing sales, and with his career in eclipse and a slow sad slide into obscurity in prospect, Tim Buckley died from a drug overdose in Los Angeles on June 29 1975, aged just 28.

In answering Willner's call, I told him excitedly that yes, indeed, I was a big Tim Buckley fan, and that I could even remember exactly where I was when I'd heard the news that one of my musical heroes had died.

I had just arrived in Taipei, Taiwan, in the spring of 1975, on the rebound from a post-graduation love affair with a much older woman in Manhattan (that's another story). I had come to Taipei to begin a new life working for my father in his import/export business and had just moved into an apartment downtown. The place didn't have many furnishings yet, but it did have a radio, which was tuned mainly to AFNT, the Armed Forces Radio English-language network that served the soldiers on the nearby base.

On the very first morning after my arrival, I rose to the sound of roosters crowing in the alleyway outside my building, turned on the radio, and heard this bulletin come over the airwaves: "1960s cult singer-songwriter Tim Buckley was found dead in Los Angeles today of an apparent drug overdose."

I felt a sharp pang of sorrow. Damn, not Tim Buckley! I will never forget that moment, as his music had really touched me. This really meant something to me. Here was a great artist and musician I loved and respected—and he'd just OD'd in LA. So gifted, so sad. What a waste.

I picked up my guitar and played a sorrowful blues for Tim.

A few minutes later, my playing was interrupted by a knock on the door. I opened it to find an owlish, bespectacled young Jewish kid, who introduced himself as Hank Frisch from Shaker Heights, Cleveland. He lived in the building, and he'd been attracted by my guitar playing, which he could hear all the way into his apartment. Like me, he'd come to the Far East to work in his dad's import/export business. He told me he dug my playing, and that he played the harmonica—did I want to jam?

Out of the ashes of Tim Buckley's death, a new musical friendship was born. Hank and I went on to form a blues duo, and later a band, and eventually had many adventures playing in Hong Kong, on Taiwanese TV, in Taipei nightclubs and recording studios, and at the National Taiwan University graduation ceremonies.

□

"I've asked Richard Hell, G.E. Smith, Syd Straw, Barry Reynolds ... let's see, who else? Shelley Hirsch, Greg Cohen, Yuval Gabay, Robert Quine, Elliot Sharp, and Anthony Coleman to be part of this tribute show."

Willner's voice pulled me out of my Taiwanese reverie.

"We're going to do this tribute in St Ann's Church in Brooklyn—a wonderful space ... just produced a show with Marianne Faithfull there ... oh, by the way, we've been contacted by Tim Buckley's son, Jeff."

"Tim Buckley had a son?" I asked.

This was news to me.

"I had no idea," I told Hal.

"Neither did we. We heard about him first through Tim's old manager, Herbie Cohen, who we had to contact for the performing rights of Tim's songs. This kid wants to come to New York to be part of this concert and pay his respects to his father. And I think you'd be a really good person for him to collaborate with."

I already had an official collaborator, a female vocalist with whom I'd been locked in a deal with for a couple years already to record an album for Columbia Records. We bickered endlessly on things like who should produce us, our group name, and the rest, and so far we hadn't recorded a note of music together. Things weren't exactly working out smoothly.

"Sure," I replied, casually. "I'll be happy to check this guy out."

Out of such moments are major turning points in life made.

☐

At the precise time Hal Willner broached the idea, I was already 38 years old—not exactly a prime cut in the voracious jaws of the music business. Still, I had recently managed to pull off something fairly miraculous for a musician my age: I'd transformed my career from that of a lowly copywriter toiling in the vineyards of CBS Records' marketing department to become a fully signed-up Columbia Records recording artist.

I had stepped out of the shadows of CBS's so-called 'Creative Services Department'—where for 13 long years I'd churned out reams of ad copy for everyone from Barbra Streisand to Bruce Springsteen to The Clash—and got myself signed to Columbia on the strength of some very well-received demos and live shows with my band, Gods and Monsters.

Over my many years working at CBS, despite or rather in the face of having a fulltime job there, I had built a reputation for myself as a superlative musician, a "guitarist's guitarist", having played and recorded on the side—while still holding down my day job—with the visionary avant-rock genius Captain Beefheart.

I'd been playing guitar since the age of nine, when my father suggested quite out of the blue that I take up a musical instrument. "How about the guitar?" he asked, which sounded good to my clueless young ears.

I began lessons on a cheap rental acoustic with strings so high off the fretboard that they caused my fingers to bleed when I tried to practice on the damn thing. I took lessons for a month and then happily chucked them and the guitar—until my folks returned from a trip to Mexico with a nylon-string Spanish-style guitar, which I found much easier to play.

Playing quickly grew into my favorite pastime, and I became proficient on the guitar rather quickly, at first mastering what passed for the folk music of the day—until my ears were warped by rock'n'roll.

Before even starting nursery school, I would listen for five or six hours a day to AM Top 40 radio, swinging back and forth in the rocking chair in the basement of our house, phoning the local radio station to make requests, memorizing every song on the hit parade.

My dream was to play the twangy solo break from Duane Eddy's 'Dance With The Guitar Man'—the title track on the first album I ever bought. I knew after hearing the song what I wanted to be in life—a guitar man.

I formed my first 'combo'—that's what they called them then—while I was still in elementary school, playing my grade-school assembly with a borrowed electric guitar plugged into the jack on the back of my father's big FM radio—that was my amplifier. I dug The Beach Boys, The Ventures, and of course The Beatles the minute they hit American shores, a few months after JFK was shot.

Then, when the British Invasion took over the radio, I became especially fixated with the raw guitar sounds of The Rolling Stones and, later, The Yardbirds. I remember hearing the siren sound of Brian Jones's Vox Phantom kicking out the hypnotic riff on the Stones' 'The Last Time'—and I was hooked. Later, Jeff Beck became my main guy, followed by Peter Green, Syd Barrett, and in the USA Danny Kalb, Lou Reed, Elliot Ingber, and Mike Bloomfield.

There were just so many awesome players on the horizon back then, re-writing the rules every day, and I dreamed of one day becoming one of them as part of the righteous elect of rock. To lay down the law with my badass guitar playing and compose anthems that would shake the world, like the Stones' 'Satisfaction' or The Beatles' 'Revolution'—that is what I aspired to in my teenage dreams.

I put together several bands to play high-school dances and mixers, eventually performing at frat parties up at Syracuse University during the psychedelic late 60s. Iron Butterfly's 20-minute 'In-A-Gadda-Da-Vida' was the big request then. I recall once stepping through pools of vomit on the floor at an SU frat-house in order to get paid the morning after a show.

I kept my hand in when I moved on to Yale University in 1970 to begin my studies in English literature, playing in some campus bands and also the infamous Yale Marching Band, where they set me up on the sidelines of the Yale Bowl with my guitar and wah-wah cranked through a 200-watt Marshall amplifier, wailing the theme from *Shaft* while the band cavorted impudently on the field and scandalized the alumni.

My first major professional experience, though, was joining the Yale Symphony Orchestra as featured guitar soloist for the 1972 European premiere of Leonard Bernstein's 'Mass,' a musical theater piece for orchestra, singers, dancers—literally a cast of hundreds, conducted by John Mauceri. The piece had originally been commissioned for the opening of the Kennedy Center in Washington, DC; now, Bernstein himself, my ultimate hero in music—I learned so much about music growing up watching his *Young People's Concerts* on CBS in the 60s—came to Vienna to supervise our premiere at the Konzerthaus.

The piece opened with my guitar chiming a celestial chord before the singing began, and I had other featured moments throughout the work—especially an extended psychedelic blues-rock improvisation over some decadent, spiky, 'end of the world' orchestral music—and Lenny himself paid me the first major compliment for my playing when I met him at the American Ambassador's party later that evening.

"You were really wailing!" he exclaimed.

My major ambition at this time, however, was to join Captain Beefheart & His Magic Band—to me, the number-one avant-rock band in the world. I first caught their act in a little club in Uptown New York in early 1971 and it changed my life completely. I vowed that night that if I ever did anything in music, I would someday play with this band.

Seeing Don van Vliet in action with his band of mutant/alien musicians sporting exotic names such as Winged Eel Fingerling and Zoot Horn Rollo made me determined to put myself in the center of that swirling maelstrom. It became my dominant obsession, and I eventually got my wish after meeting Don up at Yale the following year and bonding closely with him.

I eventually realized my heart's desire when I was invited to be a guest soloist on Beefheart's 1980 Virgin album *Doc At The Radar Station*. My performance of his complex and tricky solo guitar instrumental 'Flavor Bud Living' on that album put me on the musical map for good, with much critical ink in praise of my playing appearing in various British and American music magazines.

I even fooled the great rock critic Lester Bangs, who asked me, upon hearing the record, "What part did you play on this piece, Gary, the top or the bottom?"

"Lester," I replied, "that was all me—playing totally live, in real time and without overdubs."

Having first taken time off from my day job to work on Beefheart's albums, I soon became addicted to the joys of touring and took even more time off to go on the road with the band, coming out to play several pieces on Beefheart's final tours of the USA and Europe in late 1980 and early '81.

I wisely kept my day job, since the commercial prospects for the band were perennially thin—this was total dada blues music, and Don hated touring. But I was drafted back in a year later to become a full member of The Magic Band for Beefheart's final album, *Ice Cream For Crow*.

Critics once again took note of my playing, and my solo-guitar tour de force 'Evening Bell'—which took months for me to master and get under my fingers before recording it for that album—was praised effusively in *Rolling Stone*, *Musician*, and *Esquire*. My playing was spotlighted in the last of these, with the reviewer noting, "Magic Band man Gary Lucas apparently grew extra fingers to negotiate his way through the piece."

My bosses at CBS Records benignly tolerated my parallel career with Captain Beefheart and let me take leaves of absence to record

31

and tour with Don while continuing to hold down my day job. It actually was a source of pride to my department that they had such a motivated and creative individual on staff. Plus, Beefheart's music was art music—it hardly threatened to take market share away from CBS Records' established hit-makers.

CBS viewed my participation in The Magic Band as basically a hobby, which in a way it was—I never made any real money working with Don, but I was not in it for profit. I did it because I totally believed in it, and because I knew how important it was in a world-historical sense.

It was a joy to play with a man who had marked me out as an amazing and exceptional player—a man whose music was as difficult and demanding to play as modern classical music, which it sometimes resembled. And because I did an excellent job for CBS—my work won awards, and I always delivered it on time—they were cool with it. As long as I was dabbling in avant-garde rock with "no commercial potential" (that's what Beefheart's buddy Frank Zappa said) and it didn't interfere with me cranking out high-grade ad copy by the yard, it was fine not only for me to play with Beefheart but even record for other labels (*Doc At The Radar Station* was released on Virgin/Atlantic, CBS's competitors across the street).

□

I cruised along for 13 years at CBS, working in a kind of dead-end fool's paradise—what some might call a velvet coffin. I had no problem working in the high-pressure environment at the Black Rock—the famous black granite CBS building on West 52nd Street, designed by Eero Saarinen, which I dubbed the Death Star—as I would self-medicate throughout the work day, smoking pot on the stairwell or on the street outside the building, which enabled me to deal with the slings and arrows of corporate politics—things I felt serenely above and uninterested in anyway. Never did I aspire to be a marketing department product manager.

I was happy doing what I did, creating and writing advertising for what were, in my opinion, worthless corporate-rock bands, and it seemed ridiculously easy to me—utter child's play. I was a rebellious mole within the corporation—an update on what used to be known as the 'house hippie' in the 60s. As we were now in the late 70s and early 80s, I was more the resident hipster punk, even occasionally sneaking under the noses of my bosses such howlers as "can you take 12 inches of Judas Priest?" for the album *British Steel*.

And when I wasn't writing ads—which I would accomplish in less than an hour each day—I sustained myself behind the closed door of my cubicle with my fulltime obsessing over and micro-managing of the career of Captain Beefheart. The fact that I had unlimited long-distance phone service, thanks to the corporate WATS line, made this a very cushy situation indeed.

I probably spent at least an hour on the phone with Beefheart each and every day, talking about everything and nothing. He was a fascinating but demanding conversationalist, and once he caught your ear you would have to stay on the phone with him for inordinate amounts of time.

I had a stereo and an out-of-tune prop piano in my office, inherited from the previous tenant, and a view of 6th Avenue and 52nd Street—plus a corporate American Express card for "business lunches" and "competitive product" (that is, the purchase of other labels' records, and later CDs, for further research).

But when Captain Beefheart decided to fold his tent in 1984, convinced after a dozen critically-praised but poor-selling albums that the music business was a dead end for him, I was left bereft of my creative mainstay and phone companion, whose rococo daily conversations offset the tedious drudgery of being a staff copywriter at CBS. (Having retired from music, Don was eager now to pursue his dream of becoming a painter—something I helped along the way when I introduced him to artist and filmmaker Julian Schnabel and gallery owner Mary Boone in the early 80s.)

My relationship with Don came apart a few years after the breakup of my marriage to my first wife, Ling Ling, a feisty, brilliant Cantonese woman whom I had met and wooed in Taipei. We'd been advised to leave the island for our own safety by an American Foreign Service officer after a bloody melee broke out in a bar called the Scarecrow right after my neo-punk group The O-Bay-Gone Band had quit the stage. I married Ling in San Francisco and we subsequently relocated east. But we had grown estranged after five long years together in New York. While Ling had helped me co-manage the Beefheart enterprise in 1980, we were at each other's throats constantly by the time we broke up mid 1981.

So there I was, adrift at CBS Records, bereft of the two major loves of my life to date—Don and Ling—and trying alone to figure out what exactly I wanted to accomplish next in my life. Inevitably, the answer would be playing and recording my own music. I'd been bitten by the performing bug after touring Europe with The Magic Band in 1980. Don didn't want to tour any more after '81, which was a major drag to me.

Don and the promotion of all things Beefheart had become the central focus of my life, and the job at CBS merely something I did to pay the rent—it was easy, but ever so unfulfilling. Working with Don for nearly five years, I had been on a single-minded mission to promote his work, bemoaning the fact that, to my mind, he hadn't gotten a fair shake while the punks and new wave-sters who had fed at his trough were ripping him off blind with commercialized versions of his genius music.

Yes, I'd come up with the famous ad line for The Clash—"The Only Group That Matters"—and, back in 1978, I had really believed it. But joining Beefheart in 1980, I was embarrassed by it: hey, *we're* the only group that matters. Fuck that other shit!

Now, however, Don was all about painting—not music. So I cast about for a new musical focus—not easy after playing in what I considered to be the greatest avant-garde rock band of all time. I entertained a few offers to join bands in New York, but none of them seemed to offer the same kind of prestigious kick. It was a real climb-down to go from playing in The Magic Band to even considering accompanying the likes of cow-punk Ned Sublette, for example.

I got a few producing assignments for CBS's record division, but although the two avant-jazz albums I oversaw—for saxophonist-composers Peter Gordon and Tim Berne—got brilliant reviews, neither turned out to sell well enough to justify my services as a producer, particularly after Tim's *Fulton Street Maul* tanked. (Peter's album ended up coming out on the FM crossover label of CBS's Masterworks classical music division.)

I also did some freelance A&R work for indie labels such as Rough Trade in London and Upside in New York, signing maverick composer/cellist/visionary Arthur Russell and former Pop Group futurist Mark Stewart in the USA, but I didn't find this nearly as fulfilling as playing and performing.

I did a few sessions in the mid 80s for the brilliant UK dub producer Adrian Sherwood, US singer-songwriter Matthew Sweet, and British indie-rock darlings The Woodentops—all of which merely whetted my appetite to get back in the limelight as a player. I was given creative free rein for The Woodentops' album *Woodenfoot Cops On The Highway*, and as the music swirled around me in the headphones and I danced along with it on my guitar fretboard, I remember thinking, "Right, this is how it should be all the time. I'm born to do this—this is so much fun—this is what I should be doing with my life."

My childhood dream of becoming a fulltime recording artist had surged uppermost in my mind by then—I couldn't repress it—but how best to accomplish this? I lacked the self-confidence—not to mention the life savings—to just chuck my day job, abandon my steady paycheck and health benefits and the cushy perks of the corporate life, and throw myself into the deep end of the pool.

For years I had psyched myself completely out of the running. A double Gemini, I suffered from a weird mixture of supreme, almost arrogant self-confidence crossed with an intermittent low sense of self-esteem. Just as I was on the verge of taking creative risks, I would beat myself up with negative thoughts. "What do I possibly have worth saying as a songwriter, composer, or guitarist when there are so many talented folks out there who are already doing the job so admirably?" I wondered to myself. Have another bong hit!

Fundamentally a very shy person at heart—back then, anyway—I was content to coast on my fading credentials as a great guitar player who'd played with a legendary band, not realizing that in this fickle business and fickle world, where the average audience member has the attention span of a flea, you have to keep proving it to them over and over and over again.

For many folks, achieving a childhood dream of playing with someone like Beefheart would have provided enough ego-fuel to last a lifetime, but not for me. I knew that my reputation as "Beefheart's guitarist" wouldn't endure—but it wasn't enough in and of itself to continue to satisfy my desire to make my mark on the world.

□

My fortunes changed radically when the Knitting Factory opened its doors on Houston Street, Manhattan, in 1987. The club was founded by a couple of entrepreneurial, music-loving hippies from Wisconsin, and within a couple years—partly by accident and partly by their sheer dogged determination—it had carved out a substantial niche for itself as the hottest spot for cutting-edge avant-garde rock, jazz, and experimental music in the known universe. A major scene quickly developed around the club, fueled by avatars such as saxophonist and composer John Zorn, and seemingly overnight this frowsy little loft had become a mecca for adventurous music lovers all over the world.

The first time I went there was to check out one of my protégés, the jazz saxophonist and composer Tim Berne. Inside the narrow railroad-car of a room was a small platform stage with a picture window looking out on Houston Street at the rear. All of a sudden, in that wan evening twilight, watching Tim and his guys make some fiery music for a small appreciative crowd of hipsters and tastemakers, I could actually envision myself up there on that stage, playing—what, exactly, and with whom?

I had no group and no real repertoire of my own developed yet—just a burning ambition to Go For It before it was too late. I was already 35 years old, a rather advanced age to even begin to contemplate forging a new career in music. But that is what I was determined to do, and this club seemed like the perfect launching pad for me. After years in the service of CBS Records and in the shadow of Captain Beefheart, I had a new daily mantra. "Be your own hero!"

Three incidents in 1988 spurred me on to make a concerted attempt at a music career. The first came during a recording session with the mercurial and fiercely contrarian Arthur Russell, for which I played my ancient black '64 Stratocaster (the very same one I'd played with Beefheart). Arthur took me aside after an early take and made a very astute observation in his soft, reedy, hypnotic voice.

"Gary, you know something?" he said. "I've been watching you closely. And you're only happiest when you have a guitar in your hand. And I think this is what you should be doing fulltime."

In retrospect, he was absolutely right—which is why I dedicated my first Gods and Monsters album to him.

That notion was seconded around the same time by my friend Howard Thompson, an English A&R man and record scout at Columbia and later Elektra Records. I used to hang out with Howard in his office and bring in demo tapes of obscure artists I believed in as budding musical geniuses worthy of his patronage. He had excellent taste, having signed 10,000 Maniacs, The Psychedelic Furs, and other cutting-edge hit-makers. I'd been after him for a while, imploring him to bring me in to do A&R, since I couldn't bear my job in the marketing department much longer.

After one of these listening sessions, Howard turned to me, sighed, and said, "Gary, you're a great player—you're not just a copywriter. And you're not cut out to be an A&R man either. You should be out there doing it. Playing! Come on, already."

Finally, a very astute, very intelligent, and very attractive Korean-American girl with whom I'd become close and who worked at CBS Masterworks classical label had accompanied me to that show by Tim Berne at the Knitting Factory. Sniffing around the club, and in total sync with my own un-verbalized thoughts, she said, "This place is really cool. *You* should put on a show of your own here."

Her name was Grace.

□

It was in the air all around me at this point—a definite vibe that *now* was the time to act, to finally start tapping the crazy energy of my unfulfilled musical potential—before the rapidly diminishing window of opportunity would close and I would be entombed forever in Black Rock.

Arthur and Howard and Grace were sensitive enough to pick up on this, and they were all encouraging me, God bless 'em. And with that last little shove from Grace, I made the decision to move forward with my plan to work up a solo-guitar show—which I would then premiere at the Knitting Factory—and then see what might develop from that.

My mind was made up, and I was determined to give it my best shot. At the age of 35, what exactly did I have to lose? I was stuck in a dead-end job at CBS. I could run the clock out and stay there forever—the job was mine for life if I wanted it, and I might have stayed on there to a ripe old age, brain-dead and going through the motions and collecting my pension at the end—but I was dying on the vine creatively. After 13 years at CBS I felt sucked dry. I loathed being there. And there wasn't a strain of marijuana strong enough to hold those feelings down any longer.

I remember sitting at my typewriter gazing forlornly out the window of my office, day after day, casting a weary, jaundiced eye at the imposing Midtown skyline and then literally burying my head in my hands, my arms cradled on my IBM Selectric, overwhelmed by the utter meaninglessness of it all and the pointless futility of what I was doing there.

I was keenly aware that I was wasting my talents as a fulltime whore for the CBS marketing machine. Only once in a blue moon would an act come along to seize my imagination, like The Clash had. The rest were so typical and formulaic that my ear closed to them automatically.

There had to be more to life than this. There was a big old world out there, and I was slaving for a corporation I despised, dressing up acts I mostly despised—polishing turds is what they call it—with fancy slogans and clever, seductive imagery.

I started practicing in earnest and even went off to England to record two self-financed demos with Woodentops lead singer Rolo McGinty at Elephant Studios in the Docklands area of East London, with the very talented engineer Harold Burgon at the controls: an original co-write called 'Skin The Rabbit,' and a cover of Syd Barrett's Pink Floyd classic 'Astronomy Domine,' both of which garnered raves from my friends and co-workers at CBS.

Back in New York, I recorded an original instrumental entitled 'King Strong,' which quotes Zappa's 'King Kong,' with two members of Tackhead: drummer Keith LeBlanc helped me out with the arrangement and guitarist Skip McDonald sat at the controls. This track actually garnered some progressive FM radio play around New York, especially on WNYU's *New Afternoon Show*, on which I was a frequent guest performer, and was praised by *Billboard* magazine as "incendiary."

I figured playing solo would be the easiest and most economical way to begin to make my mark as a live performer in New York. I threw myself into woodshedding on my various guitars at home during the long winter months of 1988, practicing, experimenting, and working up a repertoire of fingerpicked blues tunes, psychedelic covers of film music, and my own original compositions.

One day that spring, I finally felt confident enough to go onstage and play this music, and let the chips fall where they may. I contacted Michael Dorf, one of the Wisconsin hippie founders of the Knitting Factory, whom I'd since befriended.

I first saw Michael wearing casual clothes and sandals, taking the tickets and serving the drinks and snacks, when I went to check out the Jazz Passengers, another downtown ensemble who were pursuing me in hopes of a Columbia Records contract. (After I'd secured major-label deals for Peter Gordon and Tim Berne, the word on the street was that I was the go-to guy at Columbia for avant-garde musicians in New York, when in fact I was all washed up as an A&R tipster after the commercial failure of Tim's album. Fuck art-jazz—CBS wanted hits, all of which was yet another sign that I should be getting on with my own music instead of trying to champion someone else's.)

Dorf had come uptown to visit me in my office at Black Rock earlier that spring, yammering a mile a minute about setting up his own record label through Columbia. I took him out to lunch and asked him why he thought he deserved his own label. "Because I'm a punk," he told me. Right.

Now, Dorf was receptive to my idea of putting on a solo guitar performance at his club ("Beefheart's guitarist wants to play at the Knit? Cool!") and offered me a Tuesday night door-gig slot at 9pm on June 7 1988. I was all set to make my New York City debut as a solo act with a concert of diverse, eclectic, and psychedelic guitar pyrotechnics.

"I'm going to give a recital," I jokingly told my friends. I did it on a dare—to impress a woman named Grace.

And there but for the Grace of God went I.

□

My first appearance under my own name in New York might well have been a nonstarter, so typically cocked-up was the publicity and promotion for it. First of all, Dorf had booked me at 9pm on a Tuesday—a terrible timeslot, Mondays and Tuesdays generally being the deadest evenings to play just about anywhere in the world.

And in the grand tradition of Knitting Factory ineptitude—back then, at least—there was no advance notice of my show at all in the club's weekly *Village Voice* advertisement. Either they had forgotten they had booked me altogether, or they didn't think the show worthy of mentioning in the ad. So I bootstrapped myself and made Xeroxed flyers and posters, which I stuck all over downtown Manhattan the week before the show. Hell, I had to let *somebody* know I was playing.

And lo and behold, by the night of my gig, the word had got out there. The place was jam-packed—so packed, in fact, that there was a line out onto Houston Street and the club had to eventually turn away folks like my musician pals Matthew Sweet and Tackhead duo Keith LeBlanc and Skip McDonald once the place filled up.

In other words, the gig was completely sold-out. It was a total triumph.

I came out, sat down on a wooden chair, and in a delirious semi-swoon—I was so nervous and yet so elated to be up there I felt like I was about to pass out—I played my 35-year-old ass off, dazzling the crowd with my virtuosic playing, showcasing the breadth of my myriad styles, from hypnotic space-guitar soundscapes to fingerpicked country-blues on my 1926 National steel to flat-out electric-blues shrieking and shredding over loops on my black Stratocaster.

In between numbers, I had the crowd roaring with laughter describing how, when I'd informed my mother some years earlier that I was going to take a leave of absence from CBS Records to run off and play with Captain Beefheart, she kvetched to my father, "The guitar? Murray! He's talking about the *guitar* again."

I totally won the audience over. After three encores, as I basked in the applause in an ecstatic haze, the club's manager, Bob Appel, came over and handed me a fistful of cash—about 600 bucks off the door— and right at that moment I knew for certain that playing music was what I was born to do with my life. I had proven both to myself and to the people in the club that I could singlehandedly move a tough New York crowd all by my lonesome—one man against the universe—and it felt really good!

Why had I waited so long to realize (and act on) this? That was my single biggest regret. But I had done it now, and that show was a real turning point in my life.

Back home, lying in bed after the show, I felt elated. I vowed that from that point I would hit music as hard as I could. I could see clearly that music was my manifest destiny. I was determined to play my way out of copywriting for CBS, and I knew for sure now that music would be my key to doing so.

I called Dorf the next day to thank him for giving me the opportunity to play at his club and described my triumph to him. (He, naturally, had failed to show up.) He booked me to appear at the Knitting Factory again a month later, as part of the club's What Is Jazz? Festival. After the show, the *New York Times* ran a rave review headlined 'Guitarist Of 1,000 Ideas.'

Three months later, I was invited overseas to perform at the Berlin Jazz Festival—my European solo debut. By coincidence, the festival coincided with the 50th anniversary of Kristallnacht—the beginning of open season on German Jews under the Nazis in October 1938. I was raised very cognizant of my Jewish identity and roots. I had no relatives living in Europe that my family knew of as they had all either fled for America or been wiped out in pogroms.

Good Jewish boy that I am, I composed a new piece the night before the concert entitled 'Verklarte Kristallnacht' ('Transfigured Kristallnacht'—a play on Arnold Schoenberg's 'Verklarte Nacht'). A grim fantasia and meditation on the Holocaust, the piece elicited gasps and then an ovation from the stunned crowd. I don't believe very many artists—especially Jewish artists—had dared to encapsulate their feelings about the Holocaust before in such a naked, personal way in what was nominally a jazz concert.

The next morning, the *Berliner Morgenpost* ran a photo of me performing at the show alongside the headline 'Es is Lucas!' ('It is Lucas!'). I was on my way.

☐

Things began to accelerate fast. My bosses at CBS couldn't handle it, displaying much jealousy and resentment with sarcastic remarks and putdowns every time I distinguished myself further in the world of music. I came back from Berlin in triumph—and with the newspaper reviews to prove it—only for one of the female kapos who ran my department to stride into my office and chuckle, meanly, "Here he is again, back in his hole."

I was determined to "fly by their nets," as the character Stephen Dedalus remarks in James Joyce's *Ulysses* (my favorite novel). They thought they had me under their thumb, working there for good, but I would soon prove them all wrong.

I continued to book myself steadily at the Knitting Factory and consolidate my New York fan base. I started playing regularly in Europe, too, and found that I was particularly warmly embraced by the Dutch. An early solo show at the Bimhuis jazz club in Amsterdam resulted in a review that described me as "the almighty guitar magician."

I also began to branch out from my solo shows into other musical areas. Over the next year, in collaboration with my childhood friend, the keyboardist and composer Walter Horn, I composed a live score to accompany the 1920 German silent horror film *The Golem*, which had its debut at Brooklyn Academy of Music's Next Wave Festival. It was praised as the evening's best work in press reviews and also by some of the influential artists in attendance, such as Laurie Anderson.

I realized my solo shows and avant-garde film-music projects, good as they were, would not be enough to bust me out of CBS Records. So, next, I decided to form a band, under the name Gods and Monsters. Deep in my soul, I knew that the inexorable power of a great electric ensemble would be hard to resist. And I knew I was capable of creating such a beast.

The name Gods and Monsters derives from a line of dialogue from one of my favorite horror films, *The Bride Of Frankenstein*, wherein one mad scientist toasts another, "To a new world of gods and monsters!"

Beginning as a purely instrumental jazz-rock band boasting two bassists and the incredible drumming of Tony 'Thunder' Smith, Gods and Monsters debuted at the Welcome Back To Brooklyn Festival in Prospect Park in June 1989, where we literally blew out their PA with our collective power.

Former Yardbirds producer, Rolling Stones manager, and general madman Giorgio Gomelsky came along to film our performance, and former Zappa/Beefheart guitarist Denny Walley showed up to check us out. Both were quite enthusiastic about the group, and we got a terrific reaction from the crowd.

We were starting to get a buzz in the press, too, with sensitive critics David Fricke (*Melody Maker*, *Rolling Stone*) and Richard Gehr (the *Village Voice*) heaping praise upon my gigs and playing style. But I knew that mere instrumental thunder was not enough to get signed to a major label like CBS in the 80s (in the 70s, maybe). Plus it would limit us to the jazz-rock category—a ghetto I wanted to avoid.

No, I wanted to make pop music—having first fallen in love with it as a little boy sitting in the basement of my parents' house in Syracuse, rocking in my chair to the rhythm of top 40 radio—and avant-garde pop music at that. It had been my aim ever since I first heard The Beatles' 'Strawberry Fields Forever.'

Coming up with actual songs with lyrics would be essential to realizing my dream—something I had hitherto dissuaded myself from doing out of shyness and fear of failure. Now, however, at age 37, I had reached the point of not giving a fuck about what people might think of my efforts in this department. If I were ever to step out of the long shadow cast by Don Van Vliet, I would have to throw the dice and make the try. Be your own hero!

I remember sitting in my office at CBS one day, forcing myself to begin the actual creative effort required to write a song.

I had recently written a neat, spooky minor-key chord sequence in an open guitar tuning during a summer holiday with my lovely English wife Caroline out at Shelter Island, and now I needed lyrics to go with it.

But hey, I was a writer, wasn't I? I'd won a National English award in my high school days, which helped me get accepted at Yale, and hadn't I supported myself for 13 years through writing? Even if ad-copy writing was writing of the lowest order. Or was that just part of my low-self-esteem problem?

After concentrating for an hour on writing lyrics and putting a melody to this instrumental, I had written my first song, which I called 'Poison Tree.' It was a doom-laden, romantic opus with haunting harmonic changes, elegant fingerpicking, and a gloomy worldview.

I had recorded some demos in England a year or two earlier with Rolo McGinty of The Woodentops, but while they were harbingers of my neo-psychedelic folk style (a hallmark of much of my songwriting), they were collaborative efforts. 'Poison Tree' was my first song with music and lyrics totally by me.

Now all I needed was a singer.

I was bursting with ambition but lacked the confidence that I could pull off the vocals myself. I had devoted so many years to honing and perfecting my guitar skills, while neglecting the development of my voice—something I probably should have been doing in tandem with the guitar playing. But I never felt all that comfortable singing.

Casting about for the ideal lead singer, I got a tip from John Warner, a former CBS Records marketing exec who lived in my neighborhood. He suggested the female vocalist and performance artist Julia Heyward, who had been Laurie Anderson's original partner back in the late 70s. Now, she mainly worked as an arty video director for bands like Romeo Void, and I remembered meeting her one day when she was up at CBS Records with her show reel.

Julia had a great look—tall, thin, and leggy, with long blonde hair and a striking, haughty face—and she had perfected a kind of demented Appalachian hillbilly yodel, punctuating her phrasing with occasional vocal hiccups in a style that Dolores O'Riordan from The Cranberries would take to the bank a few years later.

I approached Julia about performing with us, and she was game. I gave her 'Poison Tree' to sing as her signature song, and she sounded fantastic on it:

> *Mind split, darkness tripled*
> *Tree unfurled, the branches rippled*
> *And spread its banners for all to see*
> *Come and gather round the*
> *Poison tree*

And so it was that Julia joined the merry three-ring rock'n'roll circus of Gods and Monsters, which by now had expanded to a seven-piece line-up featuring drums, guitar, two bass players, a rapper, a turntable-scratcher ... and now this banshee of a singer.

I figured that a group with rotating vocalists based around my guitar playing and songwriting would make an attractive package from both a spectator's and a listener's vantage point. To have a fixed line-up seemed a bit stodgy and boring, and anyway, I was too impatient and too mercurial to want to set anything in stone at this point.

Besides, the eclectic, genre-hopping nature of the songs I was writing didn't seem to lend itself to being handled easily by just one vocalist. Gods and Monsters' early repertoire included some wicked avant-rap that was more the natural territory of a rapper like K-Rob, who had appeared in the early hip-hop film *Wild Style*. That song just wouldn't have worked with Julia.

We began gigging regularly at the Knitting Factory with this expanded seven-piece line-up in the fall of 1989, and pretty soon we were attracting an industry buzz, with write-ups in *Record World* and *Billboard* by industry veterans such as Danny Fields, who had discovered Iggy Pop.

My pal Howard Thompson, who had moved across the street from Black Rock to WEA's Elektra Records, was another early fan and advocate—it was he who recognized and encouraged me to realize my talent as a player, and he'd attended my very first solo show at the Knitting Factory. Now he was following my continuing evolution into pop-group territory with keen interest, monitoring my progress as a songwriter, showing up at gigs to scout my band, and watching the fan base swell.

Another early advocate was producer Rick Chertoff, a sensitive and brainy music aficionado and player who had scored at Columbia Records by producing and co-writing huge hits for Cyndi Lauper and The Hooters. We bonded one day in the elevator at Black Rock in the mid 80s when he buttonholed me to tell me how much he loved *Ice Cream For Crow*, the Beefheart album I had helped get the green light at CBS's Epic Records division.

I kept Rick appraised of the group's progress. In fact, I put all of CBS Records on notice by continually sticking glossy posters for my gigs all over the building. These were cleverly designed by the great graphic artist Steve Byram and printed gratis for me on beautiful coated stock by Creative Service's Joe Guarino and Artie Yeranian.

Despite the overwhelming indifference or downright hostility to my musical endeavors from the majority of my co-workers at the company, I did have some hardcore supporters there. I kept Chertoff's interest in my group piqued by supplying him with live tapes of Gods and Monsters as well as the demos I'd recorded in 1987–88.

Chertoff's rivalry with Howard Thompson—who had had an office right down the hall from Rick's at Black Rock for a few years—

probably forced the signing issue. They were now going head to head trying to sign and develop new cutting-edge acts, and Howard had just scored by signing 10,000 Maniacs.

One late October night in 1989, these two rival A&R men both showed up to a Friday night Gods and Monsters gig at the Knitting Factory—a gig that, luckily for me, was totally sold out. I had hired a guy to plaster the East Village with huge posters for the show, complete with big glossy photo of the band in action, and this visual razzle-dazzle had really done the trick.

I pulled up in a taxi to find a line stretched outside the club and around the block. Once inside, the attendees had to wait in the hot, cramped bar area downstairs while we set up our gear upstairs on a stage still littered with the synths and samplers of opening act Chuck. "Gary Lucas Hell" is how the speed-freak house manager described the chaotic, jam-packed scene at the bar.

We really played well that night, and when the show ended, Rick came backstage and told me how impressed he was with our set, how professional we sounded—and to call him on Monday. Elated, I sat out the weekend in a state of nervous anticipation and then made the call first thing Monday morning.

Rick told me that he was interested in offering us a recording contract with Columbia Records. But while he'd enjoyed the entire group—which on this instance had swollen into an eight-piece, with a second lead singer in Matthew Sweet, who was between label deals at the time—his vision of the project was to make an album with just the core duo of myself and Julia. In other words, if I wanted to make a record for Columbia, the duo alone—and not the three-ring circus— was what he wanted to sign up.

This would have made good commercial sense from Rick's point of view. Major labels mainly want a consistent product with a stable line-up and sound to better exploit in the media. My eclectic approach, while fun and enjoyable live, would have been too unwieldy to survive the journey into recording for a major—a journey that

48

would eventually translate, hopefully, into a hit record. Rick had also had previous success with strong female vocalists like Cyndi Lauper. And in my big blonde female singer, he saw a similar possibility.

I bit the bullet and accepted what I knew then was a Faustian bargain at best. It was a bit of a blow to my ego, and a major blow to my guys. It was also a rush of adrenalin and triumph for Julia, who saw this as confirmation that, indeed, she alone was the principal focus of the act—and the raison d'etre for our deal.

It was the beginning of a constant adversarial headache as I struggled to come to grips with a partner who, frankly, I never thought could or would be able to operate on the same creative wavelength as myself. She definitely had her own agenda. But sometimes you have to make the best of a situation and just get on with it in order to get to the next level.

The alternative was floundering in indie limbo with the band, making albums for smaller fly-by-night labels without any real chance of a shot at the big time. (This, unbeknown to me then in those heady days—when the world appeared to be at my feet after we signed with Columbia—was to be my fate in the long wilderness years ahead after my split with Jeff Buckley. But I'm getting ahead of myself here.)

So, in the spring of 1990, I was finally able to leave my day job at CBS Records in triumph, with a major-label deal under my belt, ready to make the music world by storm ... only to find myself drifting slowly out to sea with a reluctant, obtuse partner who fought me nearly every step of the way, creatively and otherwise.

For starters, right from the get-go, Julia pointedly informed me that she hated the name Gods and Monsters. "Too sexist," she told me. We bickered about that for ages before tabling the whole group-naming discussion to begin concentrating on writing songs.

Although I had written *all* the songs that had won us our deal, Rick had encouraged us to start writing together in an attempt to be democratic—without ever hearing any of Julia's previous solo efforts. I dutifully came up with some really beautiful instrumental music to which she could add lyrics and melodies—the underpinnings of what would become our shared repertoire.

I was on a creative roll, fueled by copious consumption of marijuana and heady dreams of finally having a platform to put my avant-pop vision on the musical map. The music, locked up inside me for so many years, just flowed out of me, seemingly effortlessly. But my partner insisted on putting some very preachy and unsubtle lyrics to my music—lyrics with a heavy feminist slant that would lead to many a cringe-inducing moment when I was forced to listen to them.

I am fundamentally on the left of the political spectrum, and a major supporter of women's rights and feminism in general. But I am not at all convinced that overt political sentiments carry all that much weight—or are even appropriate—in pop lyrics.

Take Dylan, for instance. My favorite all time 'pop musician' more or less abandoned what he called his 'finger-pointing' songs with his mid 60s breakthrough, whereupon he turned to more personal, surreal, and allusively poetic lyrics, which resulted in some of the most beautiful and indelible songs ever written.

Julia, however, was into writing 'finger-pointing' songs. I gamely stuck with the program of co-writing with her, per Rick's instructions, until a few months later, when we were to turn in to Rick our demos for his evaluation of our album-writing progress. After listening intently to the tape in his office, he turned to us and said, "I still like Gary's original songs the best." They were, after all, the songs that had won us our deal in the first place.

Julia turned red and glared at me.

□

Once we had established a halfway satisfactory repertoire—at least to Rick's mind—Julia and I then fought over who was going to produce our debut. Rick suggested Bob Dylan's Rolling Thunder backup group, now recording as The Alpha Band: T-Bone Burnett, Steve Soles, and David Mansfield.

We dutifully met with them, and I really liked the guys, especially T-Bone—whom in retrospect we should have stuck with, as he was to become a huge hit record producer a few years later—but good as he was, we didn't know why we needed three producers on our album in the first place. On top of that, these three putative producers didn't seem much interested in a key direction we intended to go in, which was to merge roots American music with a modern, technological edge via the latest innovation of the time: sampling.

The project kept getting bogged down. This dragged on and on over two years without us ever recording one note in a proper studio—only home demos. Julia and I would meet up on a nearly daily basis to rehearse our songs and work on new ones. Periodically, we'd go in and play them for Rick, who seemed to have lost much of his initial enthusiasm for the project when we balked at his suggestion of tripartite production.

And then something ominous happened. About a year into our contract, we were informed that Rick was leaving his gig as head of the Columbia A&R department to move across the street to Polygram Records. Suddenly we'd lost our rabbi, our chief supporter within the company—and we were very unsure of our future there.

Rick's replacement as vice president in charge of A&R was David Kahne, a talented Columbia staff producer and A&R man who'd signed and made some great records with The Bangles and Fishbone. Now he had been saddled with us—a hot potato of an untested act unwittingly inherited from Rick—and we were unsure that he would ever get behind our project.

We never saw Kahne after he came in; he made himself as remote as possible from the project. Instead, we were left in the care of Peter Shershin, a fledgling A&R guy who had recently been bumped up from an administrative role.

Shershin became our point man on the project, and, while superficially polite, he was always a bit stiff and frosty. He had the aura of someone who had had a bad situation foisted upon him. He

51

was not enamored of us as people—forget about our music. I felt a palpable sense of unease whenever he was in our presence—and perhaps jealousy as well, because a long-term company insider like myself was never supposed to cross the line from record company slave to record company artist. I had broken a cardinal unwritten rule.

We tried to brainstorm with Shershin to come up with an appropriate producer—somebody who might win both his and the label's support. Lenny Kaye, Mitchell Froom, Steve Addabbo, Mike Thorne, Hal Willner—all were suggested by him as potential producers. We met with most of them, but none seemed like the right fit to us.

One day, Julia and I went up to Westport, Connecticut, to meet Chris Frantz and Tina Weymouth, the former Talking Heads rhythm section who had recently scored a hit with their funk-rap project Tom Tom Club. They were Julia's friends—and this time something finally really clicked between us.

Those two really loved our stuff. In fact, I remember positively glowing when Chris asked who had come up with all the music for our songs. He and Tina pronounced themselves very impressed by the instrumental sophistication of our primitive home-studio demos. Unfortunately, they could only commit to doing half an album with us, since they were in the thick of trying to finish their next album. But half was better than none—and that was fine with us.

☐

In the meantime, I had been working a lot in the Netherlands since breaking through to European audiences at the Berlin Jazz Festival, and while touring my solo show there in December 1990 I took a tip from my Dutch friend Henk Tass, an all-around music maniac.

Henk suggested I seek out the legendary Jack Nitzsche, Phil Spector's longtime arranger and engineer, who was a producer and composer in his own right, having scored films like *One Flew Over The Cuckoo's Nest* and *Performance* and produced a number of classic records, including 'The Lonely Surfer' and Neil Young's first album. I remember calling Jack after I sent him a package of our demo tapes and hearing him drawl into the phone with his courtly Southern accent, "Ah really love your songs, maan ... they're byoootifull." He agreed to produce the other half of our debut album.

I was way over the moon. Now we had both Chris and Tina and Jack Nitzsche lined up to produce our debut: some incredible names and some very creative talents were ready to hop on board and get behind our work.

Columbia didn't exactly jump up and down at the prospect of Chris and Tina and Jack Nitzsche splitting the production chores, but we got a grudging green light from Shershin that it might possibly work out, provided we stay within our recording budget—about $150,000, which was a lot of money in those days.

We needed to get going soon. My own finances were pretty strapped, and my meager pension and employee investment fund didn't amount to very much after 13 years at CBS.

□

This is where Hal Willner entered the picture, with that fateful phone call one beautiful spring morning. Julia and I had spoken to Hal as a potential candidate to produce us when we were trying to get together a shortlist for Columbia, and while we hadn't settled on him, we had remained friends, and he had taken an interest in the ongoing gestation of our group.

By now, in March 1991, we had been under contract with Columbia for a year and a half with not one song officially committed to tape—and, in fact, we were a completely unknown quantity as a live act, since we'd done very few gigs since signing with CBS. I, on the other hand, had continued to work as a solo performer in Europe, where I was developing quite a cult following.

Julia and I were bickering on a daily basis, and the label was becoming increasingly impatient with "Chertoff's Folly," inherited in toto now that Rick had split from Columbia. Truth be told, I was at this point pretty fed-up with my musical partner and secretly dreamed of finding a male vocalist capable of executing a more rocked-out version of my more folky and blues-oriented songs than Julia was capable of.

I had been listening to a lot of Led Zeppelin, as well as The Doors and The Smiths, thinking I needed a male foil like this—a Robert Plant and a Jim Morrison and a Morrissey figure all rolled into one. A beautiful boy who could flat-out rock and not write preachy didactic lyrics—and the Devil take the hindmost.

It was at precisely this point that Hal called to invite Julia and me to perform at his Tim Buckley tribute concert at St Ann's Church—and to check out Tim's son, Jeff, as someone who might be good to collaborate with. Was Hal my deus ex machina, or was he the Devil in disguise? Either way, Hal was a good catalyst, forcing us to get off our butts in order to strut our stuff in a big public forum—and let the chips fall where they may.

It seemed a great opportunity to redeem ourselves and turn things around with the suits at CBS. In effect, the prospect of the show focused us on the idea of getting our act together, getting out on the boards in front of a large community of New York City music lovers and critics—plus (hopefully) some CBS reps—to showcase our new sound. Plus there was the added incentive of meeting and collaborating with this totally unknown mystery white boy called Jeff Buckley.

I immediately trawled through Tim Buckley's recorded repertoire to select an appropriate song for Julia and me to perform, and before long I had hit upon 'The River,' a dark, intense ballad from Tim's *Blue Afternoon*.

In light of the tragic fate that was to eventually befall Jeff in 1997, my attraction to this song has taken on very eerie overtones. I shudder to think about it, frankly, while writing this now. Yet it was only the first of many signposts along the way in the journey I will relate here that in hindsight seemed to foreshadow Jeff's early and untimely death.

In contemplating 'The River' as a great Tim Buckley song for us to perform at Hal's tribute, I knew I could overhaul it to best suit our individual strengths. I arranged it as a slow, seductive, swamp groove, utilizing open-tuned, tremelo'd, Pops Staples-type slide guitar, with my singer wailing siren-like at key junctures in the song. I also incorporated a bluesy fingerpicked motif I had been working on for an instrumental I provisionally had titled 'Stay Hard'—a motif that would eventually mutate into the main figure of the song Jeff and I wrote in early 1992 known as 'Harem Man.'

I brought my newly arranged version of 'The River' to Julia at her Soho loft and she agreed that the song would provide an excellent vehicle with which to showcase our duo at the Tim Buckley tribute show. As for what song I might work on with Jeff, Hal suggested on the phone that I take a look at 'The King's Chain,' from *Sefronia*.

On a brilliant blue-skied day a few weeks later, I took a taxi over the bridge to Brooklyn and alighted at St Ann's Church, an ornate 19th-century wood-and-stone complex whose main chapel boasts a balcony, a high vaulting ceiling, and shimmering stained glass windows that throw a sepulchral light on the dusty old chapel in the daytime.

In the space of a few short years, the church had become the preferred setting for cutting-edge music concerts, thanks to Arts at St Ann's, an organization run by two rabid music lovers, Susan Feldman and Janine Nichols, who had successfully convinced the church authorities to let them use the main altar space as a concert platform.

Together, Feldman and Nichols had produced a series of standout events, including a showcase for Lou Reed and John Cale's *Songs For Drella* project and a Marianne Faithfull concert subsequently issued as a live album entitled *Blazing Away*.

Hal Willner was involved as producer/impresario of the latter, and as Hal, Susan, and Janine were all huge Tim Buckley fans, this tribute concert in the making seemed a natural fit, complete with Hal's signature multi-artist casting and ironic juxtapositions of repertoire and singers.

I met up with Julia upon entering the church, and hung out in the foyer, a small room behind the main chapel, and we waited there with Hal and some of my compatriots from the downtown New York scene until it was our turn to rehearse.

I remember being introduced to Barry Reynolds, Marianne Faithfull's guitarist and songwriting partner, an Irishman with a twinkling eye and great sense of humor; bantering with drummer Yuval Gabay, who was later to form the band Soul Coughing; and greeting fellow avant-guitarists Elliot Sharp and Robert Quine, right-hand-man at the time of punk singer Richard Hell, who was also scheduled to perform at this concert.

I also exchanged pleasantries with Guitar Roberts, a minimalist duo consisting of guitarist Loren Mazzacane Connors and his singing partner Suzanne Langille, and G.E. Smith, the *Saturday Night Live* guitarist, who told me later that I was his favorite guitarist.

Then it was time to rehearse. I set up my effects and amplifier on the altar, got out my electric guitar, and started playing the main riff of the song. Julia locked into the groove and we swayed together as one to the deep rolling rhythm of 'The River.' The song had such hypnotic power—it required intense concentration on my part to play it forcefully and accurately. And as the music took over and became second nature to me, it felt as if time stood still. I only was aware of the inexorable pull of the primal groove of the music.

Unbeknown to me, somebody had crept into the building and was now ducked down, sitting in the pews, listening intently as we played.

After we finished the number, Hal pronounced himself very happy with our rendition. He knew it would be a highpoint of his show. Julia walked off to chat with her friend, the experimental singer Shelley Hirsch, who was also on the bill, and I stepped out into the hall behind the chapel to pack up my gear to leave.

Suddenly, this skinny, longhaired kid who had been lounging against the wall inside sprang forward to confront me, rolling and popping his eyes, intensely *vibing* me with his own personal voodoo. He looked electric, on fire—as if he was about to jump out of his own skin.

He was the very image of the young Tim Buckley—same sensual, red-lipped mouth, same sensitive, haunted, blazing eyes. He was a beautiful boy: so charismatic, so handsome, his chiseled face, both angelic and demonic.

This was obviously Jeff Buckley.

Chapter Two

He spoke first, in a soft but excited and intense high register:

"Hey man, I'm Jeff ... Jeff Buckley! And you're Gary Lucas! Really glad to know you—I'm a HUGE fan of yours—I read all about you in *Guitar Player*—I know your work, man! I LOVE what you did with Captain Beefheart—and I love what you were doing just now in there!"

Jeff gestured toward the chapel.

"Thanks, Jeff," I said. "You saw us rehearse?"

"Yeah, and it sounded REALLY cool," he replied, in a breathy, intimate tone, like he was confiding in me. "Listen ... can we get together soon and work on 'The King's Chain'? Do you know the song? From Tim's *Sefronia* album. Hal thought it would a really good number for us to do."

He was imploring me with big eyes, like a puppy dog.

"Sure. I know most of your dad's early work—I loved your Dad's stuff you know—but I've got to bone up on this one first. And I have to split now. Why don't you come by my apartment tomorrow after I've had a chance to work up an arrangement of this song? I live in the West Village, we can rehearse there."

"Cool! Sounds good."

Jeff smiled, dazzling me with a thousand-watt grin that lit up the gloomy church. Seducing everybody into his own personal orbit was very easy for him.

"How long are you in town for?" I asked.

"Dunno, not sure ... maybe just for this one show. Then I've got to go back to LA. I just came here to pay my respects to my dad—but you know, New York is SUCH a cool place."

I gave him my address and set up a meeting for the next day. I really liked the guy on first impression—what was not to like? He had such a sweet intensity. There was a touch of the ragamuffin orphan and the strange foundling about him—kind of like a young Heathcliff.

And I was really attracted to his wiry energy—he was so *on*, so present—burning with an electricity that was totally in the moment. His essential sweetness co-existed with an almost demonic intensity.

So, with those impassioned penetrating eyes alternately entreating and boring right through me, I felt compelled to ask him a very corny question, superstitious guitar magician that I am:

"So Jeff, uh—what's your sign?"

He smiled that disarming smile again.

"Scorpio—can't you tell?"

He had the reflexes and the lethal sting of the Scorpion all right—as I was to find out.

□

The next day, Jeff turned up promptly around noon at my West Village apartment. I'd done my homework, listened to 'The King's Chain' a few times, and figured out a killer arrangement I couldn't wait to try out on Jeff, who seemed totally open and respectful toward what I was going for.

My development as a guitarist had grown steadily since that first solo concert at the Knitting Factory. Three years down the line, after much daily practice, and I was on the cusp of cutting-edge virtuosity. And as my fingerpicking skills became more fluid and my aggressive, slashing electric-guitar chops evolved, I had delved deeper into the world of electronics—digital delays in particular. These functioned as mini-tape recorders with which I could achieve spacious, oceanic, almost orchestral effects in real time with just my guitar and my black boxes.

I had originally come from a folk-blues perspective—one of the earliest reviews of my playing with Captain Beefheart commented that I had "the folkiest accents since Ry Cooder." But I always loved rocking out in a totally ecstatic way. I loved to go for the Godhead every time. Couple that with my early love for electronic psychedelia in the order of Syd Barrett and Davy O'List—two mad UK guitar pioneers of the 60s—and you have an idea of some of the colors I like to fling on the sonic canvas. (You could say I was a major—although fairly unacknowledged—progenitor of the psychedelic New York freak-folk scene the world has come to know most recently through folks like Devendra Banhart and Jeffrey Lewis.)

So, as Jeff wandered around my apartment casually checking out the myriad albums and CDs in my collection, I sat in the chrome and black-vinyl armchair in the corner of my living room, from which I could commandeer the 16 effects pedals spread out before me, all wired up together—my effects arsenal.

I selected my trusty 1946 Gibson J-45 acoustic, which I had acquired a few years earlier on the advice of the late John Campbell, a white blues guitarist signed to Elektra who occasionally worked down in the Village at Matt Umanov's guitar store. John had sold it me as an instrument particularly well suited to playing "Greenwich Village blues."

I began to play an Indian-raga motif, all twisting bends and chromatic curlicues. The strings of my acoustic whined as this sinuous raga figure unfolded, and I leaned over, hit the "sample" button on one of my digital delays, set the melodic line looping endlessly, and then doubled the playback speed.

The room filled with a cascading waterfall of high-register chiming notes that sang and danced deliriously around us—and then turned inside out as I hit another switch to run the sped-up loop backward.

Jeff sat on the couch opposite me, watching intently, fascinated, as I began to strum the opening chords of 'The King's Chain' over the ambient loop texture. I handed him a mic and motioned for him to begin singing. He closed his eyes and honey poured forth:

I couldn't buy you with a hundred cattle
But you hike in shells and feathers up the African beach

Oh my God. I couldn't believe the otherworldly voice that was pouring out of this boy.

I am king here
Tied to this hut by the king's chain

All of a sudden, a full-throated wail—sounding very close to Tim Buckley at maximum throttle—was emanating from this waif-like apparition sitting across from me.

My power's like a tree ...

I sat entranced and barely registered my fingers gliding across the strings of my guitar. I was making the changes by remote control, so transfixed was I by the power of Jeff's performance.

This was way beyond mere imitation. Jeff was inhabited by the spirit of Tim Buckley.

And green taboo to me
The chameleon lies in your dusty fingers

I shook the dust off my fingers and continued playing, vibing Jeff all my prayers and love in a totally supportive way. I couldn't believe what I was hearing. The music we were producing together seemed to stop time.

And the blue flies circle your head like stars ...

What a beautiful image. And then:

Jump into me now
I must not see the water

In the light of subsequent events, I find this heartbreaking to recall.

Let me sip weakness
From your dark nipples

Jeff finished singing the lyrics to his dad's song—a hymn to Sefronia, the ancient African slave queen—with all the authority of the shaman within. I stepped on my Digital Metalizer pedal to take the song out with a fuzzed-out bluesy riff based on the orchestral line that ends the original recording.

From his innermost depths, Jeff let forth one primordial ululation after another. He was wailing, suspended in the void between purest suffering and total ecstasy, far beyond his father's lyrics now, speaking in an unknown tongue.

As I continued to play the almost Zeppelin-like riff, Jeff folded back into himself on the couch—a skinny, awkward, beautiful boy again—and gazed across at me with staring soulful eyes while my guitar loop faded out slowly.

I shook my head in disbelief and utter awe and amazement at his stellar vocal performance.

"Jeff," I said, "you're a total fucking star."

"Really?" he replied, shy and tentative. "Do you think so?"

"Absolutely."

Suddenly it became clear. Here, sitting before me, was the male lead singer I had been secretly longing for to complete my vision of Gods and Monsters. And I knew in my heart that my musical future lay not with the partner I was currently shackled to.

For months, I had been mulling over the idea of breaking off my non-starter of a creative partnership with Julia and replacing her with a soulful male vocalist. The Doors, Led Zeppelin, The Smiths—all were groups from different stages of rock history, but they were all founded on the classic formula of a compelling lead singer complemented by a guitar-hero partner and foil. Jimmy Page, Johnny Marr, Robbie Krieger—joined at the hip, if only for a moment, with Robert Plant, Morrissey, and Jim Morrison.

After witnessing Jeff's spectacular performance, I knew he had what it takes to join me in this kind of partnership.

"Hey man, let's head out for some lunch," I suggested, trying to contain my mounting excitement. "It's too nice a day to stay indoors."

□

After a ritual toke on my bong to seal our newfound friendship and shared musical exploration—and put us in the proper head—I took Jeff for lunch at the historic 19th-century White Horse Tavern on Hudson Street—the same landmark tavern where Dylan Thomas drank himself to death in the 50s, determined not to go gentle into that good night.

The White Horse had a great jukebox inside, which at one time featured the 'Ice Cream For Crow' single I'd recorded with Captain Beefheart. I'd spent a memorable afternoon there some years previously in the company of Don Van Vliet and the painter Julian Schnabel. Don loved the joint so much. His whole ethos, which he'd passed on to me, was "Rage, rage against the dying of the light!"

Jeff and I sat together at one of the outdoor picnic tables out front. What a magical afternoon. Basking in the warm city sunlight filtering through the leafy side streets of the West Village, it was one of those fecund spring days where you could almost feel the buds bursting forth and the trees throwing out new roots and shoots under the pavement.

Over an extended lunch of hamburgers and fries, we talked about everything and nothing—laughing and joking, relating our various life stories, bonding over our likes and dislikes and our similar

63

approaches to music-making. (We both believed in going for the Godhead.) We gossiped about the upcoming St Ann's concert, and Jeff, who was quite an accomplished mimic, did wicked impressions of everyone on the bill. We spoke of the quality of life in New York versus Los Angeles, where Jeff was presently living with his mom, working part-time as a clerk at the Magic Castle, a hotel with a magic theme that employed professional magicians.

Jeff told me he had studied for a while at the Guitar Center in LA, where he learned to play Yes and Led Zeppelin solos note for note. He mentioned various musicians he had hung out with in his attempts to get something going musically, including his buddy Chris Dowd of the ska-punk band Fishbone. He spoke of a childhood spent shuttling from town to town and school to school, up and down the state of California; how he had never really known his dad, except for a week they spent together when Jeff was eight years old.

Jeff had very mixed feelings on the subject of Tim—understandably so, since Tim had abandoned both Jeff and his mother—but in talking to Jeff, and of course later playing with him, it became quickly obvious that he really loved his dad's music—that he had studied it closely and intensely, and knew it inside out.

When I raised the topic of Gods and Monsters, Jeff told me how much he loved and admired the three bands I had mentioned to him as possible models of what I was contemplating going for to further develop the band. He was especially enthusiastic about The Doors. The Oliver Stone biopic was out on release at the time, and we both dug it, especially Val Kilmer's portrayal of Jim Morrison.

I recall describing the very strange feeling I had experienced in the movie theater when the actress playing the music critic and Wicca practitioner Patricia Kennealy fights with Jim over whether or not to she should abort the baby she's carrying by him. When Kennealy remarks how beautiful their baby would be, if born, Morrison replies: "Knowing me, it will either be a god or a monster."

I'd actually worked alongside Patricia Kennealy—she was the

assistant copy director at CBS Records in the late 70s, and also my friend. She used to sit for hours in her darkened office under a beautiful photograph of her lost husband, Jim, who she'd married in a secret Wiccan handfasting ceremony in 1970.

Naturally, this line of dialogue— which Patricia, who consulted on the film, swore was authentic—literally jumped out at me from the screen when I saw the Oliver Stone film. Hearing it in the darkened theater gave me an eerie sense of confirmation that yes, my instinct to re-fashion the band with a shamanistic male lead singer was the way forward.

"I love the name Gods and Monsters," Jeff said to me that afternoon at the White Horse. "And I'd love to sing with you."

It was music to my ears. Our creative partnership was born.

□

Jeff and I started to meet at my apartment on a regular basis to run over 'The King's Chain,' plus 'I Never Asked To Be Your Mountain' and 'Phantasmagoria In Two,' two songs Hal Willner had requested we perform with other musicians on the program.

Both songs were taken from Tim Buckley's magnum opus, *Goodbye & Hello*—an album I had cherished in my high school days, and the only album of Tim's to actually break into the Top 200 upon release in 1967. (Sadly, it had been all downhill for Tim from then on.)

At one of those first sessions together, I started playing a catchy, fingerpicked riff I had been developing for a while in open-E tuning. I had first provisionally entitled this instrumental 'Free At Last,' after the famous phrase from Martin Luther King's March on Washington speech—a phrase that had immediate relevance to me because when I composed the song I was actively contemplating a split from Julia.

In my solo performances in Europe during that period I had been playing it under the title 'They Can't Get It Up And I Can't Get It Down,' which described my frustrations with Columbia Records and their palpable lack of support for my recording project.

65

On one of my work tapes, recorded at home in the period between meeting Jeff and the St Ann's show, I shout out "Song for Rolo—or for Jeff Scott Buckley." Back then, I kept my DAT recorder and cassette recorder on a round table next to where I liked to sit and play—this was my guitar "workstation." I would switch on one or the other to record extemporaneous improvisations whenever the spirit moved me. I have a large collection of these tapes full of hundreds of what the Beach Boys' leader Brian Wilson has described as "feels"— mysterious, resonant motifs arising in the heat of the improvised moment on my guitar that might eventually become a building block of a major song.

In this instance, I shouted out Jeff's full name—that is how he was referring to himself professionally at this point—to help me remember where this particular song idea might be applied in the future.

As is apparent from the recording, I was not only thinking of replacing my female vocalist with Jeff but also toying with the idea of replacing her with Rolo McGinty, the Woodentops singer with whom I'd recorded one of my earliest song demos, 'Skin The Rabbit,' which had helped me get the deal with Columbia Records in the first place.

Jeff Scott Buckley loved this guitar music when I played it for him. (As far as his name was concerned, he told me that he was often known as "Scotty" at home.) When I launched into the song for the first time with Jeff present in my apartment, he immediately grabbed a microphone and started to improvise a wild blues vocal that complemented my guitar music perfectly. Fortunately, I had my cassette recorder to hand.

The tape starts with me grousing about my pet peeve at the time, CBS Records.

"I want to play extra songs, but CBS doesn't believe we should put more than ten."

"Fuck that shit!" Jeff replies supportively.

I was already contemplating out loud doing some extra songs with

66

Jeff beyond the ten mandated by the label on my projected Columbia Records album with Julia—except I hadn't broached this subject with her yet. One such song was the one I was about to record.

Then we begin.

The music starts and stops, breathes and sighs, slows down and cranks up again. Jeff starts improvising lyrics out of nowhere. He sings along with my guitar like an ancient bluesman, clapping along with the guitar at one point to suggest how the rhythm might go. "That's exactly what we need," I shout as we jointly explore and revel in the limitless possibilities of our new collaboration. By the end of this run-through, we had written our first song together.

Jeff dubbed our first joint effort 'Bluebird Blues.' The title seemed ironic, since neither the guitar nor the vocals are despairing at all (unlike most blues). Rather, the music exudes a joyous vibe—a celebration of the ease and grace we found ourselves blessed by, to be able to make music together so effortlessly and spontaneously.

Later on, in the thick of our early collaboration, we decided to record our new song more formally on my primitive DAT setup. Jeff sang into a mic plugged directly into one channel of the tape recorder, with a second mic picking up the sound of my guitar amp in the other channel. There was no other processing, no overdub capacity here—just a pure, live, two-track recording of our spontaneous combustion.

When we finished, after six or seven minutes of call-and-response improvising over my guitar changes, we listened back and heard pure magic. Despite some slow-downs where I had to stop and retune—I used light gauge strings on my acoustic, and sometimes pulled them out of tune by playing so hard—the tape ambles discursively into surprising and unexpected territory.

At one point, I summon up a real "ghost of electricity," as Bob Dylan put it—an eerie howl of feedback from my electrified Gibson J-45 acoustic that arises from nowhere and hovers in the room like a specter.

Near the end, I launch into a coda of the descending chords of 'The King's Chain,' the song that had brought Jeff and together in the first place, and after a nostalgic glance at this we segue triumphantly back into 'Bluebird Blues,' with Jeff blowing some very Dylan-esque harp.

In 'Bluebird Blues,' Jeff celebrated various unrequited loves and (mythical?) woman-troubles in the poetic metaphor of the blues, his voice swooping and soaring from angelic falsetto to raw, feral, Robert Plant-like alley-cat yowl. I always encouraged a love of Led Zeppelin in him; sometimes, in rehearsal, I would urge him: "More Robert Plant!"

This song came out as a blues, all right, but with an updated lyrical twist that was pure Jeff:

I have an angel, her eyes like the ocean blue
I have an angel, her eyes like the ocean blue
Well, someday that angel's gonna fly back home to you

He also touched upon our newfound friendship, and my predilection at the time for smoking pot:

Got this friend, his name's Gary
If he doesn't get his dope two times a day, things get crazy!

In concert a year later, at our legendary Gods and Monsters showcase at St Ann's, Jeff added an extra verse:

I went to the ocean
I wish I was as smart as you
I said I went to the ocean
I said I wish I was as smart as you
Don't need no woman for your bed
Nothing left to do

'Bluebird Blues' proved to me that Jeff was the godsend I'd been looking for—a creative partner to inspire me to feverish heights of playing and songwriting with his fantastic voice and innate musicality. To me, Jeff WAS music—he lived and breathed music. He was a stone natural; "a strange enchanted boy," in the words of the song by Eden Ahbez (aka "Nature Boy").

Looking back, it seemed that Jeff could do it all.

Besides his incredibly supple and haunting voice, which could move from a vulnerable and intimate whisper to a Wagnerian scream, he had a tremendous facility on the guitar—certainly not the result of his Guitar Center studies alone. And though he professed to be awed by my abilities in that area, and in the early days was content to relinquish the guitar and concentrate on singing, I was impressed whenever I caught him casually ripping through riffs by his favorite bands, such as Rush. (He was a bit embarrassed to admit to me, early on, that Geddy Lee & co were one of his favorite bands, probably because they held little cachet within the hip New York music scene he was slowly immersing himself in.)

Jeff was also very receptive to my overtures to him to form a band. I opened up to him right away about my dreams and always blurted out whatever was on my mind, which has been my mode since I was a boy.

By contrast, Jeff could be very guarded and sometimes silent to the point of appearing passive aggressive. He would transfix you with that brooding silent stare, and I would get a glimpse of the pain that ran deep within him. I could only guess how deep. He didn't like to open up that much.

I'd told Jeff of my frustrations and difficulties with my current singing partner, and how I wanted to put a new ensemble together that would take the music of the bands we loved and use that classic format as a template for making something new—a logical progression that would eschew mere re-creation of the sounds of the 60s and build on the past to take the unfettered energies of these bands into wilder, hitherto uncharted musical territory.

Fundamentally, however, we would still rock out—that was key, and was something I loved doing, right from my earliest demos with Rolo McGinty through the very first version of Gods and Monsters I put together in 1989. But the music I had been making with Julia was lacking the rock factor with a capital R.

I remember avidly reading Steven Davis's Led Zeppelin bio *Hammer Of The Gods* and Jerry Hopkins's book about The Doors, *No One Here Gets Out Alive*, and yearning for a shamanistic male lead singer who could catch that 60s spirit, kick it in the ass, and move it forward into the here and now—and beyond.

And now, through the divine intervention of the ghost of Tim Buckley, my pal Hal Willner, and the folks at St Ann's, such a figure had just walked into my life—just at the point I was beginning to despair of ever getting my Columbia Records project off the ground.

☐

By now, I had totally run out of patience with Julia. Despite our having lined up Jack Nitszche and Chris & Tina as our producers, she was beginning to put me down at any given opportunity, consciously or not.

When she saw Jeff and I run through 'The King's Chain' in rehearsal at St Ann's, she couldn't disguise her palpable disgust and jealousy over the way we worked so well together. Jeff's effortless vocals pointed up her own limitations in that department, and she asked me pointedly several times just who had suggested we start working together, implying an exclusive and proprietary claim on my services, and manifesting a very apparent envy at the way Jeff and I so harmoniously blended together.

Julia had ragged on me before—boasting at our somewhat lackluster showcase at the New Music Seminar the summer before about what will happen when "the folks get a glimpse of what I call 'comparative anatomy'"—that is, her (to her mind) superior, sexier physique in contrast to my implied diminished stage presence.

As a guest at my own solo show at the Knitting Factory the Saturday before the Tim Buckley tribute, she had been noticeably aloof, pointedly sitting near the stage, engrossed in reading a book and studiously ignoring my performance throughout my solo set— until the moment when I invited her onstage to sing a couple of the new songs we'd been working on, one of which was presciently entitled 'Body On The Bayou.'

This slight was the last straw, and I contemplated mentioning Jeff to the new head of Columbia A&R, David Kahne, as a potential new collaborator for me. With the departure of Rick Chertoff, no one left at the label seemed at all interested in what Julia and I were up to.

I was also virtually persona non grata with my former co-workers in the creative services department—even more so with my former marketing masters, whom I had serviced with a smile for so many years. They all seemed jealous that I had eluded their snares and was working outside Black Rock on a creative recording project for the company—one that they would eventually have to attempt to market.

I could anticipate the backstabbing knives already being sharpened for the inevitable kill and subsequent orgy of schadenfreude that was surely going to accompany the release of "Chertoff's Folly" when it eventually saw the light of day.

I made the mistake of coming back to Black Rock one day early on after we had been formally signed, and playing a cassette of some of our demos to Steve Berkowitz, a rotund, goateed hipster who was at that point a product manager for many of Columbia's artists. I'd worked with Berkowitz for a few years there and found his smug and arrogant manner extremely patronizing—once to the point of hurling a sheaf of copy in his face.

I hadn't seen Berkowitz for a year or so, but now I was back at Black Rock trying to win friends and allies in the hope of creating a hospitable environment for my new recording project. I thought he might be a potential ally—he did know something about hip music, after all—but I remember the gleam in his eye when he first caught wind of Julia's yodel wafting out of the speakers in his office.

He winced and made a face, followed by a sardonic remark—"Have fun"—that in effect reduced the project to the status of a joke. *This guy could wind up as our product manager*, I thought. *God help us.*

The writing was on the wall. With Chertoff gone, I had no real support left within the company. And the word was out there—among the folks who had heard dribs and drabs of our demos or who had actually bothered to check us out in one of our infrequent live performances—that my vocalist was a turkey.

In my experience, since first entering the music business 30-plus years ago, that's usually the way it goes in such a fetid, competitive cesspool as the record industry in New York. Too much begrudging by non-creative people ready to gleefully write you off for a loss without even bothering to listen to your music—particularly if they have not been directly involved with (or hold a stake in) the project.

And even those who *were* involved—well, consider the case of our new A&R liaison, Peter Shershin, who had never even once bothered to show up to one of our gigs, including the one on the Saturday night before the Tim Buckley tribute, where my bored singer pointedly read a book throughout my solo performance.

I had recurring dreams in this period of sitting captive on an airplane that kept taxiing down an endless runway that—despite many attempts to take off and fly—could not actually lift off more than a few feet into the air before coming back to hit the tarmac with a thud. What a perfect metaphor for my Columbia project.

Dreading the inevitable denouement, and sensing a palpable aura of failure that seemed to hang over the project like a cloud, I began to think that maybe telling Shershin and Kahne about Jeff might not be such a bad thing at all. But I didn't know how to do so without feeling like I had betrayed my partner.

The decision was taken out of my hands during the week of the St Ann's tribute to Tim Buckley after I received a call from Kahne's secretary, summoning me to a meeting to discuss the state of the project. It was my first contact with Kahne since he'd assumed command of the A&R department.

I asked the secretary when Kahne wanted us to meet him.

"This Thursday at 3pm," she replied, "and David says he only wants to meet with you."

That sounded ominous—or maybe promising. Either way, I was going to check it out. All the performers involved in the Tim Buckley concert had been rehearsing their numbers in and out of Context Studios in the East Village all week, but Thursday was a day off.

Kahne was friendly but brusque when I arrived at the appointed hour to be ushered into his office (Rick Chertoff's old digs). I had met him briefly at the CBS Records Convention in Vancouver a couple years earlier, when he was a Columbia staff producer, and found him to be quite intelligent, with a dry sense of humor—a maverick and a loner like me, in fact. He was not exactly a company man.

"I've listened to your demos," he began, scooping up a cassette of our work given to him by Shershin and holding it in the air. "It's weird."

He put the cassette back down on his desk and saw my face fall a mile.

"Just kidding," he said.

"Yeah, as weird as Fishbone," he added, Fishbone being a quirky LA ska-punk band he'd produced.

He smiled back at me.

"Honestly, Gary, I am not, shall we say, in love with your singer's voice. I really don't think a whole record of her singing will work."

"You do know that when I originally signed with Rick I had a whole three-ring circus onstage with Matthew Sweet and a rapper and a scratcher—but Rick's vision for a record was me and Julia," I said. "He insisted I co-write with her too."

I asked him if he had ever heard the demos I'd originally recorded with Rolo McGinty.

"Yes," he replied. "Good stuff."

"I'm also working now with this fantastic young singer Jeff

Buckley, the son of Tim Buckley—we're playing tomorrow night, in fact, at a tribute show to his dad."

"Yes, Peter told me," he replied. "Listen, this project that I inherited from Chertoff—it's going to cost way too much money to record it in its present shape. I heard about your producer choices. Interesting, but honestly—can't you get Julia to sing just one or two songs on it, maximum? We can use your demos with Rolo and whatever else you have to round out the album ... maybe use this kid Jeff Buckley on it as well ... let's go back to your original multiple-singers format. But we need to finish this record as cheaply as possible. No outside producers. Produce it yourself."

"But the contract calls for a designated $150,000 recording budget ..."

"You do want to keep making records, don't you?"

This was a threat but also a carrot. It was obvious that as soon as Rick was out of the picture, the company had written off the project. And Kahne did not seem at all concerned about upholding the terms of our recording contract. He was obviously under the gun to minimize expenditures as much as possible on the hot potato that had been thrust into his lap. Still, to be fair, he felt honor-bound to have an album come out in one shape or another.

"How am I going to get Julia to agree to this?" I asked. "She'll never go for it."

"Have you ever considered a career as a copywriter? Just kidding."

The meeting was over.

I walked out of the building thinking I had possibly stumbled into a fate worse even than being stuck with Julia. She had already made it clear to me that she was planning her own solo album—in her mind, anyway—once we got this joint effort out of the way.

If Kahne had his way, our album was now going to be a sonic hodge-podge of different singers and tracks recorded in different phases of my career, old tracks mixed in with new ... if Julia even went for it. And that was a mighty big if.

With a vastly reduced budget, I was not going to get the A-level production treatment I was shooting for when I started writing avant-pop songs in the first place, in the hopes of reaching the widest audience possible. Songs that would need the kind of high-tech sparkle necessary to get played on the radio.

Racked with doubts about the wisdom of meeting with Kahne at all—never mind meeting him without Julia present—and troubled by his mandate to record the album on the cheap, which implied a drastic curtailment of the budgetary funds promised in our contract, I decided not to mention any of this to Julia until after the Tim Buckley tribute concert.

□

Friday April 26 1991 dawned a brilliant, warm spring day.

As I made my way by taxi over the Brooklyn Bridge to St Ann's for our 1pm soundcheck, I reflected on the events of the past few days and then put them out of my mind, determined to play my ass off and deliver a standout performance at the concert that night. That was all that mattered.

Jeff was already there. He might have crashed in Julia's loft space the night before; I know that he stayed there once. He was doing his typical vagabond number in New York, and it was hard for anyone to resist his entreaties for temporary shelter when he trained his penetrating eyes on them.

Jeff and I ran through our number, and 'The King's Chain' never sounded better. I remember Julia emitting a gleeful chortle and grinning mockingly at me when Jeff came to the line:

And the blue flies circle your head like stars

It was as if Tim's lyric was describing me personally.

Shortly after that, Richard Hell, the former Television and Heartbreakers bassist and one-time leader of The Voidoids, came bounding into the rehearsal room wearing a T-shirt with the phrase "Acid Trash" written on it in bold letters. He had a permanent sneer on his big ugly mug, and he trained it on Jeff and I as we finished our run-through. I guess our performance was too soft and sensitive for his hard-boiled punk sensibility.

Hell's former Heartbreakers cohort and ex-New York Dolls guitarist Johnny Thunders had OD'ed three days earlier, and with Willner's blessing, Hell was going to quickly rehearse his junkie anthem 'Chinese Rocks,' written with Thunders and Dee Dee Ramone, in order to segue into it in the concert right after his cover of 'Jungle Fire,' from Tim Buckley's *Blue Afternoon* album.

Over in another corner of the rehearsal room were the attractive vocalist Suzanne Langille and her boyfriend, avant-guitarist Loren Mazzacane Connors, who performed together under the name Guitar Robert. They were doing an arid minimalist rendition of a Tim Buckley song—a vapor trail of plinks and plunks and random notes that just hung there in the atmosphere. Loren looked like he was in another time zone from his partner, hunched over in his seat, disjunctive guitar noise emanating at a glacial pace from his amp, while Suzanne gamely sang the original melody line with a pure tone and almost classical delivery. It was an interesting effort, in contrast to what everyone else was doing, but it didn't really cohere at that dress rehearsal as either compelling music or performance art.

I noticed Jeff stealing longing glances at a young intern/usher named Rebecca Moore, whom he had a crush on. Several times that day, I saw him lost in deep conversation with her. A performance artist and singer herself, and the daughter of a prominent leader of the Fluxus avant-garde art movement, Moore would quickly take on the role of Jeff's designated New York girlfriend—for a season, anyway.

I also noticed, and spoke with, another young female intern, Gisburg, the girlfriend of keyboardist Anthony Coleman. Anthony was to open the program by playing a solo version of one of Tim's songs on the St Ann's pipe organ, high up in the church loft. Gisburg, who told me she was an avant-garde singer herself, seemed smitten with her beau. Many years later Gisburg was to sing on one of my best-regarded albums, *The Edge Of Heaven*, a tribute to 30s Chinese pop.

During the soundcheck, tempers flared as various downtown egos—which are some of the biggest in the world—rubbed up against each other. At one point, I heard the voices of avant-guitarists Robert Quine and Elliot Sharp rise angrily as they exchanged words over God knows what—probably who had a bigger dick in the petty avant-guitar scene.

Quine ended up stalking off the pulpit/stage in a temperamental fit, loudly proclaiming Sharp "a total charlatan." He then repeated the insult for the benefit of the assembled musicians waiting their turn to soundcheck: "He's a total charlatan." Oy vey.

I left in mid-afternoon to go home and change, and then returned to the beautiful church around 7pm, just as the sun was setting. Outside in the street in front of the church I ran into Hal, holding his head in his hands and muttering to himself and some other people involved in the show, including the artistic director of St Ann's, Susan Feldman, and program director Janine Nichols.

"I had to do it," he said. "I just had to do it."

"Do what?" I asked.

"I just axed Suzanne and Loren from the bill," he replied. "Did you hear their soundcheck today? Horrible—just horrible. They'll sink the show." Quel scandale!

Inside the rehearsal space, I found Loren forlornly packing away his gear with his usual mournful hangdog look about him. Suzanne was near tears. I tried to console her—I felt really bad for them, getting dismissed right before curtain time, and I told her so.

"I can't believe this is happening," she said. "After all the work we've put in, the rehearsals … I'm sure Tim Buckley probably got rejected just like this in his career, too."

My heart went out to them. Cutting them from the bill at the 11th hour seemed very cruel and arbitrary. What a tawdry shallow world is showbiz, behind the scenes and up close.

It wasn't my first taste of this, and it was definitely not going to be my last. But this was the world I'd chosen to live in. It was nobody's fault but mine.

□

I glanced at the program notes in the booklet for the show.

JEFF SCOTT BUCKLEY (guitar/voice) When I was six, I found my grandmother's old six-string guitar in a closet. I loved the thing. My mother, who was a classically trained pianist/cellist, was married (at the time of the guitar-find) to an auto mechanic, Ron, with amazingly right-on taste in music. Our house was always jumping with sound: Bach, Chopin, Gershwin, Beatles, Zeppelin, Hendrix, Nat 'King' Cole. The auto-mechanic eventually found the woman he loved, and he and my mom divorced. My mom began to tell me more about my father, Tim, and when I was eight, she decided we should meet each other. The only other time I saw him was when I was two years old. I got to see him play at the Golden Bear and met him face-to-face backstage. I spent Easter vacation with him, his wife, and their adopted son. They had an apartment in Santa Monica, and I stayed for a week, a really good time. Somehow, in between my visit and Tim's death, we lost touch with him and Judy, and I never saw Judy again until '88.

I got my first electric guitar at 13. Left home for LA at 17, spent some time in a so-called music school, went on the road with some reggae acts. Escaped to NYC in '90 for about seven months; got into hardcore and Robert Johnson. Went back to LA, did a demo of some of my songs. I got a call from Carole King after she heard my stuff through a mutual friend, very cool.

We wrote a track together. More to come. Right now my band is almost complete. I'm showing up at club jams around town trying out new songs. My life is now complete and utter chaos.

This was more information than Jeff had hitherto revealed to me—especially the last bit, about coming to New York in 1990. We generally just talked about our day-to-day life and jammed music, music, music in our encounters in my apartment.

Under my name, it was written:

GARY LUCAS (guitar) Dubbed "Guitarist of 1000 Ideas" by the *New York Times* and "Guitarist Extraordinaire" by *Ear Magazine*, Gary Lucas first cut his teeth as featured guitar soloist with Captain Beefheart & The Magic Band in the early 80s. After producing albums for The Woodentops and Adrian Sherwood, Lucas began performing solo concerts at the Knitting Factory in NYC, and now tours frequently in Europe as a solo artist. His debut solo album, *Skeleton At The Feast*, which includes his music for the 1921 German silent film *The Golem* (performed at the 1989 New Music America/Next Wave Festival) will be released shortly on Enemy Records. He is currently working on an album with singer/video-artist Julia Heyward for Columbia Records.

Some factual inaccuracies had crept into my biography—I had played on, but never produced, albums by The Woodentops and Adrian Sherwood, and *The Golem* was actually made in 1920. The "debut solo album" mentioned therein, meanwhile, was the result of a compromise I had made with the Columbia Records A&R department.

Impatient with the slow progress of my recording deal with Julia, I had appealed to Shershin and the CBS legal department to allow me to get some kind of album release out into the world that represented my live solo-guitar show, with which I had been

79

barnstorming for some years in Europe (without Julia). They agreed, provided the album came out in Europe only, on an indie label, and consisted solely of live instrumental recordings. So I had struck a quickie deal with Michael Knuth, a German-American music sharpie who had started a label called Enemy Records a few years previously with the producer/bassist Bill Laswell.

Knuth and Laswell had had a parting of the ways, with Knuth retaining the rights to the Enemy catalogue, which basically consisted of recordings by Laswell's band Last Exit and the avant-jazz guitarist Sonny Sharrock. Now Knuth was looking to build up his label by signing the cream of New York City's avant-rock and jazz musicians.

I had been in a dialogue with him for a few years, initially with the idea of Enemy releasing my early recordings with Rolo McGinty. Knuth also really loved 'King Strong,' my furious Gods and Monsters mk1 instrumental. Then the Columbia deal came along, and I shelved the idea of releasing an album on Enemy, never once wavering in my belief that my music was worthy of the major-label treatment.

Now, however, two years had sped by under the Columbia contract without a note being recorded, and with my profile as a solo artist growing in Europe and much praise appearing in the press, I felt compelled to get some kind of recorded product out in the world to capitalize on this activity. So, when Columbia allowed me to seek an indie label for this project, I went back to Knuth and made a deal for *Skeleton At The Feast*.

On the night of the Tim Buckley show, I brought copies of the album along with me—hot off the press—and presented one to Julia before the show. She seemed to be in total shock when she learned I had aced her by finally getting a real record out under my own name.

In retrospect, the title of the album, *Skeleton At The Feast*—a catchphrase of the English painter and author Wyndham Lewis, from his 1927 essay 'Inferior Religions,' which appeared in *The Wild Body*—would take on an uncomfortable resonance for both Julia and me later down the line.

As the lights went down in the packed church, with folk crammed into the balconies right up to the rafters—and no sign of our A&R guy, Peter Shershin, of course—I mingled with the other musicians backstage, keeping tabs on my partners for the night, Jeff and Julia, and occasionally sidling out into the church to watch the pageant unfold. The three of us weren't scheduled to come on until the second half.

Arch-conceptualist Willner began *Greetings From Tim Buckley* by playing in the darkness a rare tape he had located of Tim speaking "from beyond the grave"—a public service radio announcement he had recorded in the 60s to endorse the Army Reserve.

"This is Tim Buckley," it began. "You know, the Army Reserve pays in a lot of ways—it pays for every meeting in each two week summer camp that you attend, extra money you can use in a lot of ways, and you get the chance to further your present skills and learn new ones—a chance that can really pay off in your civilian career."

Or, in the words of the anonymous 60s rock group harmonizing at the top and close of the spot, "It pays to go to meetings / In the Army Reserve." I had a frisson, then, in the holy sepulcher of St Ann's, of the moment I learned about Tim's OD over the Armed Forces Network in Taiwan, all those years ago.

Willner followed this with Marius Constant's well-known four-note *Twilight Zone* motif—signaling, I guess, that the musicians present would be channeling the spirit of Tim that night. Wooooooooooh! And then it was on into the first number: an instrumental ensemble version of Tim's 'Strange Feelin'' led by Anthony Coleman.

The first half flew by in a blur. I didn't pay all that much attention to the comings and goings onstage; I was consumed by the tension and anticipation of performing, but I do remember Richard Hell interpolating 'Chinese Rocks' into his set and then bounding off smugly into the night. (I still got nervous in those days, but nowadays it's more like, "When can I start playing?")

After an intermission, and some last-minute backstage chatter and bucking up of one another, Coleman led off the second half with a strange atonal organ interlude. Gradually, *Saturday Night Live* pianist and guitarist Cheryl Hardwick and G.E. Smith, cellist Hank Roberts (with whom I had first worked when I produced Tim Berne for Columbia), bassist Greg Cohen (from Tom Waits's band), and finally Jeff and I climbed up onto the darkened stage and plugged in.

The lights came up, and the crowd gasped as they got their first look at Jeff—the spitting image of the youthful Tim Buckley.

We launched into 'I Never Asked To Be Your Mountain,' a pounding, oceanic, ecstatic cri de coeur from Tim's *Goodbye & Hello*. Jeff furiously strummed his acoustic while I produced swooning seagull cries and whispers from my guitar using a glass bottleneck and my delay pedal, counterpoised against the whirlwind of sound whipped up by the ensemble.

Jeff started to sing, the lights threw his shadowed profile on the wall behind us, and the crowd went quietly berserk. I studied the faces I could pick out in the audience and watched their reactions intently as we played. It was obvious the majority of folk present were totally focused on, and transfixed by, Jeff Buckley.

And how ironic that his first utterance at his first major appearance in New York was a lyric that seemed to call into question his whole relationship with his father, an obviously troubled love/hate relationship—just as Tim's song had originally called into question his relationship with Jeff's mother and their young son.

Listening back now to my tape of Jeff's coming-out at St Ann's, I can easily see and hear him singing this song again, but this time, he is addressing the words directly to me:

I never asked to be your mountain
I never asked to fly

And there is this:

I'm drowning back to you
I can't swim your waters, and you can't walk my lands
And I'm sailing all my sins and I'm climbing all my fears
And soon now I'll fly

The song ended to deafening applause. Jeff and company trooped offstage; I remained up there and Julia came out to join me. I quickly adjusted my guitar tuning, hit the tremolo'd slide intro figure, and brought forth the deep waters of 'The River.'

In the middle of this gutbucket blues, Julia unleashed her glottal cuckoo impression—like one of those whistles with a miniature bird perched on the end that warbles and changes pitch as you blow through the opening and press the tail down. And as we spun our spooky swamp trance, St Ann's momentarily morphed into a dense, moss-covered bayou.

We received much applause from the crowd. It was a high point of the show for sure. And then Julia left the stage.

Jeff came back out in the darkness. I started up the looped acoustic raga figure that introduced 'The King's Chain,' and suddenly it was just Jeff and me, united together. He began to sing:

I couldn't buy you with a hundred cattle

It felt so good to be up there, alone together, right up front with Jeff. It felt like two kids playing together with building blocks of music. Total ecstasy.

Just as we'd rehearsed, I wrapped up the song with a fuzzed-out guitar line mirroring the bluesy orchestral vamp that closes the song on *Sefronia*. My soaring, dizzying guitar loop faded away, and we went off the stage to massive applause.

Backstage, Jeff and I hugged each other, and I hugged Julia too—it was one big love-fest for a moment.

Jeff, Julia, and I went back out later to perform 'Phantasmagoria

In Two,' joining an ensemble that featured Greg Cohen; Barry Reynolds and Chris Cunningham from Marianne Faithfull's band; and avant-garde vocalist Shelley Hirsch. I played minor-key soulful acoustic slide lines that swooped and curled around these sad, urgent voices—first Jeff, then Barry, then Julia, then Shelley—as the vocalists traded verses and united in close harmony on the choruses:

Everywhere there's rain, my love
Everywhere there's fear...

And then the flashbulbs started popping.

Off the stage again, and Jeff was absolutely on fire backstage, stalking the wings defiantly with his acoustic guitar, so eager to go out again and perform, jumping out of his skin like the first time we met.

He charged back onstage with his acoustic to sing 'Once I Was' by himself as an encore. He tore the place apart, singing and playing with such an intensity that he broke a string in the process—singing with a conviction and authority far beyond his years, inhabited not only by the ghost of Tim but by a mysterious ancient everyman soul that poured forth from him like purest honey.

And sometimes I wonder
Just for a while
Will you remember me?

The love in the room was palpable. People could not believe what they were witnessing and hearing. Heads were shaking in dumbstruck awe, smiles spreading everywhere.

And then Jeff left the stage again, and the ironic, post-modern impresario Hal Willner played Henry Mancini's famous *Moon River* theme over the PA as the audience slowly filed out of the church into the balmy Brooklyn night.

What did this schmaltzy film music have to do with Tim Buckley?

Not a whole lot, other than the fact that, yes, Tim was a dreamer who was "after that same rainbow's end"—just like everyone else on the planet.

I wondered if Hal had deliberately chosen this song to undercut the power of our performance of 'The River'—to take us down a peg or two. He seemed jealous and annoyed about our Columbia Records deal after we had passed on him as producer and had made a few put-down remarks in passing.

To this day, I do not understand him using this song as a capper on what had been a great night of music. I remember thinking something was very off as the audience left the church.

In the light of Jeff's subsequent drowning, Hal's choice of 'Moon River' to close the show is one more ominous momento mori that haunts me still, all these years on—a chronicle of a death foretold.

□

The weekend passed in a blur.

I was psyched more than ever about the possibilities of working with Jeff—he was so great and so strong at the St Ann's show. Everyone who had played and seen him perform was buzzing about him, including my wife. He seemed like just the guy to draft in to my Columbia album project, to rescue it from certain disaster. But how would I tell Julia what was going down with Columbia? She was not going to take kindly to having a severely diminished role in the album.

On Monday morning, I got a copy of the *New York Times*, which contained a glowing review of the show by Stephen Holden that mentioned everybody. There was a big photo of Julia, Jeff, and me performing 'Phantasmagoria In Two' in the early edition of the paper. By the afternoon edition, I had been mysteriously cropped out. Bummer!

I called Shershin, who of course hadn't bothered to turn up on Friday night. I had a lunch date scheduled that afternoon with Jeff and Danny Fields, a bitchy and loveable music business veteran and friend—a legendary publicist, talent scout, and manager who had worked with Jim Morrison and Nico, and who had discovered and managed the MC5, the Stooges, and the Ramones. Danny had a burning desire to meet Jeff, the "beautiful boy son" of Tim, whom Danny had worked with as a publicist at Elektra Records in the 60s.

I figured I could then bring Jeff across the street to CBS to meet Shershin, and maybe introduce him to David Kahne as well—to at least let them get a look at this possible addition to my recording project with Julia. Shershin said it was cool to stop by after lunch.

At around 12:30pm, Jeff showed up at my apartment. We exchanged greetings and hugs—he was elated about the concert review in the *Times*. We shot uptown in a taxi for our rendezvous with Danny Fields.

Jeff started talking to me in the cab about the demos he had been working on in LA—how he was so sick and frustrated by the insular, backbiting LA music scene. This was a recurring refrain whenever he allowed himself to open up and reveal his vulnerable side. He seemed really bummed out over his various unsuccessful attempts to fashion a career in music there.

Apparently, the reaction he got from his "buddies" was along the lines of: "You suck, and the only reason people are interested in you at all is because of your father." It didn't sound like a very supportive and nurturing milieu. With friends like these …

Now, however, Jeff was brimming with hope that the St Ann's show—and the attendant press exposure—would open doors and give him just the boost he needed. I commiserated with him about the LA scene, and pointedly reminded him that I had an ongoing deal with Columbia—and that he could possibly share in it. Which is why I was bringing him up to Black Rock after lunch to meet with the A&R guys. Jeff leaned over in the back seat of the cab and started straightening my collar and brushing invisible dandruff off my shoulders.

Entering the warm, expansive interior of Bombay Palace on 50th Street—one of my favorite Indian restaurants—we encountered the animated, ironic Danny Fields sitting with an older man who turned out to be Donald Lyons, a theater critic and veteran of the Warhol Factory scene. They oohed and ahhed when I introduced them to Jeff, marveling at how much he looked like his father, whom they both had known.

Danny, who had attended the tribute, launched into tales of working with Tim; Jeff basked in their attentions. He told them his name was Jeff Scott Buckley, but his friends and family sometimes called him Scotty. When Jeff left to go to the men's room, mid-meal, Danny turned to me and rolled Jeff's nickname over his tongue in delight. "Scottttttty." Jeff had won their affection in a big way.

After lunch, Jeff and I made our way across 52nd Street. I took Jeff into Black Rock, whose hallowed precincts I had not so long ago vacated. We zoomed up the elevator to the 12th floor Columbia Records offices, and then down the softly lit, carpeted corridor to Shershin's office.

Shershin began by apologizing for missing our concert, and I told him that yes, it had been a great night, and that I was really getting so much of a creative charge working with Jeff that I thought he might make a good addition to our long-stalled album project—maybe as a special featured guest?

I left the question hanging, as I didn't know how much Kahne had discussed with Shershin, or whether it had come up at all—and, frankly, I wasn't sure how much Peter was on my side vis-à-vis Julia. So I introduced Jeff and let them get acquainted.

After a few minutes of small talk, Peter put in a call to Kahne's office, but Kahne evidently wasn't around. Jeff and I got up to take our leave and I thanked Peter for his time.

As we waited by the elevators, Kahne came barreling out of his office with his hand outstretched for Jeff to shake. Apparently he had seen the *Times* that day.

Jeff then pointedly glared at Kahne and pulled his own partially outstretched hand back abruptly, as if he had been planning to shake hands with Kahne but then thought better of it. Kahne was astonished by his action—as was I.

The elevator door opened and Jeff ducked inside, turning his back on the both of us. I threw a helpless, commiserating glance at Kahne and then followed Jeff into the elevator. The doors closed, and we were alone. Going down.

"Why didn't you shake his hand, Jeff?" I asked. "That was so rude."

"He fucked with my friends Fishbone," he replied disgustedly. "Chris Dowd punched him out in the studio. I'm not going to shake that guy's hand."

"Jesus, Jeff—he's my A&R man. He's very powerful. I thought the idea was for you to meet him to get you performing on my album."

We rode down to the lobby in silence and then went our separate ways. I was livid, but wary of engaging more with Jeff at this point. I didn't want to harm our burgeoning relationship.

What a flake. I thought Jeff knew what was at stake, and he knew the drill—he'd agreed to come along with me to meet Kahne—but had thumbed his nose at the both of us, with impunity, at the last moment. Why?

I knew then for the first time—but certainly not the last—that working with Jeff was not going to be easy.

Creatively? Yes. Business-wise? No.

This was my first taste of Jeff's mercurial and temperamental side. A hard road lay ahead, as far as working and playing with Jeff Buckley was concerned, but a road that would lead to the creation of some of the most gorgeous, enduring songs of all time.

Songs we wrote together that will be spinning around the planet long after the road runs out for me, and I meet up with Jeff again on the other side ...

Chapter Three

The next week sped by quickly.

I didn't talk much with Julia, or rehearse with her. After the meeting with Kahne, I felt that my partnership with Julia was most likely not long for this world, so I concentrated on maintaining my bond with Jeff.

In the meantime, I was invited to play solo on an NPR taping for a show hosted by John Hockenberry, the paraplegic Vietnam vet and political activist. My friend Nick Hill, a DJ on the alternative station WFMU in New Jersey, had arranged my appearance on the show. He'd already had Julia and I out to perform on his show *Live At The Music Faucet* at the station's funky house/studio in East Orange, New Jersey—and he would prove to be inextricably entwined in my later dealings with Jeff.

Hockenberry's show was recorded at WNYC FM's studios at 1 Center Street in Lower Manhattan, and at the taping I was introduced to his other musical guest that day, the handsome and rakish Australian singer Nick Cave, whom I first got to know on record through his original Beefheart-influenced band, The Birthday Party. Now he had a new band, The Bad Seeds, and was in town to promote the publication of a book he had written, *And The Ass Saw The Angel*, a neo-Faulknerian Southern Gothic novel crossed with a soupçon of Flannery O'Connor and a pinch of William Burroughs.

Nick was extremely friendly and suggested I accompany him on my National steel bottleneck guitar during a reading from his book on the show, which pleased both of us. It sounded good, too, and I made a note to stay in touch with this guy, especially as he mentioned he was considering moving to New York with his young Brazilian bride, a beauty named Viviane Carneiro.

That Friday, May 3, Jeff came over and we did a run-through of 'Bluebird Blues' onto DAT. Listening to the playback, it felt strong and righteous. Jeff was a wonderful creative partner for me. With his lightning fast interpretive and improvisational reflexes, multi-octave voice, and smoldering sensual good looks, he was destined to be a major player in music—of that I had no doubt. His pedigree alone spoke volumes. It was in his genes—his whole life he had been preparing for the moment when he could bust out and show the world what he was made of.

Jeff had mentioned to me briefly the time he'd put in at the Musician's Institute in LA, formally honing his skills, and hanging out at the Guitar Center, where he learned rote versions of classic rock songs by Yes and Led Zeppelin. He could reel off note-for-note solos by Rush, who he had already sheepishly admitted were one of his favorite groups—sheepishly as he knew Rush was not a hip name to drop in downtown hipster Manhattan. (He was right.)

At this last session together at my house, I handed Jeff my Strat and he played me one of his favorite Rush tunes, reveling in the bloated prog-rock arrangement, which immediately revealed his technical skill on the guitar.

Jeff handed the guitar to me, and I dived into a freeform improvisation that touched on the psychedelic blues side of my musical palette. I then offered the guitar back to Jeff, but he waved it away.

"No, man ... I just want to hear YOU play."

I was touched. I knew he was studying my playing and soaking up as much of my technique and ideas as he could, but I felt really good about being a mentor to him. I took pride in the fact that he had called me out at St Ann's as *the* guy he wanted to work with; that he had responded so enthusiastically to my roots, which marked me in his eyes as an exceptional musician who had undergone a baptism of fire by playing with Don Van Vliet.

I felt a keen desire to share with Jeff as much knowledge and rock history as I could in order to help kick-start his musical evolution and make him my ideal counterpart in Gods and Monsters—at this point still a concept waiting to emerge, butterfly-like, from its cocoon, while Julia and I played out the death throes of our professional and creative relationship.

At age 24, Jeff was living a beaten-down existence in the music community of Los Angeles—or, at least, he had yet to connect with the right people, folks who might enable him to rise up out of the murky club scene.

He spoke of repeated attempts to get a band going out there, whether by re-inventing as everything from a jazz-fusion virtuoso in a shortlived band called Group Therapy to playing the punky neo-B-boy in another pick-up ensemble. He mentioned hanging around with Chris Dowd of Fishbone, and he had a friend named Carla who was connected to Prince's protégés, Wendy & Lisa.

But the fact remained that the four-song demo tape he had made in LA in 1990, which he called *The Babylon Dungeon Sessions*, and which was financed by Tim's old manager Herbie Cohen, was to date the first and only full-blown recording of Jeff singing his own songs—and it had not started any fires in LA.

It seemed that he was surrounded by people who scorned his background, if they even recognized his lineage at all—the type of phony friends who would tell him to his face repeatedly that he sucked. It seemed the only reason people were interested at all in him—people like Herbie Cohen—was because of his dead father.

Coming to New York to play the Tim Buckley tribute was an attempt on Jeff's part to get things going for himself, musically, in a fresh environment. And hooking up with me seemed an attractive proposition to him.

Convinced that Jeff was destined to be the singer to front Gods

91

and Monsters, I talked to him about signing on to the project as soon as my situation with Julia was resolved.

◻

On Monday May 6, the shit hit the fan.

Somehow Julia had got word that Kahne wanted to reduce her role on the album, and she phoned him up at his office to talk with him directly about it. She then called me, livid.

"*What do you mean* they only want me to sing two songs on the album?" she said. "We have a contract with them as a duo."

"Yes of course," I replied, trying to reason with her, "but they're the ones holding all the cards. Unfortunately ..."

"I can't believe this. I'm going to take this up with my lawyer."

The biggest insult, as far as Julia was concerned, was the idea of sharing space on the record with Rolo McGinty, now that Kahne was urging me to use my demos with the Woodentops singer to flesh out his vision of a scaled-down album.

We finished our tense conversation without any clear-cut resolution, and I had no idea how this situation was going to play itself out. I thought it best to keep schtum, as they say, and stay as far away from the situation as possible.

Meanwhile Jeff was about to head back to LA, with the tape of 'Bluebird Blues' among his possessions. We had one last get-together at my apartment before he left. We hugged and vowed to stay in touch. I felt sure we'd be working together again soon, one way or another.

◻

On Tuesday May 7, I was invited to go into the studio and play on several cuts on an album Rick Chertoff, my original rabbi at Columbia, was now producing for his new discovery, the ballsy rock singer Sophie B. Hawkins. Although Rick had moved on to greener pastures at Polygram, he was still the designated producer for Sophie's Columbia album.

When I arrived at the session, at Messina Music on 45th Street, Rick greeted me warmly. Then, once Sophie was out of earshot, he asked, "So how's it going with you and Julia? You are going to make that album with her, aren't you?"

No comment.

"If I were you, I'd try and make a 'quick' album."

Rick looked at me sternly. He had no doubt heard rumors of my ongoing feud with Julia, and he thought I should do the right thing here and honor the commitment I had made to her (and to him) to see the project through as originally contemplated. But for me, the situation with Julia was intolerable, and spelled certain commercial doom. I felt Jeff Buckley was my ace in the hole—my lifeline to success in the brutal arena of pop music.

I grunted a non-committal reply—I didn't want people gossiping about a situation that was still in flux, still far from settled. Maybe Rick knew more about what was going down than he let on; maybe he didn't. But I didn't want to get into it with him right then.

The session was a lot of fun. Sophie was a larger-than-life bohemian grande dame with a touch of the freakazoid about her. I remember one track had her simulating an orgasm over her supercharged music, and I dutifully stepped up to the plate to deliver an appropriately wild and impassioned guitar solo to better accent her moans and ecstatic yelps.

A few days later, I was off to Europe, the Knitting Factory having organized an extensive package tour for several of their featured artists that covered six or seven countries in a series of one-nighters—the Knit's own Caravan of Stars. I was booked to play solo alongside James Blood Ulmer's avant-garde jazz trio, the downtown indie band Chunk, and the hard-bopping Thomas Chapin Trio.

Shortly before I left for the Netherlands, where I had a few solo shows of my own booked before I was scheduled to hook up with Michael Dorf and this traveling circus, I had a conversation with Debbie Schwartz, a friend of mine and Caroline's and also of Hal

Willner's. A Jersey girl who knew Bruce Springsteen back in the early days, Debbie had met and befriended Jeff around the time of the St Ann's tribute, and he in turn had responded to her positively as a music biz insider who had managed and landed deals for several successful acts.

Feeling I needed a manager to help sort out my ongoing situation at Columbia with Julia, I met with Debbie and her then-partner, Michael Solomon, who managed a Columbia act named Parthenon Huxley, to see if they would represent me in my dealings with Columbia—and particularly with David Kahne—while I was out on tour.

Previously, I had been using my lawyer Michael Ackerman to represent me, but he had grown weary of his dealings with CBS Records' Business Affairs department. "They're animals," he said, but that gave me precious little consolation as I had to continue dealing with them one way or another. He had also recently departed for LA to work for a major law firm out there, which called into question whether or not we should continue to work together.

Debbie and Michael agreed to try to sort things out with Kahne while I was in Europe. The main thing I wanted was for them to clarify under what terms I was going to proceed on my record deal, and to act as a liaison between the label, Julia, and me—so as to at least honor the spirit of our original contract, and also fend off any possible lawsuits from Julia, if Kahne insisted on reducing her role.

□

On May 8, I flew to Amsterdam, where I played a few TV and radio gigs; visited with old friends such as my best buddy Joep Ver, a supremely gifted Dutch painter who invited me to play at his art exhibition opening to "consecrate the paintings"; sat in with my friends, the UK Marxist punk band The Mekons, at the famous Milky Way club; and eventually joined up with the Knitting Factory contingent for our first show in the Hague on May 24. I played so intensely that night that a female fan at the front of the stage literally swooned and had to be carried out of the club for resuscitation.

The next night, I played a solo show at the Para club in Breda while the rest of the New York contingent remained in Amsterdam on their day off. A prominent local politician showed up, having evidently surmised that my concert was a hip, trendy event for him to be seen attending.

There was a definite buzz about my Dutch shows. My debut solo album, *Skeleton At The Feast*, had just been released there, much of it recorded live on earlier Dutch tours, and the national newspapers and music magazines were giving it major rave reviews. "Those who love guitar fireworks will find a lot of pleasure in it," one review read, while another noted, "Lucas is a master on acoustic and electric guitar: a virtuoso who makes about every style of the American tradition his own."

The next day, the tour bus took us to Lille, France, and then on to a string of European one-nighters over the next two weeks that had us hopping around Spain, France, the Netherlands, Germany, Switzerland, and Austria, before finally making it back home on Sunday June 3.

In all of the shows on this tour, I made 'Bluebird Blues,' the instrumental portion of the first song I had co-written with Jeff, a feature of my set. With its flashy fingerpicking and joyous vibe, I would introduce it under the provisional title 'They Can't Get It Up And I Can't Get It Down'—a description of my feelings about my ongoing situation with Columbia Records and Julia, and my frustration with not being able to get my major-label recording project off the ground yet. (Ever the agent provocateur, I also introduced it in Vienna under the title 'Waldheim Must Go!' and in Germany as 'Nazis Out of Dresden Now!' in protest against Austrian President Kurt Waldheim's Nazi past and the resurgence of neo-Nazis in East Germany.)

I had a ball on the tour. It was a relief for me to get out of New

York, away from the oppressive weight of my on-again, off-again collaboration with Julia. I threw myself into the touring life with gusto and had enough adventures on this trip alone that they could fill a book. But that's another story.

Two things really stand out among my memories of this tour. One was a discussion I had with James Blood Ulmer, the black free-jazz guitarist I had known since his group opened for Beefheart in 1980 at the Beacon Theater. I had actually worked on his ad campaigns during the time he was a Columbia Records recording artist, but he had long since been let go from that contract and was now recording for independent labels.

We had established a soulful bond over the years that superseded the usual rivalries that exist among guitarists. In my experience, most guitarists act like gunslingers when they get in sight of one another. Who's the fastest? Who's the best? Who's got the biggest dick?

Instead, James and I were benign rivals, although the last rhetorical question about relative virility had come into question on this tour as we conducted an ongoing contest to see who could score the most women during our time in Europe. (We were neck and neck by the end, with about four conquests apiece.)

In any case, one day on the band bus climbing through the winding, breathtaking vistas of the Austrian Alps en route from Tubingen to Innsbruck, I poured my heart and soul out to Blood about my ongoing dilemma with Julia and Columbia.

James simply grinned and told me to "RECORD the bitch! And then you can move on."

I sometimes wish I had acted on his advice. But I felt that solution was untenable at this point, with the way Julia had reacted to Kahne's suggestion of a reduced role in the project, and a recipe for certain disaster.

The second standout recollection was making a very early morning transatlantic phone call from a hotel in a small town in Germany to Michael Solomon in Los Angeles, to see if he had made any headway with Columbia in terms of clarifying the proposed new deal—a deal that might well minimize Julia's role in the album and allow me to bring in Jeff as a vocalist.

I wanted to light a fire under Solomon and impress upon him how well my solo debut was doing in Europe, and hopefully energize him to go back to Kahne and make a case for proceeding. But he seemed unimpressed with the noise *Skeleton At The Feast* was making in the European press, and cavalier about my situation with Columbia.

It was unclear to me whether he and Debbie had even had a discussion with Kahne at all—he was that vague. He fudged giving me a direct answer and instead asked how my "hitter" (Michael Ackerman) had fared with Kahne on my behalf—even though he himself was supposed to be my "hitter" now. Hot potato!

Maybe Solomon knew more than he was letting on. I got the distinct impression that I was being toyed with. Only later did I learn that Jeff had given Debbie a copy of his demo tape to have her try to sell him to her industry contacts as a solo artist. In hindsight, it seems as though he and Debbie were more eager to drum up interest in Jeff's tape with their industry buddies than salvage my album project.

When I checked out of the hotel, I was handed a bill for nearly $200 from the front desk for one very frustrating, inconclusive phone call to my "hitter" in California.

□

I called David Kahne as soon as I got back to New York in early June. Ominously, he didn't take my call; his secretary said he was "in a meeting."

A short time later, Peter Shershin called my apartment. I excitedly told him about the great headway I had just made in Europe as a live performer, and the phenomenal reception my solo debut album was receiving in the press there.

There was a strained silence. Then Shershin cleared his throat, and in a mealy-mouthed, pinched voice, he said, "You probably realize that we've, uh, decided to drop your project at Columbia ..."

"You WHAT?"

I was genuinely shocked to hear this.

In the back of my mind, I suppose I'd known that this turn of events was a possibility, but I believed it to be a remote one, and I had successfully suppressed my anxieties about it throughout the tour.

Now, all my anxiety and feelings of betrayal spilled out into bewildered, blind-sided anger, and I suddenly knew just how Julia had felt when she had spoken to Kahne.

"How can you do this? We have a contract!"

Then, in a chilling moment of corporate sang-froid, Shershin calmly delivered his knockout punch, a real zetz of a line I will never forget—a line that has stood the test of time with me as epitomizing the ruthless and high-handed nature of the music business.

"You can't afford to sue us."

And he was right. He had us by the short and curlies. No matter how good a legal challenge I could muster, Columbia Records would have batteries of lawyers on-staff who would wear Michael Ackerman and me down and in the process exhaust my financial resources by stonewalling and/or countersuing.

I was dumbfounded. Shershin hurriedly hustled me off the phone, making some perfunctory noises about "getting together for lunch" at some unspecified time in the future. Yeah, lunch—just when I was about ready to vomit.

This was probably the single worst moment in my life up to that point. The lowest of the low—all my dreams of a brilliant pop music career had been dashed to hell. Stunned, numb, I sat collecting my thoughts, trying to figure out a way to remove the stake that had just been plunged into my heart, and I began to review my options.

There weren't many.

I could either slink back with my tail between my legs to my former bosses at CBS Records' Creative Services Department, and beg them for my old job back, or I could get out of the treacherous and fickle music business altogether, pick up the pieces, and look for another line of work—which, at age 38, would have been daunting, but not impossible. Or I could keep pushing forward on the path I had chosen.

Without a moment's hesitation, I opted for the latter course of action.

Number one, I'm not a quitter—my motto is "never say die."

Number two, I knew I was damn good as a guitarist and a songwriter, and that I had the raw talent to make it if I stuck with it. I was also a firm believer in Woody Allen's maxim that "99 per cent of success is just showing up," and I was determined to keep showing up, to keep shoving my mug in other people's faces until they had to take me seriously—just to show *them* up.

Number three, I had my secret weapon waiting in the wings.

□

I spent an hour or so trying to calm down Caroline, who seemed much more devastated by the bad news from Black Rock than I was, and who intuited immediately that, without an ongoing record deal or some kind of steady employment, our meager savings would barely be enough to stave off the wolf at our door for even a few months.

And then I rang Jeff in LA. I relayed what had just gone down with Columbia, and how I had resolved to go forward with the band and find another major label for the project—and would Jeff be interested in joining me in the group as my fulltime singer?

Leaping easily over the distance of the many miles that separated us physically, but not spiritually and creatively, I heard Jeff's excited, high-pitched voice ring out loud and clear.

"I'll be your singer!"

This was music to my ears.

I hung up and relayed the good news to Caroline, but she hardly reacted in one way or another.

She seemed not to have heard me at all, imploring me instead to reconsider going back to ad writing. As if they'd take me back there.

I could well imagine the smug schadenfreude at the spectacle of me crawling back on my belly, looking to resume my old job.

Caroline suggested I at least consider seeking some freelance copywriting to tide me over in the interim, while I recovered from this devastating blow to my music career.

"No one will ever take me seriously in this industry if I split my focus on being a fulltime musician with copywriting again," I replied. "I'll always be 'that copywriter who dabbles at being a musician.'"

I strongly believe that if you do too many things too well, people will invariably choose the least impressive of those things and focus on that as your major "identity" in their minds. It's plain jealousy that makes most people actively begrudge artists for going out there and daring to be different, to do something creative with their lives— particularly struggling artists on the cusp of making it.

Once you're proven successful at doing what you do—and in America, that means mega-bucks, never mind brilliant reviews—well, that's another story. Then, those people will bow down before you. Some of them, anyway. For a while.

For now, there was nothing else for me to do but continue the course and go the distance. Pick myself up, brush myself off, and start all over again, as the song goes. But this time, I would be going out there with the most exciting, talented, charismatic, good-looking young singer I'd ever encountered.

Jeff's verbal commitment strengthened my resolve to get busy and write more songs for the two of us as Gods and Monsters mk3. I went to bed that night with a sense of grief at the loss of my Columbia deal, but also with a warm feeling of contentment and hope at the prospect of working fulltime with Jeff Buckley. Fuck Columbia and my Faustian deal with Julia.

☐

I never did hear from Julia in the aftermath of Shershin's bombshell. She had obviously received the bad news and was as upset about the collapse of our deal as I was. But after squabbling with her for several years I was not inclined to try to patch things up now. There was nothing more to stay to one another.

Now, though, with Jeff in my group, I'd been given a chance to be reborn and to shine. The road wouldn't be easy. The music business had proven treacherous, fickle, and unforgiving, and the thought of mounting another assault on the major-label citadels was frankly scary. But the thought of collaborating with Jeff made me feel like I was protected in a cloak of unassailable magic armor.

There was something about Jeff's aura and youthful brilliance that surrounded and bathed me that night in a kind of healing balm. It soothed away my troubles and helped dispel my cares, making me feel protected and secure at my worst moment of doubt in my entire life. I felt touched by grace.

The very next day, late in the morning, I sat in my black vinyl chair in the corner of my apartment and picked up my black '64 Stratocaster, ready to work on new music for the two of us. I was in my groove, at my workstation—the same spot where I had composed all of my songs to date, and where I had recently worked with Jeff on 'The King's Chain' and 'Bluebird Blues.'

As I've mentioned, my composing technique on the guitar resembles the way my hero Brian Wilson writes on the piano. My fellow June 20 Gemini has spoken of how he likes to sit at the piano and absentmindedly pass his fingers over the keys, playing randomly until he hits or stumbles upon the right "feels"—those magic chord changes and motifs that strike a resonant chord within. He then plays them obsessively, over and over, gradually modifying, developing, and shaping the raw musical material into fully-fledged compositions.

On this sky-blue sunny day in early June, the light bouncing off the Hudson River and streaming into my apartment, bathing the room in a warm iridescent glow, I absentmindedly began fingerpicking. The sound echoed out of my open window across the 180-degree panorama of the Hudson River and the Hoboken skyline beyond it.

I have always found that for me to successfully compose, it's good to try and get into the Zen mindset that John Lennon urged the world to adopt in his magisterial anthem 'Tomorrow Never Knows':

Turn off your mind, relax and float downstream

My fingers moved gracefully over the strings of my guitar—the same guitar I had acquired for 200 bucks in the last month of my senior year at Yale from a couple of shady entrepreneurs calling themselves Guitars Unlimited; the same guitar I had gone on to play with Captain Beefheart.

I detuned my low E string down to D and started playing 'Evening Bell,' the solo guitar tour de force from Beefheart's *Ice Cream For Crow* that had put me on the musical map. I had recently worked it back into my repertoire, and had played it at shows on the Knitting Factory European tour. It was one of those pieces that I really needed to practice fairly regularly in order to be able to pull it off successfully.

I moved on from 'Evening Bell' and began to improvise in this dropped-D tuning, my fingers wandering restlessly over the fretboard. I got up after a bit and took a hit from the bong resting on the round glass table across the room—self-medicating with marijuana being something I did a lot of in those years.

Now I was really relaxed and floating downstream.

I don't make any special claim that drugs (particularly marijuana) enhanced my creative abilities in any way in this period—just that I liked to have some around, like so many other musicians. I have composed just as effectively without drugs in my life, and I have been drug free for well over a decade now.

Back then, however, I found that grass frequently served to relax me, and allowed me to listen to my music from alternative perspectives—which would sometimes kick me into new directions. And that's what happened that morning. .

In the midst of my random improvisations, I heard something

new emerge on my guitar—an Ur-melody that suddenly appeared on my internal radar screen and struck a vast resonance within; a sad, insistent progression that moved from a yearning, questioning motif based on a diminished chord to a definitive answering motif in A-minor as my fingers explored unknown musical terrain.

This music sounded so fantastic and so right. I kept playing this question-and-answer motif, astonished and bemused by my own invention. My random improvising had magically unearthed a haunting fingerpicked progression that delighted me, that just sprang into being without any conscious subjective intellection on my part. A Q&A with its own definitive logic that sounded eternal and righteous, like some ancient spell that had been inscribed in stone and then buried for eternity, and that now only needed me to bring it into the light and shake the dust off for it to work its magic again.

This motif soon pervaded my waking and dreaming thoughts, an insistent query that wouldn't leave me—the quarry—alone:

Dah-dah-dah-dah DAH? Dah-dah-dah-dah DAH?
Dah-dah-dah-dah DAH! Dah-dah-dah-dah DA-DAAAAH!

This wistful figure would later become the famous opening leitmotif of our song 'Mojo Pin.' But it was as if I didn't find it—it found me. I played this ancient, melancholy phrase over and over again in a hypnotic trance, awed by its ghostly power. It seemed freighted with a centuries-old aura of pain and resignation.

The fingerpicking required to play this passage did not come naturally to me, but after some hours, the years of practice that had enabled me to master Don Van Vliet's insanely difficult compositions kicked in and allowed me to pull it off effortlessly, until it became second nature.

The work tapes in my archive reveal that I kept plowing this obsessive music furrow until ultimately resolving the A-minor chord into a D-major flourish. This incorporation of major and minor key changes within the same song is a hallmark of my songwriting. Mixing the bitter with the sweet—just like life.

I was transfixed by the rhythm of my own passes on guitar. I could hear in my mind's ear Jeff's incantatory voice gliding over this repetitive, skeletal intro. It was shaping up as the underpinnings for a possible verse section, and as I played on, the mesmerizing figure tap-tap-tapping at my chamber door, it sounded like a spell—not mere music. It was a spell that would unlock mysteries behind many doors, a spell hinting at extremely strange days to come.

Over the next few hours, I worked hard on composing another fingerpicked section. This part seemed to function as a chorus in my nascent new instrumental—the part where Jeff would later sing:

> *Don't want to weep for you*
> *Don't want to know*
> *I'm blind and tortured*
> *The white horses flow*

I often wondered whether this was a reference to our meeting at the White Horse Tavern, where we had first decided to join forces.

This second section of music surged up out of the sad resignation of the hieratic verse section, and suggested to me a sense of striving forward positively, shrugging off the claustrophobic sense of doom generated by the intro/verse music to rise up, amble forward—and groove.

> *Memories fire*
> *The rhythms fall slow*

It would then resolve to a D7 chord in a wild shout of exultation, bringing all the erotic heat of the previous music to a head as the rhythm underneath accelerates, faster and faster … and then the music gallops forward, pell-mell into a headlong rush that is the clipped, strummed bolero section of the song: four stop-and-start cluster-bursts of 16th-note chords that ascend skyward, then dip down back into minor key hell, and finally resolve in a grand, fermata'd D-major chord, bringing sweet relief.

This instrumental evolved over several febrile days of intense concentration and experimentation where, sitting entranced like a yogi, I worked over the sections incessantly and obsessively on my guitar like a sculptor chipping away at a solid block of marble until the contours of the form beneath make themselves manifest and the work is finally finished as a fully realized product of creative imagination.

□

Periodically, Caroline would appear in the room, observe me working, silently raise a finger in the air to say hello and then give me a sublime, silly smile that would never fail to cheer me up.

She knew that although I was in the throes of composing, beneath my efforts to mine this musical diamond I was seriously suffering from the humiliation of being dropped by Columbia Records. Underneath my defiant air of artist-at-work, I was naturally more than worried about my suddenly and seriously challenged financial prospects.

Both of us were now freelancers. Caroline did freelance casting out of our bedroom, and while her business would occasionally thrive, she also suffered the vagaries of the feast-and-famine vicissitudes of the artistic life, while I did not have many pending bookings or many prospects of steady employment on the horizon.

The crutch of a major-label deal that might have led me down the path to fame and fortune had just been kicked out from under me by my former employer. There were no more corporate perks to come, no more expense-account dinners to look forward to.

In truth, these had vanished a year and a half previously, when I signed with CBS as a recording artist. Worse than this, we no longer had the safety net of corporate health insurance—plus we both had very little in the way of savings to lean on in these suddenly lean times.

So, although Caroline left me alone pretty much over these last days of spring as I worked on the raw material that had emerged from the depths of my despair, her occasional comic walk-through appearances while I worked, and her sympathetic and supportive air during this period, were like oxygen to me. I loved her dearly for all her tenderness and understanding, which helped get me through this protracted long night of the soul.

□

Back to the work at hand.

My criterion for the composing of a memorable song has never changed. First and foremost, it has always been about the underlying guitar instrumental. If, after composing a new instrumental on the guitar, I sleep on it, wake up the next morning, and the music I had written the day before is still running through my head, then I know I have a keeper—the framework for a full-blown song.

I knew that I had the makings of an epic after the first day of working on this music. It was some of the most powerful music I'd ever written. To listen back to my work tapes reveals that, after finishing up each discrete section of the instrumental, I kept trying out several different directions and tangents until I eventually hit on the one that felt the most right.

Invariably, my instinct would guide me on the correct path as I aimed to wring the maximum emotion out of each emerging section in order to make the entire flow of music pay off and bring the song to a gut-wrenching conclusion.

Finally, after three or four days' work, the music was finished. And as I played it from the top, the song slowly unfolded itself like a peacock displaying its luxuriant plumage. The dramatic arc of the piece just felt right, each section complementing and contrasting with the section before it.

The music had its own internal logic—hovering and moving from major to minor, the stop-start push-pull of the recurring question-and-answer figure gave it a feeling of claustrophobic oppression ... before the shadow-figure cast by the music throws off the imprisoning shackles that weigh it down, rises up and moves forward in a defiant swagger, faster and faster, headlong into the rush of ecstatic revelation and the exultant promise of freedom—only to plummet back down into the dungeon of disappointed dreams in an eternal ricorso before revving up one more time to plunge head-long into the mystic, resolving finally on a note of sublime grace.

It was a mini-symphony. I'd never composed such dramatic, pictorial music before. It was music with a tale all of its own to tell. Music that cried out for Jeff's soaring voice over it—to make it whole.

I gave this music the title 'And You Will.' It was a message, a prophecy, and a little bit of Zen encouragement for both Jeff and myself. As in: "Come to New York and join me on this band project. Come to complete and be a part of this song. And you will realize your true potential, fulfill your manifest destiny, and truly become the star that you are."

☐

Almost immediately after starting work on 'And You Will,' I began working on a second epic instrumental I'd begun months earlier, before I had even heard of Jeff Buckley.

I kept juggling the two pieces over this very fertile creative period. I'd go back and forth from one to the other each day over this week and a half of feverish composing. I had written the opening arpeggio'd, fingerpicked progression and an ascending chordal section several months earlier, in the winter of '91. They were inchoate fragments of a greater whole that was due to come later, and I wasn't sure at that time how they fit together, or where to take the music to next.

I was anxious about the future but impressed by the resolve of my young hero to come to New York and join me. Jeff was my shining knight in LA, ready to travel east to light the lights of my music, do battle with the A&R gods, and slay the dragon/gatekeepers of the major labels.

I always kept in mind what my father had taught me: "Whenever you're handed a lemon, make lemonade."

Summoning all my strength from the depths of my anguish, my thoughts flashed occasionally while composing this instrumental to all the false trails and right and wrong moves I'd made along the way in putting a solo show and then a group together.

How I'd forced myself to begin writing songs to secure a major-label deal. How I had actually forged a career in music for myself at a relatively advanced age. How I'd then left the security of my day job to scale to the pinnacle of a dream deal with Columbia—only to have that mountain crumble, and to see all my dreams dashed on the rocks below.

I started playing the pensive fingerpicked progression I had composed some months earlier—a sad, tense, funereal waltz in 6/8 time that ascended from F-minor 7th to G-minor 7th and then crashed and burned in the black hole of E-minor:

Dahdahdahdahdahdah dahdahdahdahdahdah
Dahdahdahdahdahdah dahdahdahdahdahdah?
Dahdahdahdahdahdah dahdahdahdahdahdah
Dahdahdahdahdahdah dahdahdahdahdahdah?
DAAAAAAAAAAAAAH!

It was another riddle, another question answered by a resounding "NO!" And then, out of the Stygian depths, the music soars into the blue empyrean with the D-major peel of chiming, silvery church bells resounding over the blasted wasteland below.

The music mirrors the archetypal flight from death into Eros—a major motif of my own personal philosophy—fleeing inevitable annihilation in a positive and joyous embrace of life. The doomed minor-key intro moves into a major key in an ecstatic, whirling dance that celebrates the rich possibilities of love. Then, after a sweet taste of this heaven on Earth, the music plunges back again into the depths of E-minor hell.

Bittersweet, like life itself.

I called this second piece 'Rise Up To Be.' It was another self-help mantra directed at both Jeff and myself: "Rise up to be! Leave LA and come to New York and join me in this group odyssey to become the rock god that you are."

It was a defiant shout of liberation, hurled in the face of Columbia Records' cold abandonment of my album project. I refused to be defeated, and I wanted a title that would inspire both of us.

It was also an affectionate ribbing of my old boss, Don Van Vliet, who had continually belittled any aspirations of mine (or my fellow Magic Band members') to make my own music. Back in the 80s, Warner Bros had suggested compiling a double-album Beefheart "best of" collection.

I remember Don contemptuously asserting that he would only give his blessings to the album being released if the folks at Warners allowed him to title it *Rise Up To Be Discontinued*—a backhanded slap at the company that had empowered him as an artist by signing him twice—and then had dropping him unceremoniously (also twice) when his records failed to sell and there was no prospect of recouping their investment.

Now the company was asking him to cooperate in the recycling of his old work—a gesture he viewed as a complete insult. ("Didn't I put enough music out there in the first place?" came his incredulous response.)

This music became the instrumental template for 'Grace,' the title of Jeff's one and only album for Sony, and probably our best known song, and in analyzing it, I can clearly see that its embrace of the twin polarities of experience—the yin and yang of all the pain and joy of the universe manifest in a four-minute pop-song—was a breakthrough in my writing.

Perhaps it's my double-Gemini nature that accounts for this. A close analysis of the musical progression of both this and 'And You Will' reveals that both move from minor to major and back again through the course of the song. This gives them their underlying harmonic tension and resolution in recurring cycles of sadness and happiness, which I think most closely mirrors the actual conditions of most people's lives.

It also places my writing in the tradition of one of Jeff's greatest musical influences: his father, Tim Buckley, whose two most creatively successful albums were called *Goodbye & Hello* and *Happy/Sad*.

This tension and resolution helps transports these songs out of the mundane realm of bland, one-dimensional, saccharine pop music. These songs function both as objets d'art and as popular music—which, since the advent of The Beatles, is what I have always believed a cutting-edge songwriter should aim to do: namely, write an avant-garde hit.

These two songs do not sound like typical Top 40 radio fare—or conventional modern-rock album fare either, for that matter. Yet they have proven themselves to be enduring and popular with many folks all over the world, and have secured their place in musical history. ('Grace' especially has made all sorts of critical and listener polls, with *Mojo* magazine citing its parent album as the #1 Modern Classic Album of the 90s over albums by U2, Radiohead, and others.)

Years later, Jeff would introduce 'Grace' at Royal Festival Hall in London, England, where he was performing as part of the 1995 Meltdown Festival, as curated by Elvis Costello. Jeff mentioned to the crowd the difficulty he always had playing this particular intro figure accurately on his guitar. He told them that it was instrumental music composed "by the New York luminary, Gary Lucas."

"I tell people I carry you with me always in my fingers," he later told me.

☐

After ten days or so of what I recall as a sunny, golden period of Zen concentration as I hunched over my guitar and teased out the lines of these songs—my music reverberating in my mind all night while I slept, and still sounding fresh and beautiful upon awakening each day—I was finally satisfied.

This burst of creativity had resulted in two most mysterious and ghostly instrumentals. They functioned beautifully on their own, but at the same time they called for Jeff's voice to make them come fully alive as songs. I took a stab shortly after composing these pieces at writing some of my own lyrics for 'Rise Up To Be':

> *What is this voice I keep longing to hear?*
> *No fear*
> *What is this place I keep longing to see?*
> *Torn free*
>
> *Rise up to be*
> *Stronger than you or me*
> *Rise up to be*
> *Free*

I also attempted a lyric for 'And You Will':

> *And you will come this day*
> *And you will rise this way*
> *And you will hear them say*
> *You have to change your ways*
>
> *But you will not obey*
> *And you will never stay*
> *And you must try and sway*
> *The path of life that's here today*

I rejected them almost immediately as vague, simplistic bromides, and figured that Jeff, as the singer, would most likely be able to come up with more poetic and personal lyrics—words that would be meaningful to him—as he would be the one singing them. This is a rule of thumb I've followed in all of my subsequent collaborations with other singers.

I called Jeff shortly after composing these instrumentals to communicate my excitement about them, and the possibilities they might bring as the foundations of the new Gods and Monsters sound we had spoken of developing at our initial bonding lunch at the White Horse Tavern in May.

I got his answering machine. His high-pitched voice audibly sighed and then declared slowly and sorrowfully a message on the order of, "Man, there's *nothing* worse than the A&R puppet show in LA." Beeeeep! I left an excited message about how I had written and recorded two spectacular instrumentals for him to tackle as new songs for Gods and Monsters, and requested he call me back with his mailing address.

When Jeff called back later, he sounded upbeat, though obviously bummed that nothing had happened with his solo demo tape (which would explain his rueful message). He told me he'd been working part-time at the Magic Castle hotel in Hollywood, and that it looked like he'd be coming through New York in mid-July as he'd just landed a gig playing bass in a traveling covers band playing promo parties to plug the music from *The Commitments*, Alan Parker's film based on Roddy Doyle's novel about a young Irish band with great potential who rise up out of the slums of Dublin and then break up a week later, just as they're on the verge of getting signed (one more harbinger of things to come).

Jeff promised to start working on our new songs once he received the cassette I was about to send him, and we'd have a chance to connect and further develop them when he came through town in July. I was thrilled about hooking up with him again.

I asked him to send me back a copy of the cassette I had made of the two of us playing 'Bluebird Blues,' plus some rough ideas I had put down for him of possible future songs, as I had not made a backup version, and he had the only copy.

Some of my earlier instrumentals on this cassette—which were tabled by Jeff in favor of working on the two new compositions I had just composed specifically for him—were remnants of earlier songs I had been developing with Julia.

One was 'Peep Show Bible,' which finally came out in 2011 on my Gods and Monsters album *The Ordeal Of Civility*. Another, which I referred to as "that hillbilly song," later became 'Handful Of Gimme,' which I recorded as part of my Killer Shrews project a few years later. One other was later developed for Gods and Monsters post-Jeff under the title 'Ultra-Shark,' finally appearing on our 2006 album *Coming Clean*.

☐

A few weeks later, I received the cassette I'd requested from Jeff in the mail. On the flipside, he had included a solo home-demo version of The Smiths' classic 'The Boy With The Thorn In His Side.'

It was a telling choice. Morrissey's lyrics—"How can they look into my eyes / And still they don't believe me?"—must have had a very personal resonance. It seemed to underscore Jeff's profound disillusionment with the LA music scene.

In July, I was invited out to dinner at a Chinese restaurant on Bleecker Street by Susan Feldman, the artistic director of St Ann's who had put together the Tim Buckley tribute with her partner Janine Nichols and Hal Willner.

A small, pugnacious woman, Susan was full of encouragement for my plan to continue working with Jeff. She seemed particularly disposed to my idea for bringing Jeff into my band, and proposed on the spot a concert at St Ann's to showcase the new Gods and Monsters line-up on Friday March 13 1992.

She laughed when I winced at the date. I tried to explain to her that I was a bit superstitious about such things. She shrugged it off and said that she could not think of a more appropriate date for a band called Gods and Monsters to be given a showcase.

Susan and I really got on well at that dinner—I gravitated to her passion for music and her feisty spirit. She seemed like the kind of person who got things done, and she filled me in with more details about what she knew about Jeff's background and struggles in Los Angeles. There was no mention of the various abortive band projects described in the posthumous *Dream Brother* biography—as far as she knew, he had never had played in any group. She confided that she really didn't believe he was capable of putting a band together on his own, and told me she was glad I was trying to involve him in mine. I would provide him with a readymade framework in which to showcase his talents and would act as a valuable mentor.

Like everyone else in New York who had spent time around him, Susan was smitten with Jeff. She spoke warily of his so-called LA friends who continually put him down, and felt that bringing him to New York—where he could escape their influence, start afresh, and blossom anew through working with me—was a wonderful idea.

Rise up to be.

One moment gave me pause, however. Describing her vision of our projected St Ann's showcase, Susan proposed a segment during our program that would be a tribute to "Timmy and Jimi": Tim Buckley and Jimi Hendrix. I thought this was a corny idea, and I knew that Jeff would hate it as well. I told her I'd think about it.

I walked out of the restaurant truly glad to have such a powerful ally. Susan knew quite a few people in the music business from several years of mounting shows with Lou Reed, John Cale, Marianne Faithfull, and others. But I also had some trepidation. That "Timmy and Jimi" idea struck me as insipid, and I wondered if there were other hidden agendas at work.

114

I suspected at the time that beneath her friendly manner, Susan's motives in booking a showcase for the group were mainly about helping Jeff, whom she felt needed someone like me to help him pull his scattered energies to the fore. She acknowledged my talent, for sure, but I'm not sure that she didn't ultimately regard me as anything but a stepping-stone for Jeff, until such time as he could walk on the water himself.

I remember giving her a copy of *Skeleton At The Feast* in the restaurant that night, hoping to get some positive feedback, but when I spoke with her a few days later she barely registered an opinion. She didn't seem to respond to my own music at all, but I consoled myself by thinking that, although Jeff was her darling, he was key to my vision of Gods and Monsters now, so any support that came our way would ultimately help with the development of the band.

❑

Later that month, Jeff arrived back in New York with the *Commitments* touring band.

He swung by my apartment around 9pm and told me he'd literally just jumped off the band bus. He looked fit and determined, with those same burning eyes, but also a bit melancholy. He had grown his hair out longer, and there was a sadness and a seriousness to him. He wasn't smiling that much. The recent rejection of his demos in LA had obviously scarred him, but at the same time made him even more steely.

It was a hot and steamy summer night in Manhattan, and my apartment provided a chill haven from the sticky streets. I'd arranged for Jeff to come over when Caroline wasn't around so we could talk about the new music I had written for us in relative solitude.

We sat together, shared some water and juice, and spoke about Gods and Monsters. We smoked some strong grass, and then he proudly pulled out the *Babylon Dungeon* cassette of his demos and asked me to play it on my system.

Jeff was eager for my approval, but frankly it was difficult for me to get a handle on the songs. They didn't hang together for me—each song sounded radically situated in its own universe, having little to do with the song following it. It just did not make much of an impression on me, other than Jeff demonstrating his ability to skillfully perform and sing in widely disparate styles and settings. Plus there were no obvious hooks there that I could immediately discern. One jangly song seemed to owe a heavy debt to The Smiths; another was pure hardcore thrash in the style of one of Jeff's favorite groups, Bad Brains.

Not wanting to hurt his feelings, I tried to summon up some enthusiasm. I knew how much his tape meant to him, as a declaration of his musical independence, but I was a poor dissembler that night. Jeff looked visibly hurt by my lukewarm response to his music—it was yet one more rejection, this time coming from someone whose opinion (and music) he respected. And I don't think he ever quite forgave me for it.

Here he was, playing me the first fruits of his own creation, in the hope perhaps that I would show some enthusiasm for adapting one of his songs for our new project—and I had unintentionally dumped on it. It just wasn't happening in my mind, and the ever-so-sensitive Jeff had picked up on this.

In retrospect, I really regret not being more generous with Jeff that night, and not making the effort to encourage him to contribute his songs to Gods and Monsters. Things might have gone down differently with us later. Blame it on my ego and self-centered faith in my own music—after all, hadn't my own songs won a record deal for Julia and me with Columbia? Blame it also on my tendency to be a control-freak sometimes. This was not the first time, nor the last, that I've shot myself in the foot.

My apparent rejection of Jeff's own music was, along with Jeff's snub of David Kahne up at Black Rock, one of the first real cracks in our relationship. A fault-line had appeared now between us, and would always be there, henceforth, as much as I tried to paper over it. It would continue to deepen as time went by.

After a long, awkward silence, I switched the subject to the tape I'd sent him. Jeff said he'd been digging it and reaffirmed his interest in joining Gods and Monsters. He asked me if I had any other music to give him, and I played fragments of several other instrumentals I'd been working on.

Jeff listened intently and then told me he would continue to work on the music I had sent him, as he liked those two pieces the best of anything I'd played for him so far.

A sullen silence descended on the room. Our desultory conversation more or less broke down altogether, drifting away from our usual intimate dialogue. I felt detached from Jeff and the whole scene in my apartment, disembodied and a bit nauseous, as if on the verge of passing out from the smoke and the heat—until Jeff brought me back to earth abruptly by suddenly snapping angrily at me.

"Come ON, man ... don't be a fucking human waste."

He was incensed, like a spoiled child demanding attention— pissed that I had momentarily allowed my attention to lapse away from him and our plans for the project. Underneath his caustic remark he was seething with rage, his anger probably stemming more from the short shrift I had given his tape than from my momentary space-out.

Embarrassed by my brief slide into a semi-vegetative state, I willed myself back from my psychedelic reveries to concentrate on our group game plan. After smoothing things over with some tension-diffusing jokes and gossip, we resumed our conversation and made plans to get together to work on the songs in August, which was only a few weeks away.

The plan was to further refine the songs by adding Jeff's currently formulating lyrics and vocal lines in rehearsal in my apartment, then teach them to my band in a formal rehearsal studio. After that, we would go into an actual recording studio and commit them to 24-

track tape as the first new Gods and Monsters demos with Jeff as lead singer—demos my lawyer Michael Ackerman would then shop in hopes of securing a deal for us.

The demos were to be recorded on my dime, Jeff seemingly being in a more impecunious position. Plus I thought I'd demonstrate a vote of confidence in our collaboration by underwriting these sessions myself, precarious as my own financial situation was at the time.

Jeff departed shortly thereafter, perhaps to rendezvous with his new girlfriend, Rebecca Moore. Their innocent flirtation, which had begun at the Tim Buckley tribute, had blossomed by now into a full-blown romance. The thought of being with Rebecca again, the prospect of coming to New York, where he felt fully alive, and the promise of working on our new songs together gave Jeff all the incentive he needed to return to New York as soon as he could.

Chapter Four

A few weeks later, on Wednesday August 14, Jeff arrived at my West Village apartment in the late afternoon of a sunny summer day. He was back in New York and staying with Rebecca.

We greeted each other warmly. Jeff settled onto my sofa while I took my usual seat facing him. He pulled out the coffee-stained notebook he had brought with him, and I glanced through it for the first time. I had previously shown him the blank-paged notebooks I had been keeping for some time now since before I began working with Julia—black hardcover notebooks containing blank white pages, where all my lyric ideas, aperçus, business contacts, and manic stream-of-consciousness ideas were jotted down in a sequential jumble.

Jeff's notebook was similar, and he had been filling it with poems, lyric ideas, random thoughts, journal entries, sketches—the kind of notebook that writers and creative artists often carry with them to write in the moment when inspiration hits. This notebook was to become ubiquitous with Jeff. He would carry it with him everywhere he went.

He got right down to it.

"You know that instrumental piece you sent me you called 'Rise Up To Be'?" he asked.

"Sure," I nodded.

"Well, now it's called 'Grace,'" he said willfully.

OK, I thought.

I handed him a microphone, turned on my guitar amp, and

119

started fingerpicking the rising-and-falling opening arpeggio motif. Jeff watched my hands closely as I hit the definitive E-minor "chord of doom" that closes the beginning section before launching into the chiming church bells section that follows.

When I returned to the E-minor chord, Jeff turned to a page from his notebook and began singing:

There's a moon asking to stay
Long enough for the clouds to fly me away ...

I ratcheted up the tension by moving from E-minor to F-minor and then back to E-minor. On "fly me away," I hit a dissonant chord—E-flat minor against E minor—and Jeff flashed his brilliant smile across the space between us. His voice and lyrics sounded so cool against my guitar.

On this first taped run-through of 'Grace,' Jeff tentatively tries to fit the lines of his lyrics into my music for the first time. He has trouble scanning the lyrics, for starters. Eventually, his words and his inchoate, evolving melody lines will flow seamlessly to mesh with the guitar music. Jeff asks me to play my instrumental verse music over and over while he works out his vocal approach, searching for the right phrase and melody that will complement the mysteries of this music and pull him deep inside the song.

His pitch wobbles at times as he wanders slightly off-register but then pulls himself back, determined to match and master the flow of my guitar music with his voice. He tries various approaches, singing lyrics in places where they just don't belong, eventually finding sweet spots where his voice nestles comfortably in the dramatic arc of the piece—the places in the song he's most comfortable with. Places that were soon to be codified for all time as he worked up the definitive version.

It's all there aborning, on this tape ... the Ur-'Grace.' And as I write these words here in the apartment where this all went down, nearly 20 years to the day after recording our first 'Grace,' I pull up the window that overlooks the Hudson River—my river view having become more occluded in the passing years due to the grotesque modern high-rise apartments that have shot up in my neighborhood in a rush of ill-considered development—and I thrust my head out the window and drink in the humid scent of early morning summer.

Memories fire.

And then a sudden chill in the room as the sky darkens. And the rain comes—screaming down from heaven—hammering my windowsill, absolutely soaking it, threatening to flood the apartment as I sit hunched over my laptop writing this. I have to get up to close the window before too much water gets in. I feel another chill as Jeff's ghostly presence seems to fill the room.

And the rain is falling
And I believe
My time has come

It reminds me of the pain
I might leave
Leave behind

Wait in the fire
Wait in the fire

'Grace' as the world has come to know and love it was truly born that day, 20-odd years ago. The vocal pyrotechnics, the daredevil swooping leaps were to emerge shortly as Jeff honed his parts. On our first ever run-through, Jeff tries out alternative lyrics to flesh out his glimpse of an angst-ridden and star-crossed lover wearily resigned to his fate.

He chants the word "chained" repeatedly where the line "Wait in the fire" would go later, eventually to predominate as the main lyrical hook in our song. There are other variants too, such as when he sings:

My love's inside my heart
Ooohhhh
Walking to the bright lights in sorrow

At one point on the third run-through, Jeff's voice drops down to a baritone level—surprisingly so, as I don't recall him ever really attempting to sing in this register before. Maybe he was emulating Jim Morrison. But the low-pitched crooner's voice didn't suit him much, and soon he is back to his soaring tenor.

This take also features the first introduction of Jeff's Dylan-esque harmonica flourishes in the "church bells" section that proved such a shock to fans when the 'Grace' demo finally saw the light of day with the release of the *Songs To No One* album of our early work in 2002.

Faintly in the background, you can hear Jeff occasionally pick up and strum my Gibson J-45 acoustic guitar, which had been resting off to my side. He had asked me to teach him the chords, and he probably wanted to try them out for size while we ran down the tune, to see what they felt like. Perhaps he was even envisioning playing this song solo, without me, somewhere down the line.

The take ends abruptly, and then Jeff says excitedly, "Got another verse ... do the verse again in exactly the same way." I begin the descending chords, and Jeff starts to sing "It's my time" awkwardly (and ultimately incorrectly) against them and then stops.

"Is that the end?" he asks quizzically, in a high-pitched voice.

"Oh no, I think we should go on to do one more of these," I reply assuredly, and continue the song by playing the ascending motif that occurs in the "rain is falling" section.

I think this exchange is instructive as it demonstrates the give and take of our songwriting process. Jeff never modified my original instrumental template and motifs beyond asking me to repeat or shorten a section in order to make it conform to his lyrics. And I often lobbied successfully with him to get him to shift his lyrics around to conform to what I felt was the underlying "rightness" in how the music—and hence the song—should unfold.

Following these three attempts to put 'Grace' on tape, it was time to tackle my other opus, borne out of the flames of my deal with Columbia Records.

I start to play the opening fingerpicked question-and-answer motif of 'And You Will,' instructing Jeff to wait for "two complete lines—and then you come in."

Jeff starts to mumble a line against my insistent motif about watching the lips of a lover move as she talks:

They seem like an entrance into heaven

He seems to falter with the lyrics after that, and I direct him to repeat the verse with different lyrics, as I felt the song needed a hypnotic, hieratic repetition of its opening musical statement.

I start playing the motif again, and Jeff says, "Oh no wait—I know some cool lyrics I've been writing ... it's called 'Mojo Pin.'"

He begins to intone the words in a low voice:

I'm lying on my bed
The blanket is warm
This body will never be safe from harm
Still feel your hair black ribbons of coal
Touch my skin to make me whole

I start the question-and-answer sequence again, and Jeff continues singing:

I don't want to wish for you don't want to know

I'm blind I'm in torture the white horses flow
Don't want to stay here I don't want to know
Black beauty, I love you so

His lyrics didn't seem to fit over the music, so I switched to the second section of my instrumental as Jeff repeats his lyrics again—and this time they fit like a glove.

Then comes the push-pull intro motif again:

And all these strangers that walk outside
All the sleeping city wet with pride
Remind me of huddled flocks of lambs
Holy stoned and flung to find

I sail into the second section of music again, and then Jeff stops me.

"Do it, do it four times," he says, and then, thinking better of it, "Three times of it, man—three times—and then the climb."

I dutifully follow his lead here. He was really loosening up now vocally, trying all sorts of falsetto scat glissandos and liquid phrasing throughout this section, improvising like a jazz singer.

When I get to the climb, my bolero section, Jeff lets out a high scream of ecstasy:

Blaaaaaaaaaaaaaaaaaack Beau-tyyyyyyyyyyyyyyyyyyyyyyyy!

He recites rather than sings the next section in a rush of words, which sound like:

Send the stinging whips of opinion down my back
Give me more
The sting of your opinion my love
Give me more
It's you I've waited so long to see

124

It's you I've searched so hard for
And there's so many plans at my door

Jeff then launches back into the "Don't want to wish for you" section before taking the song out over the bolero part with a repeated "Black, Black, Blackkkk!"

I had prepared a musical surprise for Jeff at the end. Inspired by the hardcore song on his *Babylon Dungeon* cassette, and determined to forge common musical ground, I had composed a violent, thrashing double-time coda, which I appended after the bolero section resolves to the peaceful, stately D-major chord for the second time—the formal close to the song.

Now I unleashed, for Jeff's approval, my new surging, aggressive coda with a fuzzed-out wah-wah attack, and it delighted him. He howled and moaned along with the music. It seemed to take the song into dangerous territory.

After finishing up this first romp through the hitherto uncharted musical terrain of what Jeff was now calling 'Mojo Pin,' I had a question for him.

"What's a mojo pin, Jeff?" I asked, in all innocence, having never heard the phrase before.

Jeff mimed a junkie grimacing and injecting his arm with an imaginary syringe. I instinctively recoiled from this dumb show, and I remember the sinking feeling as I thought to myself, oh, shit, he's put a drug lyric over my beautiful music!

I never did ask Jeff outright if he ever had tried heroin after he told me what a mojo pin was. I had never shot up heroin or any other drug. I still haven't, and I don't intend to. I had snorted heroin once in college in 1970, out of boredom and sheer curiosity, and I found that it made me feel numb and lethargic. I felt no need to do it again. Pot was definitely my drug du jour.

Now, I have compassion for heroin addicts, and I believe that opiates in general should be legalized. But I have always been ambivalent about musical commemorations of the act of shooting up, from Lou Reed's 'Heroin' to the Stones' 'Sister Morphine,' whether their lyrics are meant as ironic or not.

I believe in free speech, of course, and that an artist has the right to sing or celebrate anything. I just don't have to listen to it.

In truth, I don't think that Jeff was necessarily condoning heroin here in his lyric, which seems to describe a protagonist who is taking it as a palliative for his lost love—or maybe not. It's a poem, and is of course open to multiple interpretations.

Still, I was made uneasy when he mimed shooting up to me that day. He was freighting my music with a heavy lyrical message and image that just was not in my mind at all when I composed it— something that might be construed as condoning heroin injection, which was not exactly a message I wanted our song to convey. But as Jeff was the lyricist/singer, I let it pass without comment. I'm not a censor or into censoring my collaborators.

I knew that somewhere down the line, a casual listener might conclude that I was the lyricist on this song, or that Jeff and I were junkies. People like to project all sorts of things. As beautiful as the song was now, it also now seemed fraught to me—not a good omen.

□

The following day, we taped another run-through of the two songs in my apartment. Jeff's vocal parts and lyrics had really started jelling— he sang them with much more confidence, as if he had spent a good deal of the night working on refining them.

There were more variant lyrics he tried out. From the work tape of 'Grace':

Drink a bit of wine
We may both go down tomorrow ...
Wait for the fire, wait for the fire

From the work tape of 'Mojo Pin':

If only you would come to me, if I could only hold your face
I wouldn't need my little bottles daily
To wipe out the pain

Don't want to weep for you
Don't want to know
I'm blind and I'm tortured
The heart bruises grow

Give it up for my smile
'cause my love's coming down like the
Devil's on trial

During the hardcore break in the new coda of 'Mojo Pin,' Jeff chanted: "Shoot! Shoot! Shoot! Shoot!"

We also did a definitive run-through of our first ever collaboration, 'Bluebird Blues,' with renewed bluster and confidence. The song leaps out of the speakers as Jeff whoops and struts over my aggressive fingerpicking.

I knew we had the right stuff now. Our music was on fire.

I scheduled a full band rehearsal with Jeff and my rhythm section for the next afternoon at Countdown Studios on West 26th Street, between 5th and 6th Avenue.

The bass player Jared Nickerson had been my longtime cohort in the group since I first formed Gods and Monsters in 1989. A funny, sweet, and good-natured black man from Dayton, Ohio, Jared could play the hell out of the bass in a funk-inflected Larry Graham style. He could rock out, too, and had been a member of indie darlings Human Switchboard. I first saw him play in the mid 80s at a Black Rock Coalition showcase at CBGB's with his own group, the rock and soul band J.J. Jumpers, and I was mightily impressed.

127

Jared was my first choice to hold down the bass chair in Gods and Monsters, and he'd stuck with me through all the twists and turns of the last couple years, including our all-instrumental phase, the multiple singers with DJ incarnation, and the pared-down group with Julia.

I kept him informed about my burgeoning relationship with Jeff, and he was eagerly monitoring our progress. He had put in a lot of time in the band already, and like me he was hoping that this new incarnation, with Jeff, would prove to be the ultimate payoff.

Tony 'Thunder' Smith had been hired out from under me by Lou Reed, so I had brought in the black jazz-rock and solid groove specialist Tony Lewis to fill Smith's considerable shoes in the drum chair after seeing him play with Arto Lindsay's Ambitious Lovers. A super nice guy, he had soul, fire, and technique to burn. He proved very easy to get along with, and he played like a motherfucker with Jared.

One musician friend later questioned my choice in assembling a black rhythm section for my early Gods and Monsters bands, calling it a form of "reverse racism." Truthfully, I wanted a solid funk/jazz underpinning for my guitar and songs, and these guys had that.

Having an interracial band with players from disparate sonic backgrounds mixed up the colors of the music nicely. Plus I was dedicated to the idea of projecting an image of spiritual unity with an integrated, multicultural ensemble. So much of what I saw on the bandstand in rock music of the day was overwhelmingly lily-white, and I wanted to subvert this image and demonstrate the joy of working together in harmony across the color line. Plus, from a purely aesthetic viewpoint, I thought it looked cool.

At the rehearsal session on that Friday afternoon, I introduced Jeff to Jared and Tony and quickly ran down the music. They grasped the essence of it immediately, and very quickly the contours of full-band renditions of 'Mojo Pin' and 'Grace' emerged, with Tony adding splashy free-jazz cymbal accents to a new intro for 'Mojo Pin' I composed on the spot—an electronically sustained drone fermata on the open bottom four strings of my guitar (tuned to DADG).

Through the use of my eight-second digital delay I was able to loop and sustain this yearning, melancholy chord infinitely, in medias res, over which I added high, harmonic chimes that shimmered with a flourish of my whammy bar.

My idea was to have the basic song begin with this drone and then add the fingerpicked motif, with Jeff's keening, wordless melismatic voice fading up and emerging from the primordial musical mist. The opening electronic drone cast the whole song in an aura of longing and lamentation.

Jeff clutched his notebook, turned, and began singing disconnected phrases with his back to us, which suited me fine. I didn't feel like paying close attention to what he was doing at that moment, concerned as I was with leading my guys through the tricky stops and starts of these songs.

I knew instinctively that the best policy at this point, now that we'd worked out the song structures back in my apartment, was to leave Jeff alone to further refine his vocal parts on his own. He had consistently demonstrated his natural musical gifts to my complete satisfaction, and I saw no reason to ride herd over him now.

Besides, I have always been a democratic bandleader, as regards to giving my players a large amount of leeway to develop their own parts, only really pulling rank to change things if anything they subsequently played in my songs struck my ear as inappropriate.

This was the opposite of Don Van Vliet's bandleader-as-dictator approach, and was illustrative of how, having had a problem with authority figures and bosses all of my life, I would often follow the opposite course of whatever such a figure demanded of me or demonstrated to me as the 'correct' approach, in order to subvert the status quo and assert my own independence. Hence Beefheart's *Rise Up To Be Discontinued* became my 'Rise Up To Be,' and his tyrannical bandleader model was supplanted by my kinder, gentler, "we're all in this together" approach.

It's an Oedipal thing, I suppose, this rejection and symbolic murdering of the father figure as authoritarian baddie. To cast off perceived restrictions and inhibiting shackles in order to stand up and fight the good fight on one's own.

And as I was eventually to learn, to my sorrow, Jeff proved to have very much the same mindset toward me as I did toward Don.

Don't get me wrong—I did often speak up loudly to fight to get my various bands over the years to change their parts when they clearly didn't seem to work in the scheme of my songs, and often I would make them play specific lines note-for-note as I composed them and heard them.

But I liked a bit of give-and-take in allowing them the freedom to fully engage their own creative processes in coming up with the 'right'-sounding parts. I believed it made them feel more comfortable, and more at home with my music—part of a creative team, rather than mere contract players.

Jeff seemed to really get along with Jared and Tony, laughing and chatting with them amiably when I introduced them. And he actually got down with Tony on his kit to demonstrate the hardcore beat required for the new thrash coda to 'Mojo Pin,' in the process revealing his own marked skills as a drummer.

□

After a couple of hours running over the two songs, we broke for the day. The band was sounding good. The plan was the rhythm section and me to cut the basic tracks the following afternoon at 1pm at Krypton Studios in Soho, without Jeff. He preferred to keep away until we were ready for him, so I scheduled him to come in around 5pm to do his vocals.

Krypton was a small basement studio located at 150 Mercer Street, owned and operated by a soulful Jewish songwriter and producer named Murray Weinstock, whose production company was called Lovenotes Music. While not an 'A'-grade New York studio, Krypton was capable of quite high-quality productions. Most recently, the singer Shawn Colvin had recorded tracks for her hit debut album for Columbia there.

I had been introduced to Murray through my old friend Jon Tiven, a rock critic and talented guitarist/songwriter/producer I had befriended at Yale while he was still in high school in New Haven. He originally introduced himself to me as a fan who listened regularly to my radio show, The *Sounds From England (And Other Delicacies)*, wherein I regularly spun Tim Buckley and Beefheart tracks. Now living in New York, he had recommended Murray's studio to me when my Columbia Records deal with Julia materialized as a place to possibly record our album.

I finally checked the place out with my producer pal Steve Addabbo in early 1990. Though small, it had a homey feel to it, and I quite liked Murray, who was definitely one of the handful of 'good guys' I had encountered in my somewhat tortuous dealings with the music business so far.

I rang Murray once the songs with Jeff started to come together, and he offered me a spec deal to record at Krypton. He knew I was down on my luck at that point, after being unceremoniously given the boot by Columbia, and was kind enough to offer me studio time with payment deferred.

I had to pay his engineer, but the rest was gratis until a deal came through. I would also have to cover the costs of paying my guys for performing on the date. This was typically known as a demo deal, and it is thanks to visionary, generous people like Murray Weinstock that many indigent artists were enabled to record in the first place and have their music see the light of day.

The stage was set for recording demos of our two new songs on Saturday August 17 1991. It would be quite possibly the most momentous creative afternoon of my life.

□

It was a typically humid, overcast August day in Manhattan.

I kissed Caroline goodbye for the afternoon and loaded my Roland JC-120 amp, my '64 black Stratocaster, and my Monster case full of effects pedals and cables into the back of a Yellow Cab. I arrived in Soho just after noon, and the house engineer, a wiry, bearded Irish ex-pat named Johnny Byrne, helped me down the steps leading into the studio.

I'd been there once before, in January '91—some time before I'd ever met Jeff—to record two new Gods and Monsters songs sans Julia. I was already in despair about working with her at this point, and had just come back from a second successful solo tour of the Netherlands. Rolo McGinty was in town visiting his American girlfriend, and I drafted him in as vocalist to record the two new songs I'd written on tour.

I called up Jared Nickerson and Tony Lewis55, and invited the very talented percussionist Michael Blair to come along and add hand percussion to one of the tracks. Michael was a good friend of Hal Willner, a great traps drummer, and an omnipresent figure on the downtown scene—someone I really wanted to work with.

Those two days of recording at Krypton were a good and satisfying experience. Thanks to my great ensemble, the capable engineering of Johnny Byrne, and Murray's overall presence on these sessions, we emerged with two really hot tracks—a rousing, rustic singalong gallop entitled 'Glo-Worm,' and 'Whip Named Lash,' a driving, moody psych-rocker with African overtones—a kind of pocket opera that unfolded in several distinct movements, with lyrics concerning the first Gulf War, to which I was opposed. (Both of these tracks can be heard on my second album, 1992's *Gods and Monsters*.)

Krypton was thus a natural choice of place to record my new songs with Jeff. Both Murray and Johnny were eager to meet this brash young singer of mine. They'd heard the buzz on the street courtesy of the *Times* review of the St Ann's show.

Jared and Tony arrived at 1pm, just as I had completed setting up my effects rig, and after settling in and gulping down some coffee they quickly got acclimated to the studio situation. Jared and I would be playing live together in the small main room, with my amp miked up in isolation in the corridor outside and Jared plugged directly into the board. Tony and his drum kit were in a glassed-in isolation booth directly in front of us.

Over the next four hours, we cut several takes of the backing tracks for 'Grace' and 'Mojo Pin.' It seemed to take an especially long and tedious amount of time, as studio sessions often do. I broke a couple strings, which spoiled several promising takes and kept interrupting the flow, as I'd have to stop and re-string/re-tune my guitar each time. (I purposely never changed my strings until they broke of their own accord, in order to let them get stretched-out satisfactorily for bending purposes—a tip I picked up from the great axe man Tommy Bolin in a *Guitar Player* interview.)

We took a lot of time initially to get properly positioned in the room, and we kept having to adjust our overall placement, as the guys needed to have eye contact with me in order for me to lead them through the tricky changes and rubato time shifts in both songs.

I decided to play sitting down in a folding chair to ensure more accuracy in performing my tricky and complex guitar parts—the opposite of the 'Glo-Worm' session, where I played my driving acoustic parts in a standing position. Sitting also enabled me to reach my effects pedals more easily at critical junctures in the songs. I was able to conduct my guys with raised eyebrows and nods of the head whenever it was time to cue them to slow down, pause, or resume playing.

After punching out several good takes of both songs, I doubled a few of my guitar parts to further enhance their tensile strength, building up the arrangements so as to move from quiet, solo fingerpicked passages at some points to a walloping wall of guitars in others.

We worked a long time on the effects-laden intro section to 'Mojo Pin,' recording it as a discrete standalone section of 30 seconds or so, which Johnny then expertly spliced onto the head of the basic tune right before where the fingerpicking, and then Jeff's vocal, commences.

I was still working on the guitar overdubs at 5pm when Jeff showed up, all ready to sing. Tony had had to split earlier for another gig, and Jared left soon after, but it wasn't a problem as I was already more than satisfied with the high level of their performance and the overall energy on the two master takes we had chosen to keep.

Now it was Jeff's turn to grace these songs with his presence. He seemed in good spirits but slightly nervous, not at all the jokester he occasionally transformed himself into. He'd been working assiduously on these parts over the last three days since we'd first demoed them as duo performances in my apartment, and he was approaching this real-deal recording session with a certain amount of gravitas.

And now we were coming to the payoff. It was his turn to step up to the plate.

□

After gulping down a coffee (Jeff was a caffeine fiend, a fact he acknowledged by putting coffee-stain rings on the cover of his *Live At Sin-é* EP), he sat with me on the couch in the control room with his notebook, reviewing his lyrics. He occasionally read me a line or two and asked how I thought they sounded.

"Let's do this," I said.

Jeff moved into the main studio room and propped his lyrics up on a music stand in front of him. Johnny set him up with headphones and placed the mic carefully in front of him, and I sank into the leather couch in the control room, relaxed and ready to receive whatever Jeff was about to throw down.

First up was 'Mojo Pin.'

I have to say again here that I had never listened all that closely to Jeff's vocals and lyrics in the three days since the song had first come together for the two of us. I deliberately made myself relatively oblivious to them, afraid that too much attention would spoil the results—kind of like the Heisenberg Uncertainty Principle.

I trusted totally that Jeff knew what he was doing, based on our playing together live and recording the rough demos in my apartment, and like many guitarists, I had been concentrating primarily on my guitar sound and getting my own performance up to snuff.

As the producer of these sessions, however, I had a sense of what I wanted the overall soundfield to be like, and how Jeff's vocals would fit within the sonic tapestry of guitar, bass, and percussion. I was aware of his overarching melody, but in truth had not really paid much attention to his lyrics, beyond noting the 'mojo pin' connotation. I had also not volunteered too many of my own opinions in our rehearsals as to whether certain lines scanned better than others.

Basically, because of my innate respect for Jeff's ability, I was happy to take the leap of faith regarding whatever it was he was about to commit to tape. I had absolute confidence that, when the time came to record, he would rise to the occasion and deliver the goods, lyrically and vocally. That was the most beautiful part about working with Jeff Buckley.

And away we go …

As the sighing sampled drone of the bass strings of my guitar kick the song off, speckled with high, plucked harmonics like diamond drops of rain, you can hear Jeff let out a breath close to the mic in a world-weary sigh, like a lover taking a drag on a post-coital cigarette.

My wistful guitar figure starts up, and from the depths of his 24-year-old soul, Jeff brings forth the anguished moans that begin the song, a wounded cry for help that would hook his legion of fans—young and old, and primarily female—tight by the heartstrings and clutch them close for all eternity. The universal message here is "I'm hurt, feel my pain"—not that far from what James Dean, Montgomery

135

Clift, Johnnie Ray, and later Scott Walker were selling in its pure wordless distillation of romantic, adolescent angst.

Jeff nailed the 'Mojo Pin' vocal in a couple of takes. I more or less lay back and let it happen, in total awe of the transcendent power of his sinuous voice and the dramatic octave-leaping technique that showed off his gifts in full effect. It was obvious that he had really done his homework here, delivering an assured vocal performance that astonished me with its nuanced sensitivity and passion.

When Jeff reached the first bolero section and was about to hurl "Black black black black black black black black Beauuuuuuuuuu-ty!" in the face of the gods, he paused for a moment and I told him to really bear down on it:

"More Robert Plant! More Robert Plant!"

I was grinning and rooting him on. It was no secret that we'd spoken of fashioning Gods and Monsters into a modern-day Zeppelin, with Jeff as the shamanistic lead singer. And Jeff willingly twisted the lead-off of "I love you so ... soooooo" into his own approximation of the Plant ritual mating call, changing the vowel sound at the end to "ow!"

When we got to the final hardcore coda, Jeff shouted "Suck!" and then "Jet!" repeatedly as the band pounded furiously and my guitar shredded and shrieked like a Valkyrie, with Jeff moaning in low, agonized resignation as the song sputtered to its final death throes.

In retrospect, it is clear to me that this rave-up section represented to Jeff an aural/musical apotheosis of shooting up, especially the "jet!" part, which was like heroin spurting through a needle into a vein, or at the very least a rush of adrenalin or an explosion of defiant energy. I certainly didn't plan it to come out that way—it just seemed like an effective coiled-spring tension-and-release mechanism with which to bring the song home to an unexpected and super-charged finish. Jeff's lyrics came later.

Whatever the case, when it came time to record 'Mojo Pin' for Jeff's Sony debut, this hardcore coda was deemed too wild, too dangerous, too provocative, and too messy. It was cut from the song's otherwise immaculate arrangement—whether by Jeff or his handlers, I don't know.

Perhaps he decided to cut it himself because it depicted an experience that was just too painful and too intense and too jarring for him, whether it was real or imagined. Perhaps he just wanted the song to resolve on a peaceful yet unresolved note, with my wistful, misty guitar-drone coming back from the intro to suggest the eternal circle of existence. We never did discuss the reasons for dropping it.

Back at Krypton, we'd finished our little four-and-a-half-minute epic in a matter of a couple of hours—a song that takes you from the bottom of a well, scales the heights of ecstasy, and then plunges downward on a breakneck rollercoaster ride straight back to oblivion.

And as I write these words, it occurs to me that this song of ours, as laid down in its original format, is a near mirror image of Jeff's career trajectory—a crystallized portrait of his meteoric rise from the depths of obscurity in Los Angeles, rising out from under his father's shadow to blaze as a star in his own right—until his terrible, final crash back into the waters from whence we all came.

☐

Next up was 'Grace.'

On the demo we recorded that day, I unfurl my arpeggio'd intro figure, and then Tony, Jared, and I pull away into the 'church bells' section like the Three Horsemen of the Apocalypse in an insistent, propulsive waltz meter. It sounds kind of like a waltz for the end of the world, taken at a much faster tempo and with much more urgency than the version eventually recorded for *Grace*.

Jeff then enters the stage, singing spookily in his lower register, moodily intoning this song for haunted lovers with a spectral cast to his voice.

There's a moon asking to stay
Long enough for the clouds to fly me away

I doubled and even tripled his voice in places, such as on the "wait in the fire" refrains, which Jeff sang in octaves with himself on the last repetition of the line each time. It gave the recording such power, to hear this army of Jeffs marching through the windswept clouds like the Phantom Regiment.

He forcefully howls through his harmonica to punctuate the driving rhythm on the turnarounds, which occur twice more in the song. His bluesy, Dylan-like harp playing came as a shock to many listeners when this demo was released in 2002 on *Songs To No One*.

I had Jeff harmonize with himself on the bridge section. The wordless melisma he sings here over the instrumental section that occurs between the second chorus and the third verse is particularly eerie, Jeff squeezing every bit of torment out of the cry of the doomed lover-protagonist of the song. His dual voices voluptuously entwine themselves in minor-key harmonies that rise to a ghostly falsetto as the band gallops furiously alongside them like a stagecoach to hell, reminiscent of the phantom horseman in Schubert's lieder 'Erlkonig.'

We managed to get two different rough mixes of this song on tape that day before we had to clear out of the session. The first one has a less accomplished lead vocal, with Jeff straining and missing some high notes, and rhythmic harmonica bursts throughout the song.

The second mix boasts a much more confident lead vocal, Jeff handling the hair-pin vocal twists and turns with aplomb, his harmonica only audible in the church bell sections. This is the take that appears on *Songs To No One*.

Here, Jeff really cranks up his vocal to deliver a defiant, heroic reading of the final verse:

And I feel them drown my name
So easy to know and forget with this kiss

I'm not afraid to go
But it goes so slowwwwwwwwww
Ohhhhhhhhhh Ohhhhhhhhhhhhhh

As I play the demo back in my apartment on this overcast, humid afternoon, 20 years after the fact, Jeff's voice reaches out from beyond and rivets me with this chilling presentiment of his—and all of our—fleeting mortality. I am gripped by the palpable aura of a tormented soul with a spirit that yearns to soar high and free, yet finds itself condemned, bound for what seems an eternity on this island earth.

And yet Jeff could also be an extremely happy-go-lucky, fun-loving guy who loved life. These two signature songs of ours are the flipside of this manifestation of his personality: dark and brooding, mysterious and sorrowful—yet they manage to pack quite a punch, and still they rock out.

So how to account for this duality within Jeff? In *Dream Brother*, author David Browne claims that Jeff was bipolar and given to brooding depression. I did see glimpses at times of someone who seemed to have the weight of the world on his shoulders. Like his father, Jeff was *Happy/Sad*, Prometheus bound, the eagle of Zeus pecking at his liver (a good metaphor for the music business).

As a double-Gemini, I can relate to this. Like many artists, I have suffered serious bouts of depression too. It kind of goes with the territory.

☐

Back to the 'Grace' demo, and as a final fillip, the last vocalizing Jeff did that day was to overdub (at his own instigation) a myriad of bewitching, whispering, high-pitched elfin voices that seem to engulf and bedevil the lead vocalist as he struggles and wails through the final moments of the song, with their mocking, lilting repetition of "Wait in the fire."

139

These spirit voices have an Irish lilt to them, like leprechauns.

Than it was over. We were bumping into the next session, so we had only enough time left to make some hurried rough mixes to DAT from the two-inch multi-track, pack up our gear, and get out of the studio.

Jeff wandered into the control room, looking spent and almost sheepish with embarrassment after exposing his soul so nakedly to us.

"Was I any good?" he asked. He had the uncertain voice of a little boy—the opposite of the bold assertive doomed lover in the song he'd just sung.

"Are you kidding?" I replied. "You were incredible."

I motioned for Johnny Byrne to begin the playback, and we listened to Jeff's stirring vocal wash clean the room, like the strains of a new anthem from some mysterious and distant land. I turned to Jeff in sheer awe at the power of his voice, melody, and lyrics. In awe of the miracle he had just delivered.

Yes, I'd had faith that he would deliver a great performance. But he had far surpassed my every expectation, and I told him so.

"Jeff, that was the most amazing vocal I've ever heard from you— or from anyone else. You totally lit the lights of my music—our song is fucking incredible."

Right then, the jazz drummer Kenwood Dennard entered the control room. He and his group were booked to start the next session at 7pm, so we had to break down hurriedly and split without getting a chance to fully mix both songs.

Johnny busied himself with laying down rough mixes of the two songs for me to leave with as references. And as the eerie outro of 'Grace' played back in the room, I caught a glimpse of Kenwood's face. He looked totally spooked by what he was hearing: Jeff's unearthly wail from beyond surrounded by mocking spirit voices whispering over a bed of demonic, descending, dissonant chords that refused to resolve but repeated endlessly.

Kenwood's expression simply said, "What the fuck is *that?*"

□

I thanked Jeff, Johnny, and Murray for their time, and promised to make Jeff a copy of the two tracks. Then I packed up my gear and dragged it upstairs.

I caught a taxi and headed back home to the West Village, the DAT tape of the two songs safely tucked away in my pocket. I felt as if I was literally carrying the atomic bomb on my person. That's how righteous and beautiful and intense these two tracks sounded to me— even more so when I played them back on my system after I got home.

This was explosive, powerful music that I knew was going to shake the world when these songs eventually surfaced for all to hear.

And I was right.

Chapter Five

When I got home that evening, I listened to the tracks over and over, marveling at the sinuous melodies Jeff had come up with, and the way they snaked and coiled around the dense thicket of music I had created underneath.

In certain cases, Jeff's melodies directly derived from my guitar figures—in the "weep for you" section of 'Mojo Pin,' for instance, his vocal melody is nearly identical to my fingerpicked motif, while in 'Grace,' his wordless vocalese over the mid-section bridge precisely dovetails with my ascending and descending guitar chords.

But in most instances, the range of his melodic invention and flights of vocal derring-do seemed to come out of nowhere. His risk-taking arabesques seemed to grow organically from the harmonic movement of my guitar lines and chord patterns in dazzling spires that go far beyond mere scalar technique into the realm of pure enchantment.

Like his hero Nusrat Fateh Ali Khan, Jeff was truly capable of singing in tongues, with vocals that touch upon the sacred, the spiritual, the devotional. To this day, he remains the best vocalist and most creative collaborator I've ever worked with.

I knew after playing back these songs that no matter how complex or thorny a guitar instrumental I handed him, Jeff would invariably come back with a beautiful and appropriate melody for it—one that would sound absolutely right within the musical framework. And lyrically, I felt his words, like his melodies, fit my music like a glove. His imagery—startling at times—and narrative tropes showed him possessed of considerable poetic gifts.

Some cynics have criticized his lyrics as juvenile, dealing as they do with many adolescent romantic clichés of doomed lovers, falling rain, blind and tortured souls, and so on. In truth, I do find some of the lyrics on *Grace* a little bit cringe-inducing (especially the "I love you ... but I'm afraid to love you" part of 'So Real,' which I remember Jared Nickerson and I snickering at after the album came out, feeling that Jeff had deliberately created a "pussy moment" for his considerable female fan base).

But not 'Grace,' not 'Mojo Pin'—and not the many other songs we wrote together. Perhaps I am being partisan here, but I find the lyrics to these songs to be of a very high quality. They serve the music superbly.

My wife fell in love with these songs too when I played her the finished studio demos, and she too was convinced that I was on to something momentous in collaborating with Jeff. The two of us, like so many others, had fallen under his spell, seduced by his waif-like aura and the passionate and soulful grain in his voice.

I told Caroline that I was convinced that I had finally found the singer who would enable Gods and Monsters to soar out of the ashes of my Columbia deal; that I totally believed in Jeff and our collaboration together, that this was just the beginning of a brilliant collaboration—and that I was ready to seriously dedicate all of my energies to making the band fly.

❑

The day after the demo session, I flew off to play with my pal Nick Cave at the Ein Abend En Wien (A Night In Vienna) festival in Rotterdam, the Netherlands, in a reprise of our radio duet of a couple of months previously, where I accompanied him on improvised National steel guitar while he read from his book *And The Ass Saw The Angel*.

I remember carrying a cassette of 'Mojo Pin' and 'Grace' with me to the Netherlands, debating whether or not to share it with Nick. In the end I decided not to, for fear that he might dislike the music and subsequently dismiss our collaboration, as he was known for some very tart opinions about performers, or pilfer some of our musical ideas before we had a chance to get the tracks out into the world!

This was mostly just paranoia on my part, although Nick's use of *Trout Mask*-style vocal mannerisms and discordant slashing guitars in The Birthday Party gave me pause for reflection. Pop music is a well-known playground, where wholesale borrowings and outright thievery constantly go on (these days under the post-modern name of 'appropriation') as a means of keeping up with the latest pop fashions and musical trends.

Still, my most certain hunch was that, at the very least, Nick—like most pop stars a supremely competitive and cocksure fellow—would instantly sniff out the fact that he faced a formidable up-and-comer in the form of young Jeff Buckley. And since I didn't want to jeopardize my burgeoning relationship with Nick—or let him know what I had on the drawing board at that point—I decided to keep schtum about Jeff. For the time being, anyway.

Someone I did play the tape for, though, was Hal Willner. Arriving back in New York a week later, I got a call from Hal inviting me to visit him in his new apartment off Tompkins Square and to bring along my demo tape with Jeff, which he had heard about through the grapevine.

I went over to see him on a late August afternoon. After surveying Hal's stylish new digs in the fashionable East Village—plus his voluminous vinyl record collection and miniature statues of comic icons Laurel and Hardy—I proceeded to get stoned with Hal, and then I played him the tape.

He was seriously impressed, both by the songs and the way the tape caught Jeff in perfectly impassioned, angst-ridden voice. He did, however, sardonically raise an eyebrow at Jeff's soon-to-be-patented 'doomed lover' persona, which did not quite square with the generally cheerful if not manically gleeful cut-up we had both grown to love.

Caroline also remarked on this. In the few times she had met Jeff, she had really taken to him. There was something about his little-boy looks and the insouciant spring in his gait that brought out the nurturing, mothering instinct in her and many other women. Jeff was a born charmer and seducer of just about anyone of either sex who crossed his path—all he needed to do was train those big Scorpio eyes on them.

His acute awareness of the hard fate that had befallen his father informed not only his singing style, which bore obvious traces of Tim's swooping falsetto and risk-taking vocal acrobatics, but also in his obsessive use of the junkie metaphor in his lyrics to 'Mojo Pin,' which in my opinion can most likely be traced to his obsession with his father's overdose—as can the defiant but gloomy worldview that permeates the lyrics to 'Grace.' Because of his close connection with his dad, drugs and tragic death seemed like touchstones in his central lyrical mythos.

This was the melancholic other side of Jeff Buckley—the side that most pre-dominates these songs. And while he certainly could be gloomy, depressed, and moody offstage, he was known for the most part as a very 'up' kind of guy.

Hence Hal and I just shook our heads, marveling on listening back to the songs at the acute dichotomy between Jeff's singing persona and the relaxed and for the most part fun-loving kid we knew.

Hal told me to stay in touch and keep him closely informed of our progress. He was plainly interested in producing us, once I had secured a new recording deal.

I soon got the tape to my lawyer Michael Ackerman, whom I empowered to shop it aggressively in pursuit of a new label deal. Michael was very impressed with the music on the tape and excited about the band's potential now, with Jeff as lead singer and his old friend Jared Nickerson on bass.

Meanwhile, I stayed in fairly close communication with Jeff back in California. I was plotting our next move, which naturally enough meant showcasing Jeff live in New York with the band, and to that end I arranged for us to play in October at two key events in the city: a benefit at Tramps for the listener-supported freeform radio station WFMU, and a closing spot at the CMJ Convention, an industry schmooze-fest focusing mainly on underground indie bands, as well as non-mainstream major-label acts—and thus a good place to be seen and scouted by A&R people.

While pondering whether or not to come back East for these shows, Jeff dropped a bombshell on me, telling me that he was going to audition soon for Mick Jagger's touring band (coincidentally, I had helped recommend players to Mick's manager, Tony King, while I was still working at CBS).

"When you get the call from Mick, well—you just have to go," he nonchalantly explained, while a tremor of anger and despair shook me to the pit of my stomach.

This was the second time I had felt a sense of betrayal in my dealings with Jeff, or at least an indication that we were not totally on the same page together (the first being his grandstanding refusal to shake hands with David Kahne at the Columbia offices that spring), indicating that he was not 100 percent committed to Gods and Monsters.

"I see," I said, biting my tongue but thinking, what about *my* group you told me you were committed to joining? Here I was, trying to pull strings for us in New York, engaging my lawyer to hunt down a deal, revving up for another assault on the labels with Gods and Monsters mk3, and Jeff was ready to fuck off with Mick.

But this was the music business, where people routinely and casually flaked out of commitments right and left, always seeking to improve their position from moment to moment. And hadn't I done this myself with Julia, when Kahne had dangled the idea of transforming our collaborative album project into what would essentially be a Gary Lucas solo album?

146

To be fair, that was after two years of working with Julia, and after a good-faith effort on my part to follow the company dictum to work together with her as a team had turned into a fiasco. Here, on the other hand, Jeff seemed ready to gallop off in another direction, just as we had taken the first baby steps toward working together—and when we hadn't even gotten out of the gate yet.

I silently prayed that Jeff's audition with Mick would come to nothing, and sure enough it fizzled out. I could well imagine that Jeff, with his type-A personality, charismatic looks, and considerable musical gifts, would have generated just a little too much heat in the room for Mr Jagger to handle.

In any case, Jeff lined up another trip to New York for October, in order to play with us and visit Rebecca. Meanwhile, Ackerman got busy talking-up our tape to his various industry contacts.

I busied myself in September working on a side project called The Killer Shrews, a kind of post-punk super group with Jon Langford from The Mekons and Tony Maimone from Pere Ubu. We recorded an album in Chicago and played well-received shows at Tramps in New York and Maxwell's in Hoboken, but my heart was with Gods and Monsters throughout. I just couldn't wait for Jeff to return and really fire up our band.

❑

In October, I got my wish.

Jeff returned to Manhattan with even longer hair than before and eagerly jumped into band rehearsals for our upcoming showcase gigs. The idea was to take the stage without Jeff and then bring him on in the middle of our set as a special guest—a Dylan-like 'mystery tramp.' We would first perform 'Bluebird Blues' as a duo, and then do full-tilt band versions of 'Mojo Pin' and 'Grace.'

At the Tramps show in late October, I'd been invited by my friend, WFMU DJ Nick Hill, to perform with the full band on a bill that included Syd Straw, Eric Ambel, and Marshall Crenshaw. We kibitzed for hours in the packed club, watching bands and solo artists come and go off the tiny stage, waiting to go on, until finally, late in the evening, it was our turn, and we were to be introduced by WFMU DJ Jim Marshall, aka The Hound.

The Hound was a loveable misanthrope, a fellow pothead and a tart connoisseur of Iggy Pop, rockabilly, and old 50s blues who did a Saturday afternoon show I listened to regularly. He had me up there once, we got high, and when we were on the air I made the mistake of playing one of my electronic soundscape pieces when I should really have been rocking out, which he ribbed me about mercilessly. Still, whenever my name came up he would refer to me on his show as "Gary Lucas ... he has the GOOD pot."

This time he introduced me as "the Rupert Pupkin of rock'n'roll," Rupert Pupkin being the deranged fan (played by Robert DeNiro) who runs an imaginary television chat show in Martin Scorsese's *The King Of Comedy*. So when I took the stage I zinged The Hound back: "Hey Hound, wasn't Rupert Pupkin that guy who made fake broadcasts out of a basement in New Jersey?" This was a reference to the WFMU studios, which for many years were located in the basement of a building on the Upsala College campus in New Jersey.

Gods and Monsters sans Jeff opened with a heavy metal fanfare of Wagner's 'Ride Of The Valkyries,' which segued directly into the propulsive instrumental 'King Strong,' which had already received a lot of airplay on WFMU. The crowd was really receptive to our performance, and after Jeff came onstage the temperature in the room rose another couple of notches. After zipping through 'Bluebird Blues' we stormed through 'Mojo Pin' and 'Grace' and got quite an ovation. Jeff was especially flushed with triumph at this, his first major outing on a New York City stage in a high-profile venue after the St Ann's tribute show.

I knew we were doing something right when hip indie singer-songwriter and industry darling Marshall Crenshaw, who was emceeing the show, took the stage immediately after our set and said sarcastically, "Well, folks, just like on WFMU, we sure have heard *all kinds* of music playin' up here tonight," rolling his eyes on the words "all kinds."

This gratuitous putdown, reminiscent of Dean Martin's infamous digs at The Rolling Stones on his TV show during their first US tour, reminds me today just how potent we must have been as a new band, threatening the rock status quo in New York, to warrant such an unprovoked, backhanded jibe from Mr Laidback Good Vibes.

Crenshaw's insult—and The Hound's previous attempt at one— served to illustrate the routine jealousy and resistance I encountered during this period in my efforts to re-establish my presence, my music, and my new band in the tough, competitive atmosphere of New York. It was not all that different from what Jeff had experienced in Los Angeles, except I was older and theoretically wiser (which likely made it even more difficult).

I did have pedigree back then for having played with Captain Beefheart, but this also seemed to mark my own music as 'weird,' causing people to dismiss it without even bothering to check it out. I write this today in a somewhat more satisfied mind, in light of having been profiled recently by the *New York Times* and the *Wall Street Journal*, but it took about 20 years of concentrated hard work to achieve these accolades.

There's a song on the latest Gods and Monsters album, *The Ordeal Of Civility*, that sums up my philosophy pretty well. When I perform it live, I usually preface it by saying:

"When everybody says you're through, what you gotta do is CHIME ON."

As Woody Allen said, 99 percent of success is just showing up— and, I might add, showing others up. Rise up to be, indeed! Still, rising in the cut-throat music business by playing non-mainstream music has never been an easy climb for anyone—nor is it without its pointed setbacks.

At the end of the WFMU benefit concert, we were all invited to come back onstage to jam on Neil Young's 'Fuckin' Up.' I rushed to pull out my '66 cherry-red non-reverse Firebird with the special leather strap I had had custom-made with a metal clasp in the shape of a phoenix, symbolizing my rising from the ashes of the Columbia deal.

When I reached for the guitar, however, I discovered that some asshole had stolen the strap clean off it.

Chime on ...

□

A couple of days later, on Friday November 1, Jeff made his second appearance with Gods and Monsters at the CMJ Convention, at a gig held in my old stamping grounds, the Knitting Factory.

This was to be a crucial showcase for us. CMJ was a magnet for various industry movers and shakers, as well as the many underground rock fans that flocked there every year from all over the world to attend panels and see myriad bands in venues all over New York during the three-to-four days of the festival.

As an underground event, CMJ had replaced the earlier New Music Seminar; the same idea would later be copied and expanded upon at South by Southwest. It was organized by the *College Media Journal* (hence CMJ), a tip-sheet for college radio station personnel that operated like a mini-*Billboard* or *Record World*, with charts and gossip columns touting supposedly 'happening' new bands.

Nick Cave was in town with The Bad Seeds, and having finally told him about this fantastic new singer I was working with, I'd invited him to come and check out the new lineup of Gods and Monsters. Nick of course knew all about Tim Buckley. He promised he would try to show up with some of his band, and presumably they were sitting somewhere in the back of the packed club now, near the bar, along with Susan Feldman, who had said she was going to bring along a special friend of hers.

To set foot back in the Knit was strangely satisfying to me. It was eerie to be revisiting the place where I had launched both my solo career in 1988 and Gods and Monsters mk2 with Julia the following year—but it felt right. Now I was ready to showcase the new Gods and Monsters and my best singer ever, and the Knit gave us a high-visibility closing spot around midnight.

Tony Lewis couldn't make the gig, so I drafted Michael Blair in on drums, and we rehearsed with Jeff the day before the show at Countdown. Pony-tailed Michael, who had recently come off the road with Lou Reed, fell effortlessly into the sway of the music, and he more than made up for Tony's absence that evening.

We weren't going to get the benefit of a soundcheck, so it wasn't until about 11pm that I arrived at the club. It was a frigid November night, and I recall dragging my Roland JC-120 amp, my Monster case of effects, and several guitars into the cramped foyer outside the stage entrance with the help of my roadie for the night, an older rock fan named Dennis.

Dennis and his longtime partner Lois were famous on the local music scene as avid concert-goers, die-hard fans, and basically gophers and slaves for many of the British rock groups visiting New York, including The Mekons, The Fall, and Happy Mondays, who wrote a song about them entitled (naturally) 'Dennis And Lois.'

Jeff and the guys joined me shortly thereafter to wait in the unheated hall outside the main stage door, where we sat, anxious to play, for what seemed like hours, all of our gear splayed on the floor in front of us, including our amps and my guitar effects, which I had set up on a portable table.

These club gigs invariably ran late, and at about 12:45pm The Microscopic Septet, a twisted jazz-rock instrumental group led by the bespectacled, short-haired saxophonist/composer Phillip Johnston, came trudging through the door, fresh from the stage.

I recall Phillip jeering at us with a typically sarcastic departing musician's remark along the lines of, "Too bad about running over your time allotment, man, but hey, we were great ... and what's the name of *your* band?"

It's funny to recall this now, as Phillip and I later became good friends, and are now co-leaders of the Captain Beefheart tribute band Fast 'N' Bulbous. But back in 1991, although we'd never been formally introduced, we were ostensible rivals on the so-called downtown scene. (I've always subscribed to Rip Torn's philosophy as espoused in the final scene of Norman Mailer's paranoid-conspiracy film-cum-home-movie *Maidstone*: "Don't you know the one leading with the insults is the one eating the shit?" I never lead with insults in my encounters with anyone, even people who I know to be malefic enemies.)

We got onstage and set up as quickly as possible in sight of everyone. Michael Blair luckily had the benefit of using the house drum-kit, and Dennis helped me out as best he could with the heavy lifting, but as usual there were no roadies. We didn't have the luxury.

After a brief test of the mics we began with a free-form space improvisation before launching into our signature opening instrumental, 'King Strong.' A video shot from a stationary camera set up at the soundboard in the back of the Knitting Factory shows me dressed all in black—black silk shirt, black Levis. Jared is dressed in a black muscle shirt, showing off his weightlifter's physique.

After a couple of numbers I announce to the crowd that I've brought a special guest with me that evening, and Jeff strides out, clutching his notebook, from the side foyer entrance, wearing a thrift-store black jacket with white panels that hugs his skinny frame.

He faces the crowd, his long hair framing his sensuous face and pouting mouth, and while I plug in and tune up my acoustic Gibson J-45, Jeff squints at the audience and says, "Hey, this is a blues that Gary came up with ... that's like the first thing we ever came up with ... and it's in G." And away we sail into 'Bluebird Blues.'

I begin fingerpicking my rolling-and-tumbling, happy/sad riff, and then Jeff starts singing:

I'm a stone-cold loner
I'm as hard as a man can be

I am a stone-cold loner
I'm as cold as a man can be

Hearing Jeff begin with these lyrics (instead of his customary "I have an angel") sends a chill down my spine.

I am busy busting out my rippling guitar riffs, but I am screaming inside; what the fuck is Jeff saying, and why? Here I believed he was joining my group, yet the first lyric out of his mouth seemed to be a way of separating himself from us. By singing "stone-cold loner," he was declaring himself to be exactly that: not a member of my band but a solo artist.

I feel like I've been kicked in the balls, but I continue to play on seamlessly, giving no visible display of the anxiety that has been set off internally by Jeff's new lyrics.

What game is he running on me, I wonder. What exactly is he trying to say here?

We finish the number to hearty applause and whistles, and Jeff and I shake hands. Maybe my fears are groundless.

I switch over to electric guitar for the next song.

Jeff seizes the moment to address the crowd while I tune up.

"Yeah ... shall I tell that joke, that I told the other time?" he asks, turning to me.

I don't know what the hell he is talking about, so I say nothing.

"Got this ... there's this thing I learned—and it was really an important lesson—OK, when you're listening to the radio, and this song comes on, and it's a band, and it's really old, and you think, I know, what is that band? I know that band. But you don't know what the band is ... is that Crosby Stills & Na—? No! Is that like, old? But you don't know what the fuck ... what the fuck IS that? Stop torturing yourself, man, because it's ... the Grateful Dead."

There are titters from the hipster crowd, for most of whom the Dead were considered anathema and of an earlier hippie generation.

"I was at this guy's birthday party, man, and ... what *is* that?" Jeff

153

continues. Then, in a strangulated parody of Jerry Garcia's voice, he sings the opening line of the Grateful Dead's well-known song 'Casey Jones.'

"Drivin' that train ..."

I cut Jeff off here by playing the wistful intro to 'Mojo Pin.' The bass and drums kick in, and Jeff segues smoothly into his mellifluous moan. We perform a muscular rendition of the song, climaxing with a spasmodic thrash in the "shoot 'em up" section, Jeff shrieking wildly and then emitting a coy moan as the song shudders to a close in a welter of fuzz guitar and a splash of cymbals and drums.

But my paranoia button had already been pushed. I was hardly a major Grateful Dead fan, although I liked their first couple of albums, but I wondered now whether in his spoken introduction Jeff was trying to associate Gods and Monsters' earlier instrumental playing with the Dead. Maybe it was a backhanded putdown, another way of disassociating himself with the band, along the lines of his "stone-cold loner." (I soon dismissed this thought, as I didn't really see the link, although more than a year later, in his four-star review of *Gods and Monsters*, Robert Palmer would note that the instrumental basis of many of the songs reminded him of the Dead. Go figure!)

The crowd at the Knitting Factory scream and shout after 'Mojo Pin,' the song having functioned as a collective catharsis after Jeff mimed his mini-breakdown at the end. He then steps up to the mic one more time while we retune.

"All right, this song is called, um, 'Grace.'"

I launch into the intro, hit a false major keynote (to which Jeff says "nah"), and then execute the intro correctly. Jeff punctuates the opening chords with quick upper-register swoops from his harmonica.

It's a hard-charging rendition, Michael Blair kicking out fancy tom-tom polyrhythms, Jared adding ghostly harmonics and strummed chords on his Pedulla bass. Jeff's agonized wails of "wait in the fire" seem to come from deep in his gut. We close on the fermata'd E-flat over E-minor dischord to an equally fervent response from the crowd.

"Thanks," says Jeff. "That's all."

He turns and goes back over to shake Michael Blair's hand as I announce him again.

"Jeff Buckley!"

Jeff then moves toward Jared and me on his way to stage door, whispering sharply and intently to us. "That's it! That's it!" As in, "I'm done here—now get off."

But we have one more number to play: 'Right Off,' the instrumental funk/boogie theme from Miles Davis's *Jack Johnson* album, which segues into a psychedelic rave-up version of Suicide's 'Ghost Rider.'

I pointedly ignore Jeff's admonition to split the stage with him—who does he think he is, trying to order us off the stage like that?—and signal Michael Blair to begin the solo shuffle that counts down our instrumental blastoff. And then we really do blast off, pulling out all the stops and getting the crowd on its feet by the end of this number (which you can hear in its live entirety on *Gods and Monsters*).

We weren't trying to upstage Jeff by playing 'Right Off'/'Ghost Rider' after his incandescent version of 'Grace.' The medley had long been planned to finish our set; Jeff knew this and our agreed set order well in advance. But something within the stone-cold loner made him rebel that night when it came time for him to leave the stage while we carried on without him.

Whether it was his ego asserting itself or just petulance on his part, I'm not sure. Perhaps it hurt him to leave the stage at that point. Perhaps it made him feel that he was not a real part of the band, but rather an appendage. Whatever.

In retrospect, I blame myself for not trying to integrate Jeff in the band more fully at that point. Perhaps I should have had his vocal numbers conclude the show. But as we had only written three songs together at that point, I thought to keep his appearances in the center of the show, as a cameo, which would whet the appetite of everyone in the crowd for more Jeff Buckley with Gods and Monsters down the line.

I was also back to running the band without Julia as primarily a showcase for my playing, so I had opted to go out on a spectacular display of guitar pyrotechnics. And I wasn't about to turn command of the band over to Jeff at that point when he implored us to leave the stage with him. I had founded the band, and I had been leading it since 1989, so his attempt to herd us offstage by imperial fiat seemed pretty cheeky—on a par with his behavior toward David Kahne at Black Rock.

A year later, the *Wall Street Journal* cited *Gods and Monsters* as one of the best albums of 1992, and the writer, Jim Fusilli, singled out this instrumental as a standout track. (Jeff, having long since quit the group, was not present at all on the album.) So I still believe I did the right thing here by finishing the set the way I'd originally planned.

After the show, many well-wishers came to say hello as we packed up our gear in the little hall backstage. Jeff went to the bar to say hello to his friends, including Susan Feldman. He came back to report that she had really enjoyed the show and had brought her special guest along with her: John Cale, whom Jeff described as looking like a seedy version of the Ancient Mariner, dressed in a full-on sailor suit.

There was no sign of Nick Cave or any of his Bad Seeds, but their names had been crossed off the guest list, so they definitely were in attendance.

I shrugged off Cave's not coming backstage to say hello, but Jeff took it to heart as a personal slight—a rejection of his performance from one of the so-called rock royalty he respected and from whom he wanted approval—even though he had never met Nick before.

"What happened with Cave?" he asked. "Why didn't he come backstage? Oh man, I must have sucked."

I attempted to console him. "Jeff, it doesn't mean anything. He probably had someplace else to go with his band after our set. Or, more likely, he took one look at you, saw a younger, more talented singer staring him in the face—and he didn't like it. He probably views you as a competitor. No wonder he didn't want to acknowledge you—*if* he saw your performance at all. Maybe he split before you came on—who knows?"

Nothing I said could allay Jeff's depression over this imagined slight by Cave. He brooded about it for days. It seemed to further reinforce whatever negative feelings he had been forming in his mind about becoming a member of Gods and Monsters. It was something that added to the general aura of discontent that seemed to be coalescing under the surface of his stated willingness to collaborate with me.

In retrospect, it occurred to me that one of Jeff's most poignant lyrics from 'Grace'—"I'm not afraid / Afraid to die"—also appears as a key lyric in Nick Cave's magnum opus, 'The Mercy Seat.' Was it an unconscious quote on Jeff's part? For sure he was a Cave fan. Perhaps he thought Nick had noticed this refrain in 'Grace' at the Knitting Factory, and left in disgust.

I never did ask Jeff after the show why he sang that he was a "stone-cold loner," or why he had attempted to pull us offstage after we finished 'Grace' that night. I knew something was up with him, but I was in denial, preferring to paper over these nascent signs of dissatisfaction on Jeff's part and move forward.

□

A day or so later, Michael Ackerman called from Los Angeles and said that he had some good news on the label front.

He and I had both been actively shopping our demo tape. I had dropped a copy off to Peter Wright, head of Mute Records America, in the hope that he would recommend it to the CEO in London, Daniel Miller, whom I'd met back in the 80s while doing A&R for Upside.

Ackerman was the first one to get a solid bite, however. He had sent our tape up to Kate Hyman, the head of A&R for Imago Records, a new boutique label distributed by BMG and run by British record man Terry Ellis, one of the co-founders of Chrysalis Records.

It turned out that Kate was a huge Tim Buckley fan, and she had been knocked out by our demos. Now she wanted to set up a meeting with Jeff and me as soon as possible. No doubt the buzz about Jeff's live appearances with Gods and Monsters in New York was starting to spread through the industry.

I leaped at this news and told Michael to schedule an appointment with Kate as soon as possible. I then called Jeff, who seemed elated.

A few days later, I made my way up to Imago's midtown offices and waited for Jeff to join me. As I surveyed the typically glitzy reception area strewn with magazines and framed posters of Imago's current signings Henry Rollins, Paula Cole, and Aimee Mann, I felt the déjà-vu of entering once again into the slippery and treacherous major-label world.

I had heard a lot about Kate Hyman, but we had never been introduced, and I was quite looking forward to meeting her. I had seen her once at CBGB's and found her to be exceptionally attractive.

Jeff soon showed up and I rose to greet him with a hug and a handshake as he ambled off the elevator. Out of the corner of my eye I spotted Kate semi-hidden behind the main door to Imago's suite of offices, peeping around the corner of the door and studying the two of us intently but surreptitiously, no doubt trying to size up our relationship before our meeting so as to try and best figure out how to deal with us. I glanced directly at her but she quickly moved away before I could make eye contact.

Jeff and I sat together, waiting to be called into our meeting. I remember him making disparaging remarks about Henry Rollins, whom I'd shared a bill with solo in Eindhoven the year before, when he was doing his spoken-word thing with Lydia Lunch. Henry, Lydia, and I had had breakfast together the next morning in our hotel, and he told me he really dug my playing. I thought he was a good guy and an OK poet, but I didn't exactly love his hardcore thrash music.

Eventually, we were called into Kate's office, where she greeted us warmly and with mutual respect. She proudly pointed to a large photo of Tim Buckley that hung on her wall and said that he had been her favorite artist ever since her college days. I think this was supposed to reassure us that she was the most sympathetic A&R person we could ever hope to find, given her love of Jeff's dad, but Jeff hardly reacted to this information at all.

Early on, I could sense a dichotomy in Jeff's view of Tim. On the one hand he loved Tim, and Tim was obviously his biggest musical influence. Tim's incredible talent was part of his DNA. On the other hand, he was wary of people who were drawn to him simply because of his being Tim's son. He wanted to be his own man and his own artist.

Plus Tim had left an enormous legacy for Jeff to try to live up to. Tim had six albums under his belt by the time he turned 24, which was Jeff's age at the time. And Jeff was still waiting to jump into the game.

Kate really put on the charm; she told us she loved our demo tape and was very excited about the two of us working together. She said she was sorry she had missed us at the Knitting Factory and wanted to know when we were playing again.

I told her I had invited Jeff to join me back at Tramps a few weeks hence for the official record release party of my first solo album, which since the demise of my Columbia deal I was rushing to put out in the US through Enemy. In the meantime, I invited Kate to come over to my apartment as soon as possible to hear the two of us perform live and up close for her alone.

Kate thought this an excellent idea, and we made plans to have her drop by to hear us. She showed up a couple of nights later with her friend and fellow Imago marketing exec Jim Leavitt, whom I had met previously, and a young British friend of Kate's who was now working as her assistant. Caroline was in attendance too. Our guests were sitting on the couch in Jeff's usual spot, so he pulled an ancient wooden folding chair up close to me, and together we ran through our three numbers.

They seemed delighted with our performance. I then invited them to take a look at a VHS tape of our show at the Knitting Factory CMJ showcase. Kate seemed strangely perturbed at this, perhaps because she feared that we had another tool with which to scare up a deal with a rival label, but she promised to be at Tramps the following week for my record release show, where I would again feature Jeff.

□

On Thursday November 7, Susan Feldman, who was keeping abreast of our developing situation, invited Jeff and me to come with her up to the Ethical Culture Center on 64th Street and Central Park West. The occasion was a poetry reading by Lou Reed from his new book *Between Thought And Expression*.

Susan had stayed in close touch since our summer dinner and had become one of my confidants regarding my ongoing situation with Jeff. I had ready access to her and found her to be supportive of the notion of further developing Gods and Monsters with Jeff as lead singer.

However, she bridled when she heard about Kate Hyman entering the picture, and she told me that she thought that Jeff and I could do better than Imago Records, which at that point had no real track record, and certainly no current hit-makers. At best, they offered major distribution through BMG. Instead, she casually mentioned that she had met David Kahne and was very impressed with him, and maybe it would be a good idea to get our tape over to him at Columbia.

"Are you crazy?" I replied. "Kahne is the asshole who wrecked my Columbia deal. Now you expect me to climb back in bed with him with Jeff? And why would he have me back, after booting me out of there in the first place?"

"Gary, if you always think negative thoughts, sometimes they can turn into self-fulfilling prophecies. Why do you think people are out to get you all the time? Have you always been like this?"

I admitted to her that I had more or less learned to expect the worst from the record business, based simply on prior experience (especially recently). Following this philosophy, if something good was then to occur, I would be pleasantly surprised.

I'd grown up a sunny, optimistic child, and seemed always to be a winner—getting into Yale, working at CBS, beginning a late entry into music professionally with a slew of amazing reviews—but the latest fiasco with Julia had really shaken my faith, and I was now doubly wary of any potential pitfalls. Kahne seemed like an utter snake to me—why go back there?

These thoughts continued to prey on my mind when Jeff and I went up to hear Lou Reed, although I didn't voice them to Jeff. Susan brought us back to meet Lou after his reading, and he was very friendly. Jeff stayed on to talk to him privately after Susan and I left.

□

During this period I was extremely prolific in writing new music.

I soon gave Jeff the gift of a new instrumental I'd written that I'd dubbed 'Fool's Cap'—a reference both to medieval writing paper (foolscap) and the invisible cap I often felt I was wearing by risking a fulltime career in music this late in the day. It was one of my best acoustic pieces, jazzy and swinging, with a driving Afro/Latin chorus.

In one of our rehearsals the week before the Tramps show, Jeff came over and said he'd written lyrics to the song, which he proceeded to sing twice through. I taped both run-throughs to DAT. Jeff utilized his Nusrat Fateh Ali Khan qawwali vocal technique to stunning effect, and I thought his performance was breathtaking. I found the lyrics very revealing, yet also a possible harbinger of more trouble to come:

And though the door was open,
There's nothing left for you now

161

But to hide your dreams away
Till they come into play

Show this song to no one

In my mind, Jeff was indirectly signaling that he was hedging his bets by only half-heartedly throwing in with Gods and Monsters until something better came along for him. Lyric aside, however, I thought it was a very catchy song with great potential, and I was keen to add it to our live set, but despite my many entreaties to that effect, Jeff never agreed to sing it live—not even once. Perhaps it was too personal; perhaps he was aware how nakedly it revealed his agenda.

In any case he always refused to perform it. Opened once ... and once only.

☐

On Sunday November 10, Jeff and I played a dream gig on our friend Nick Hill's radio show *Live At The Music Faucet* at WFMU's new digs in a suburban tract house in New Jersey.

We smoked some pot together to get into the mood before the broadcast, and then we sat facing each other on the plush studio carpet, which was really the front room of the house. We had them dim the lights so that the space was mainly illuminated by the glow from the console of the glassed-in control booth built into the room.

Jeff had brought some Nag Champa Indian incense along with him, and now proceeded to light it. He had also brought along a pair of tiny finger-cymbals and his harmonica, and he found a big African drum lying around in a chest of percussion instruments and dragged it out onto the carpet.

It was pretty hot in the room, and as the sweet-smelling incense began to waft and curl around us, Jeff pulled off his shirt. The red light went on, signaling that we were on the air, and Nick introduced us as "Gods and Monsters—Gary Lucas and Jeff Buckley."

It was a holy, magical moment that seemed frozen in time. We were both very, very stoned.

We did four numbers that night: 'Bluebird Blues,' 'Grace,' 'Mojo Pin,' and a new addition to our repertoire, Bob Dylan's 'Farewell Angelina.' Dylan's original version had recently been officially released as part of Columbia's *Bootleg Series Vol. 1* boxed set, and I thought it was a cool song for us to cover. I don't even remember us rehearsing it; Jeff had just jotted down the lyrics earlier, when I'd suggested playing it, and had brought them along with him to the taping.

I tuned my acoustic to an open E chord, capo'd up to G, and we just sailed into it, flying by the seat of our collective pants. Jeff began by blowing a bluesy melodic paraphrase of the song's main melody on his harp, and then I leaped in with a waterfall-like dancing raga figure reminiscent of 'The King's Chain.'

I looped it, sped it up, and ran it backward—and then declared the melody of the song in full chords on acoustic over this swirling loop, setting a rhythmic groove. And then Jeff starts to sing ...

We groove on smoothly over a couple verses, Jeff thumping the drum in time to my guitar and delivering a beautifully restrained vocal, without his usual octave-leaping tricks. After four or five verses, I start improvising a single-string lead line while Jeff blows soulfully on harp. Then I pull out my E-bow, adding infinite sustain to my psychedelic arabesques, and then I hit my bass octave pedal, and at one point it sounds like a temple full of chanting monks.

The ending is one of the coolest ever.

The sky is interrupting
And I must go where it is quiet

I switch my two 16-second delays to their slowest speeds and an electronic tidal wave of sound floods the room. I then speed up the remaining decaying original raga guitar loop, and the last notes

163

bounce in stereo from left to right and back for a long, long fade-out that must have made a lot of the stoned folks that were tuned in very happy.

We took a collective deep breath at the end and looked across at each other with big grins on our faces—we'd done it. It was the first time we had ever attempted to play this song, and we had improvised our way through it, pulling off some really magical sounds, totally in the moment. It really doesn't get any better than that during a live radio broadcast.

It was also Jeff's first time singing on the radio, and he'd handled it superbly. We bantered back and forth in the interview that followed, and at one point Jeff told Nick:

"I knew that where Gary was coming from was a lot like what I liked to listen to all my life."

Total positive vibes.

It felt like all systems go at that point. It was a very loving and friendly atmosphere—and, in retrospect, one of the nicest times we ever had performing together.

Our live on-air performance of 'Farewell Angelina' was included on a 1992 WFMU CD anthology entitled *They Came, They Saw, They Blocked The Driveway*, which was given as a free gift to folks who had sent money to the listener-supported station during its annual fundraiser. Still officially unreleased aside from that, it has acquired the status of a legendary performance in our collective history.

□

My record release showcase at Tramps a few days later went smoothly. I performed solo after a set from my friend jazz guitarist Jean-Paul Bourelly and his band, and Jeff joined me for our now standard three numbers.

In attendance that night was Mike Knuth, the head of Enemy Records, and his Girl Friday, Rosalie Sendelbach. I had given Knuth a copy of the 'Grace' and 'Mojo Pin' demos shortly after recording them, but he was the only person I played them to who had a negative reaction to them.

"I don't dig this guy's vibe at all, man," he had said. "Why don't you try and work more with Rolo McGinty? That's the singer for you."

Jeff disappeared into the crowd after we performed our duo numbers together. When I finished my solo set, Knuth was the first to come forward, smiling, eyes glinting.

"Really good set, man," he began, "but I still think that guy does nothing for you ... now that I've seen him live, I'm more convinced of that. Really, you need to find another singer to work with. I wouldn't want to put those songs you did with him out even."

As Knuth stepped off, Kate Hyman came forward with her Imago entourage. Her eyes were glinting too.

"Gary," she said, "you and Jeff were fantastic."

She reached her hand up and stroked my cheek.

"And you wrote the music for those songs ... you're such a genius."

I blushed. She seemed totally genuine. I was flattered, of course, but I tried to act nonchalant. Kate asked what my next move was, and I told her I was leaving in a few days to start a two-month solo tour of the UK, the Netherlands, Italy, and Belgium to promote my new solo album.

She said she was going to try and push through a development deal with Imago for Jeff and me, and that she'd been in touch with my lawyer Michael Ackerman about it.

Jeff and I left the club that night in high spirits. We were finally on our way.

Chapter Six

My month-long UK solo tour was fairly dire.

In my eagerness to get out there to tour, I'd let my guard down and let a British agent recommended by one of The Mekons sweet-talk me with promises of high-paying gigs all over the UK, culminating in a solo showcase at Ronnie Scott's famous jazz club in London.

I foolishly hadn't bothered with contracts—I was still very green back then—and when I got over there I found that the majority of promised lucrative gigs the agent had enticed me with had morphed into 'door deal' shows without guarantees, just a percentage of the night's receipts.

It is generally the death-knell for relatively unknown artists like myself at this point to accept such gigs—especially with a low-budget indie label releasing my work and a lame UK distributor that failed to get any product in stores while I was working over there. They wouldn't even answer the phone. This after several excellent reviews of my live show at the Berlin Independence Days Festival the previous winter, plus a major profile that spring in *Melody Maker*'s 'New Faces' section, courtesy of *Rolling Stone* editor David Fricke, a friend and supporter since my Beefheart days.

It turned out to be a very unprofitable month for me. I had to shell out for a driver and tour manager, plus a hire car and backline, only to be run up and down the British Isles like a hamster in a maze in order to play far-flung and poorly promoted gigs in dodgy venues.

The worst was in Glasgow. It took the better part of a day to get up there from a gig the night before in Hebden Bridge in Yorkshire, only to find out that the Basement Jazz Café was exactly that: a basement room in a dingy pub. The only promo for the gig was my name chalked up on a blackboard outside the pub: "An Evening of Jazz with Gary Lucas"!

This rather silly posting goes to the heart of the question of my identity as a musician. Many folks persist in putting me into the 'jazz' category, when in truth I have the soul of a rocker. Yes, I am capable of playing traditional jazz, but I don't much like to. I am coming much more from a rock, blues, and folk sensibility, with a healthy dose of classical, avant-garde, and world music influences thrown into the mix. Putting labels on music often serves as a shortcut to thinking about it. Or, as Don Van Vliet so memorably put it, "Lick my decals off, baby."

As a guitar virtuoso, I can pretty much play any music I set my mind to. Hence the 20-plus albums I've released since 1991 cover everything from traditional and non-traditional Jewish music to 30s Chinese pop and Indian blues fusion on *Rishte*, the album I made with Najma Akhtar, my most gifted collaborator since Jeff. I have also released albums of experimental improvisation, eclectic solo acoustic material, solo guitar arrangements of classical music, and psychedelic rock.

But how would you classify my music, and what section of a record store would you put it in? That may be a moot point now, given the virtual disappearance of most brick-and-mortar record stores over the past decade, but back in 1991, *Skeleton At The Feast* was displayed in the rock, jazz, and country sections of the flagship Tower Records at 4th and Broadway. Go figure.

The nature of a lot of what I do has caused headaches for the folks attempting to market my work, but it has been a blessing in terms of my ability to keep myself working. Whenever one project slacks off, I can usually segue neatly into another.

But I am getting ahead of myself here. At the end of this very sparsely attended Glasgow gig, the promoter stiffed me out of my rather meager guarantee, mockingly asking in a thick Scottish brogue, "You got a roof over yer head tonight, doncha? Yer gettin' braikfast tomorrah mornin', aintcha?"

There were a few good things about this UK tour, however, the main one being that I got some excellent write-ups in the music press—including an interview in *The Wire*, and also a very nice review and profile in *Melody Maker* by David Stubbs (another strong supporter over the years). David's profile had me plugging my brilliant new singer and promising to return to the UK with him and Gods and Monsters as soon as possible. It was the first time the name Jeff Buckley ever appeared in the British press.

The tour was also good in terms of me coming up with new music for our project together. One night at the start of the tour, I was dozing in the back seat of the car on the way from the seaside town of Whitstable, where I'd been staying on my days off, to Oxford, where I was due to play at the Jericho Tavern. (Little known to me was that the members of Radiohead were coalescing at the very same venue under the name On A Friday at the time. I have a strong feeling that some of them may have seen me perform there that night.)

My tour manager, who was driving me there, was a stone reggae fanatic, and he had a reggae mix tape going full blast in the car. I remember waking up in the back to the strains of a heavenly high register voice singing a song of such sadness and resignation that it touched me deep in my soul. The protagonist of the song was pining for his lost love (who now scorned him) to the accompaniment of sweetly weeping strings in the background. It was 'How Long Will It Take' by Pat Kelly, who possessed the highest voice I'd ever heard in reggae outside of Junior Murvin. I lit up in a joyful Eureka! moment.

Jeff would be great singing this, I thought. *This is the perfect song for us to cover!*

It was one of the most beautiful songs I'd ever heard, and I was surprised I hadn't heard it before as I am a great fan of reggae.

I couldn't wait to share this song with him. And indeed, we would work it up into our live act shortly after I got back to the States.

Meanwhile, I was feverishly writing new music for Jeff and me on this tour, mainly because Michael Ackerman had called me from New York with some good news. Kate Hyman was offering us a small development deal with Imago Records—enough to bring Jeff to New York to write with me, and enough for the two of us to live on for a while.

We were to rehearse our new songs and preview the results with Gods and Monsters on Friday the 13th of March in a public showcase at St Ann's Church—Susan Feldman's longstanding date for our new 'coming out' show. And if Imago liked what they heard, they would have the first option to fund, record, and release our debut album.

I threw myself into writing new instrumental music in my spare moments during the tour—music I thought would appeal to Jeff, and that he could add lyrics and melodies to. I also began to think about songs we could cover. 'How Long Will It Take' was one; Van Morrison's 'Sweet Thing' was another.

After a frustrating and money-losing month in the UK, I took the ferry to Antwerp and then journeyed up through Belgium, where I had a few dates booked, and then to some shows in the Netherlands. These were much better gigs. On the continent, musicians were for the most part treated with much more respect than in the UK. We were generally well taken care of—and, most importantly, well paid. It was like night and day.

In mid December, I took a ten-hour train trip from Amsterdam to Germany for a great last-minute booking at the Tacheles, a former Yiddish theater in East Berlin that was now a huge, raw, unheated industrial space that had recently started booking avant-rock and jazz. The Berlin Wall had just come down, and East Berlin's new-music fans welcomed foreign musicians with open arms. I had never played there before, but I was regarded as a living legend there, thanks to my work with Captain Beefheart.

I had booked three consecutive nights at the Tacheles, and there

169

were huge posters all over Berlin announcing my appearance. When I set up the first night, I became aware of just how chilly the bombed-out theater was, despite the long fire-truck-type hoses snaking around the space jetting plumes of hot air into the hall. Despite this, the East Berliners that came out for the show kept themselves bundled up tight in their winter clothes throughout—it was fucking COLD!

They shuffled in like zombies from *Night Of The Living Dead* and stayed mummified in their seats throughout while I played one solo piece after another—and then rose to their feet at the end with a collective roar of approval. What a reception! It was a real turning point after what had been pretty much a downer of a tour so far.

I stayed in Berlin for a week at the sumptuous loft belonging to Monika Doering, the legendary rock promoter who was packing off to Brazil for a winter holiday. I'd been given the run of her place thanks to our mutual friendship with Irmgard Schmitz, who booked shows at the Loft, where I had performed during Berlin Independence Days a year earlier.

I worked constantly on new music during that week, which coincided with a particularly frigid Christmas.

Shortly after Christmas, I took the train back to Amsterdam, where I had a final show booked right after New Year's at the Paradiso, the famous church-turned-venue that had hosted concerts by The Rolling Stones, the Sex Pistols, Nirvana, and The Velvet Underground. It has been pretty much my favorite place to play in the world ever since I performed there with Captain Beefheart in 1980. To date I have played there more than 25 times. It's a magical space.

I spent New Year's with my best friend in the Netherlands, the painter and bohemian Joep Ver, who had carved out a beautiful studio and man-cave inside a former mustard factory on a canal. His workshop was filled with his immense, colorful abstract paintings, thick gold and silver leaf impasto encrusted on the canvases. They looked like glistening dreams, shimmering in the half-light of the late winter afternoon.

Joep's loft was my favorite place of refuge in Amsterdam for many years. It had a palpable aura of enchantment about it. I recall waking up there on New Year's Day 1992, after a wild night spent trawling the canals and the clubs and hash bars that lined them in Joep's boat, the Poepejantje, with the music to what later became 'Dream Of A Russian Princess' playing in my head, all by itself.

Then, after my solo concert at the Paradiso (posters for which still hang in the windows of several houses lining the leafy side streets of Amsterdam) brought a close to two and a half months on the road, it was finally time to come home.

☐

I embraced Caroline as I walked through the front door of our apartment. She was happy to see me but could barely hide her annoyance at my long absence.

I'd explained to her many times that if you really want to have any kind of sustaining power or longevity of career in music, you needed to make as many appearances as possible, in as many territories in the world as possible.

You also had to release as much new music as possible, continuously and relentlessly. That's about the only way to stay a player in this game, especially as an indie artist. Otherwise you will be swept under the rug by the long broom of history. That often means being away for a while.

But she has never gotten used to this, and to this day she still has never gotten used to it—even after 28 years of marriage!

I kissed her hard.

"Honey, don't hate me," I said. "I know I had some dodgy gigs on this tour, but I had some good ones as well, especially on the continent—they love me there. The main thing is, I worked like a son of a bitch on new music for me and Jeff, and I really have some cool new music for the band now."

Now that I was back in New York I was eagerly awaiting his arrival from LA—a move that was underwritten by Imago but which also handily dovetailed with his burgeoning romance with Rebecca.

He called me the day he arrived in mid January to say hello and make a plan to come over the next day. He sounded thrilled to be back in New York and eager to start work with me. When I rang him back about something else later on I got Rebecca's machine, which now had a brief message on it from Jeff—and then a long excerpt from Led Zeppelin's languid 'The Rain Song' before the final beep.

Jeff came cheerfully around to my apartment the next afternoon and we picked up where we'd left off. I had a lot of new instrumental music to give him. I would record it onto DAT as I played and then give him a cassette copy so that he could work on his lyrics and melodies back at Rebecca's.

As a mentor and friend, I would also play Jeff as much music as possible by other artists that I liked, to try to speed up his evolution as a musician and creative artist. Even the greatest of supposed sui generis musicians, such as Charlie Parker, had a vast knowledge of the history of music—Parker himself would sometimes warm up by blowing his sax along with recordings of Stravinsky and Bartók—and I believed that the more cool music I could play for Jeff, the better it would enrich and widen his overall musical palette. He was super-attentive and embraced all the music I played for him like a sponge, with the exception of one of my favorite groups, The Fall (although Mick Grondahl did tell me later that Jeff and has band had got into them on tour).

A case in point was Van Morrison. Jeff had only a cursory knowledge of Van the Man's music when I met him, most of which was derived from the few singles he'd heard on classic-rock radio in LA. I remember playing him *Astral Weeks* in its entirety, and how it stunned and delighted him.

We quickly worked up a duo arrangement of 'Sweet Thing.' It was Caroline's favorite song, and she was really impressed by our version, with Jeff's finger-cymbals tingling on the beat. We debuted this song at my solo show on Sunday February 2 at PS 122, the East Village performing artist's space, on a bill with avant-dance choreographers Eiko & Koma. Jeff joined me onstage, as usual, as my special guest. It was a warm-up for our big Friday the 13th showcase at St Ann's, where we would formally debut our new Gods and Monsters project.

In the meantime, our rehearsal ritual continued, with Jeff coming over to my apartment every few days. By now, Caroline had really bonded with Jeff. She would usually be home when he arrived, and would love to chat and flirt with him. He really liked her, too. Despite our Imago advance, Jeff and I were both in fairly impecunious positions back then, and Caroline helped out by finding Jeff some work as an extra in Hungarian director Gabe Von Dettre's new film *The Diary Of The Hurdy-Gurdy Man*.

While they bantered, I would go to the kitchen to make soup and sandwiches for us before we got down to playing. Sometimes Caroline would cook simple meals for the three of us. She and I had a strong nurturing instinct toward Jeff, who had the air of the skinny, undernourished orphan. I wanted him to feel comfortable and relaxed at our rehearsal sessions, and I also wanted to feed him the right stuff music-wise at these sessions to help speed up his evolution as a budding rock star.

Meanwhile, I was getting positive feedback on our studio demos of 'Grace' and 'Mojo Pin,' which I'd circulated amongst some key tastemakers, including my old friend David Fricke. Another strong supporter was Bill Flanagan at MTV, who also wrote for *Musician* magazine. He was really taken with Jeff.

On the other hand, prior to Imago stepping in with the development deal, our demos had fallen into a black hole at the two places Jeff and I had considered as desirable homes for our project. I had personally taken the tapes to Peter Wright of Mute Records America, and I had mailed a copy to 4AD, home of the Cocteau Twins (with whose singer, Liz Fraser, Jeff would later have an affair). I never heard a peep back from either place, but that was it. Contrary to the various stories that have circulated about hip A&R folks being keen on our tapes but failing to act, I never sent the demos anywhere else.

□

Some serious magic occurred over the winter months Jeff and I met to write and rehearse at my apartment.

On the night of Wednesday January 22nd, Jeff came round in the early evening. It was a black wintry night with newly fallen white snow gleaming on the icy streets below. We got very stoned together, and I started playing a recurring bass note figure on my E-string, which I had detuned to D.

Many of the songs I wrote for Jeff are centered in the key of D and are played in this dropped-D tuning, which holds a special mystic place in my heart. I can't explain it really—it just felt right, then and now. It also fit Jeff's vocal range perfectly.

I looped my slow, recurring bass motif and began floating minor-key space-guitar lines over it, stark, doom-laden, and melancholic.

"That sounds so cool," Jeff whispered.

I turned on my DAT recorder and began taping us, starting over and fading in the looped figure from dead silence, out of the ether ...

I start weaving filigreed sonic spider webs over the recurring bass pulse, and Jeff begins a wordless wail, holding and caressing a note in his high plaintive voice. And then begins singing:

If the sun
Should tumble from the sky
If the sea
Should suddenly run dry

If you love me
Really love me
Let it happen
I won't care

My guitar entwines itself around his voice in near-orchestral crashing waves of sound as Jeff continues to sing his version of what at that moment was unrecognizable to me but turned out to be Edith Piaf's 'Hymne A L'Amour,' pitting the melody to this classic French chanson against my D-modal hieratic bassline.

Midway through this spontaneous improvisation, I switch on the wavy chorus effect built into my amp, which is pumping out both Jeff's vocals and my guitar—and suddenly Jeff is singing underwater. Here he goes off script and starts riffing:

My dream brother
I miss you so

He then delivers a rush of poetic stream of consciousness imagery that's hard to make out, ending by repeating the words "dream brother" over and over. My guitar erupts volcanically in a shrieking maelstrom of sound, a vortex spiraling downward, and then into final peace as Jeff calmly restates the opening verse of 'Hymne A L'Amour.'

Let it happen
I won't care

Together, we had created an indelible and haunting soundscape that would remain one of the most affective and effective pieces we ever recorded or performed live.

Hal Willner, who edited the DAT tapes that comprise *Songs To No One*, selected this piece to lead off the album, editing it down to 11 minutes and 35 seconds. (It may not have been the most obvious choice to open the album, but people seem to love it anyway.)

There was a whole other section that Hal cut out, where Jeff started riffing on a poem he had written, but what is left stands by itself as a haunted and transcendent piece that I number among the finest of our surviving work, and one that displays many of the qualities I consider hallmarks of my own solo music. Although the track is credited solely on *Songs To No One* to Piaf and Marguerite Monnot, who co-wrote 'Hymne A L'Amour,' the underlying music is mine.

Many of my compositions seek to take the listener on a trip outside their body and the mundane everyday existence. They are truly psychedelic—that is, mind-manifesting—in the best sense of the word, and have an otherworldly quality about them, which is no accident, as for many years I have tried to summon forth the spiritual and the numinous in my art.

My earliest years were spent absorbed first by Greek, Roman, and Norse mythology, and later by horror, science fiction, and fantasy literature and films. Perhaps it's my general alienation from the world at large that accounts for this love of the other, of the other side.

Although I obviously love life, I have been on a mission throughout my life to connect with what lies beyond this veil of tears through my music. I've always wanted to pull aside the curtain and connect with what lies beyond through my music. And since I first began to compose I have tried to manifest and bring back images from the other side in ghostly, haunting music.

The music I am most attracted to for my own listening pleasure I would define as transcendental and spiritual—especially the blues. I have been quoted as saying that the voice of God speaks through a bent note—whether it be vocal or instrumental, these sliding, wailing pitches embody the essence of spirituality to me—the sound of human struggling.

Consider the name of my group and the titles of various albums and projects of mine: Gods and Monsters, *Skeleton At The Feast*, *The Golem*, *Beyond The Pale*. These are signposts.

My favorite author is Isaac Bashevis Singer, the Polish-Jewish Pulitzer Prize winner whose fantastic novels, folk tales, and short stories deal with great metaphysical issues in a world filled with angels and demons, dybbuks and wandering spirits.

His protagonists constantly scan the landscape for signs of divinity, and signs of deviltry. And so do I.

In Jeff Buckley, I found the perfect foil and collaborator to express these celestial and demonic visions. His voice could move from the purest choirboy falsetto to an erotic caress, to a streetwalker's snarl, and his imagination was unfettered, his lyrics elliptical and allusive, romantic and Byronic.

There's a moon asking to stay
Long enough for the clouds to fly me away

In creating, rehearsing, and performing music with Jeff I always tried to give him the absolute best within me. I believed in this music totally—and I only offered to Jeff music I could imagine his voice inhabiting a space within.

This included our cover versions of other artists' songs. As predicted, Jeff fell in love with Pat Kelly's aching 'How Long Will It Take,' and we quickly worked up a cool duo version, with me looping the loping reggae riddim underneath, and then voicing on guitar the weeping string section of the original over the top using my volume pedal and whammy bar to mimic the swelling tides of emotion that surge in the song. Jeff handled the falsetto lover's lament magnificently.

Jeff also fell in love with 'Sweet Thing,' of course. Van Morrison's Irish gypsy soul spoke profoundly to him, and appealed to his sense of romantic adventure. And then there was a song on a Dylan bootleg I had picked up in Rotterdam in 1990, labeled on the CD as 'If I Had Wings.' It had a stomping, righteous, bluesy feel and built to an undeniable crazy joy, with an unforgettable refrain of "Fare thee well my honey."

Jeff loved the song and we quickly worked it into our repertoire. It totally rocked. Later, Dylan scholar Nick Hill informed us that its true title was 'Dink's Song,' with Dylan having apparently learned from Dave Van Ronk.

The instrumentals I'd composed for Jeff over the last few months also quickly took shape as songs after Jeff took them away to work on them. He gave some of them his own titles too, after first putting lyrics and melodies to them, while others retained my working titles.

My instrumental 'Malign Fiesta,' named for one of the last novels by the English modernist Wyndham Lewis, became 'Malign Fiesta (No Soul),' a folky hardcore thrash number that remains one of our most popular co-written songs among Jeff's fans. I went deliberately in that hardcore direction while writing it, knowing how much Jeff loved these primitive four-to-the-floor stomps.

I also composed a beautiful and ecstatically strummed acoustic instrumental with a decidedly Spanish feel to it, which I titled 'In The Cantina' after the legendary lost section of Brian Wilson and Van Dyke Parks's 'Heroes And Villains.'

Jeff loved the title and added appropriate lyrics about sitting in a cantina somewhere in Spain or Mexico in a delirious haze, raising a glass to his lost love. It is one of our loveliest numbers, with Jeff displaying his extravagant vocal gifts and singing peacock-like, à la Nusrat Fateh Ali Khan.

Another dark instrumental started out as 'Voluptuous Cruelty.' The title was a variation on the theme of Chaucer's poem 'Merciless Beauty.' I've had an interest in femme fatales (intellectually only, of course!) since falling in love with Barbara Steele's witchy Princess Asa in Mario Bava's *Black Sunday* (*La Maschera Del Demonio*), which scarred me for life as a boy. The music I wrote seemed to summon forth images of a dangerous, haughty bitch in heat.

With Jeff's approval, I retitled the song 'Story Without Words,' a reference to Franz Masereel's graphic novel of the same name, composed entirely of woodcuts without texts. Jeff's lyrics are appropriately furtive and fraught with anxiety, mirroring my music, and depict a jealous lover's agonized plight.

And then there is 'She Is Free,' perhaps the catchiest and most mainstream of all of our songs, a soft introspective ballad with lyrics that could melt your heart. They seem to describe Jeff's troubled itinerant youth—always moving from town to town, friend to friend—and how he was determined to set free the woman he loved, as if his devotion to her dragged her down and got in her way:

She is free
A shadow crossing the sky
Free from hope
And this misery
She's beautiful
Away from me
She is free

I composed the music for these four songs, along with the aforementioned 'Fool's Cap,' on my trusty 1946 Gibson J-45 acoustic—my favorite guitar, and one I still play every day of my life—and wrote the rest of our songs on my '64 Stratocaster.

'Cruel' was a classic rocker with some of my most hypnotic fingerpicking, an unexpected bridge, and an explosive slide solo near the end. Jeff added biting lyrics about a woman who keeps picking up and then ditching men:

Well you're movin'
Movin' on again
Baby, you're so cruel

'Distortion' was a psych-rocker with a tricky, complex guitar figure and a double-time chorus. "I love to sing this song so much," Jeff told me shortly after we started playing it.

Don't you want somebody cool sometime?
Don't you wish that confidence could take a body over?

179

'Harem Man' was a down-and-dirty Zeppelin-ish blues-rocker with slide guitar and another million-dollar fingerpicked riff that rose from the ashes of my arrangement of 'The River' for Hal Willner's Tim Buckley tribute show.

At one point, Jeff did a scat singalong with my guitar, George Benson-style—a section both of us loved to play together. (This was inexplicably snipped from the master by Willner when he assembled the *Songs To No One* album, against my incredulous protests.) On our work tapes, Jeff fiddled with the flanger effect on my amp, and was delighted with the eerie vocals that emerged.

The pièce de résistance, though, was 'No One Must Find You Here,' which I had composed in early January after returning from Amsterdam, shortly before Jeff arrived in New York. I remember Irmgard Schmitz, who had recently brought me to Berlin to play her club The Loft, coming to visit me at my apartment shortly after I had finished writing it. I played it to her in a hypnagogic trance.

"You really love this person, don't you," she said when I finished.

This song was a real epic, cinematic in scope, and with many different movements. I had poured my heart and soul into writing it.

It expressed all of the emotions I was feeling toward Jeff at the time—all my joy and hope and fear in the struggle to make this project work. It keeps tugging at the heart, with a bittersweet repeated theme that shifts gradually into dissonance and back again.

Like 'Mojo Pin,' it opens and closes in media res with a looped harmonic drone played on the bass strings of my guitar, moving from contemplative resignation to a bold scream of assertive triumph, and then fading back into the eternal slipstream.

□

One February afternoon, Jeff and I were working together at my apartment. I momentarily turned my back to him to sit at the dining-room table to check some lyrics I'd transcribed by ear from my recording of Van Morrison's 'Sweet Thing.'

Suddenly, Jeff came up behind me and wrapped his arms around my shoulders in a big hug.

I froze, blushed furiously, and then rose up out of my chair, too embarrassed to do or say anything but move over to my guitar. I started playing 'Sweet Thing' as if nothing had happened.

Now, people have projected all sorts of things on me for years about my own sexuality, particularly as I look a lot like my mother! But I can assure readers I am a confirmed heterosexual who loves women (probably a little too much). And in the pursuit of female affections, suffice it to say that Jeff and I had a definite rivalry going on there.

That Valentine's Day, for instance, I took Jeff and Caroline out to lunch at one of my favorite Indian restaurants, Mitali West on Bleecker Street. Caroline later told me that Jeff had grabbed and held her hand under the table while we dined—the cheeky bastard! She loved the attention, of course, and having been up and down with her for many years I didn't take it too seriously at the time, except to duly note Jeff's rather caddish behavior.

But back to that hug. I think everyone is to some degree bisexual, but they rarely act on it. Outside of one sleepover with a famous record producer during the glitter-rock era for experimentation purposes—which amounted only to kissing and holding each other close in bed—I never had any desire or inclination to further explore my options in this department.

Whether or not Jeff had any gay experiences I really don't know, and I never asked him. There was kind of an invisible wall between us in this regard. I didn't think it was my business, and I just never went there with him.

So this may well just have been an innocent friendly hug on his part, although both Susan Feldman and Janine Nichols at St Ann's had said to me several times during this period that in their minds, the key to the ultimate success of Gods and Monsters would be for Jeff and I to fall in love with each other—which we did, of course, upon first meeting and playing together. That much is obvious. We loved each other for sure, but never in the way they were driving at.

That said, Jeff obviously loved playing with and subverting straight notions of sexuality, as did I. On one occasion, Jeff came over in the early evening, when Caroline was home, and before we got down to rehearsing he begin merrily rummaging through her closets, eventually selecting a variety of her frou-frou Laura Ashley print dresses. He then stripped down to his underwear and started modeling them for our delectation.

"I'm going to wear one of these at our St Ann's show," he exclaimed, to our general amusement.

This was in the great rock-drag tradition harking back to the Stones dressed as women on the cover of their 'Have You Seen Your Mother, Baby, Standing In The Shadow?' single, as well as The Mothers Of Inventions' *We're Only In It For The Money*. And of course Kurt Cobain had recently worn a dress on MTV. I didn't take this very seriously, but I encouraged Jeff to do it—why the hell not? I am all for outrageous statements in rock. It goes with the territory. After all, I had graduated from Beefheart University. But of course Jeff never followed through on it.

Another thing Jeff seemed to be intrigued with, besides my wife, was my penchant for exploring the other side in music, and this carried through to many of his own songs (and cover choices) once we split. One day, while we were working in my apartment—then as now stacked wall-to-wall with records, CDs, books, and guitars—Jeff noticed a copy of Gershom Scholem's famous treatise on Jewish mysticism, *Kabbalah*, that I'd been perusing.

"You know Hendrix's 'Voodoo Child'?" he said. "To me, Gary, you're the 'Kabbalah Child'."

Many years later, Jeff was to title his last live go-round the Mystery White Boy Tour. I felt I had encouraged and inspired him in that direction. Jeff had a thing about Judeo-Christian mysticism; in fact, in many of the photos of us together, he is wearing a T-shirt with a crucifix prominently displayed on it. (On another occasion, after we had split up and I became a member of The Killer Shrews for a spell, Jeff grandly told me, "I'm going to name my new band The Christ Killers!")

□

During a break from writing and rehearsing together, Jeff and I paid a visit in early February to the home studio of photographer Jack Vartoogian, who took the photos on the front and back of the *Songs To No One* album, as well as the one used on the cover of this book.

We had a fun time clowning around; Jack and his wife really made us feel at home. We were there to get a decent publicity photo to advertise the upcoming St Ann's Show, and as you can see from the resulting photos, Jeff and I were pretty happy with one another.

It was right about this time, however, that a pronounced schism in our relationship developed and served to drive us further and further apart.

Ken Hurwitz, one of my oldest friends from when I first moved to New York, had been following my career avidly since the Beefheart days. He was a year older than me, but we had been at Yale around the same time, although I didn't know him then. He was now a lawyer, and had subsequently become just about my best friend in New York. I went to him often for career advice. He had witnessed all the ups and downs of my struggles with Julia and CBS, and he was rooting for this project with Jeff to succeed.

He advised me to ask Jeff to sign a basic partnership agreement, and helped draw up a one-page, two-paragraph draft. Jeff balked at signing it, however, and simultaneously informed me that he was now being represented by a friend of Susan Feldman's named George Stein, the son of Lou Reed's attorney.

When I enquired with Susan as to the particulars, she informed me rather smugly that not only had she and Janine steered Jeff to George Stein but that she had also just heard from Jeff himself that he had just come from a meeting with Kate Hyman and Imago's major domo, Terry Ellis—a meeting to which I had pointedly not been invited. Jeff hadn't even told me about it.

My heart sank. I was incensed, naturally, and intense feelings of betrayal and paranoia began welling up. *Oh my God*, I thought, *here we go again, another power struggle with another unreliable singer* ... Just one of the many dirty, petty, aggravating little contretemps of showbiz.

When I confronted Jeff about this that night, asking him why he hadn't insisted I be there with him at this important meeting, he broke down and started crying.

"I didn't mean anything by excluding you," he said. "I feel really bad—I'm sorry."

But honestly, these seemed like crocodile tears. Jeff was always a pretty good actor. He certainly could do 'sincerity' when he chose to, simply by opening those big eyes of his and vibing you.

Frankly, I didn't buy it, but I gave him a pass on this one so as to try to smooth things over.

Jeff seemed to recover from crying mode pretty quickly. When I pumped him for more information, he was pretty vague as to what actually went on at the meeting. I will never know exactly what was said to him, or what he said in return, but I can imagine.

The writing was on the wall. In theory, we were equal partners, and we had split the Imago money down the middle, but Jeff was the one being invited to meet with the CEO. I began to feel insecure about both our deal and our relationship, but I chose to put a brave face on it, just ignore it and soldier on. What else could I do? Withdrawing was not an option, but nor was falling out with Jeff over this. We had a big and important show to put on, worlds to conquer.

Nothing more was said about this, although privately Caroline and I both felt Jeff had betrayed me here. But then I'd had that meeting with David Kahne without Julia, hadn't I. Turnaround is fair play. Instant karma. Or, as The Band put it, "Just be careful what you do—it all comes back on you."

□

We continued rehearsing at my apartment, and then in the second week of February began band rehearsals at Montana Studios in Midtown, for which I summoned my rhythm section of Tony Lewis and Jared Nickerson, who had played so well on the 'Grace' and 'Mojo Pin' demos—the tapes that had won us our development deal with Imago.

They began to learn our new songs in earnest, and I thought they were performing brilliantly, but something was amiss.

On our third rehearsal, Jeff brought in a giant boom box he'd borrowed from someone, and pointedly played a track by the 60s black revolutionary spoken word group The Last Poets over and over. It was called 'The White Man Has A God Complex.' It felt like Jeff's way of currying favor with Jared and Tony, to show them he (not I) was down with them, as it were—and a less than subtle slight on my leadership of the band and, by extension, my decision to draft in these two black players. Jared and Tony were not amused by Jeff's antics, however, and seemed more concerned with the difficult business of trying to master the twists and turns in the complicated music I had brought in for them to learn.

On our fourth rehearsal, Jeff brought with him a brand new Sony Legacy boxed set of Mahalia Jackson CDs. He conspicuously displayed it in front of us, once again showing off his 'Soul Brother Number One' credentials. But he didn't say how or where he had come by it. I wondered about that then, but I didn't say anything. I couldn't imagine him buying it. It was pricey, and we hadn't gotten that much money off of Imago. Later on, all the pieces would fall into place.

After the fifth rehearsal, Jeff pulled me aside in an arrogant manner and insisted we go to a bar near the studio for a drink. His usual fun-loving playfulness was absent, and he was in a stark, hyper-aggressive mood—something I had never before witnessed. Whether it was something that had been inspired by his new manager, the women at St Ann's, or his friends, I don't know. But the mask had dropped.

"Jared and Tony have to go, man," he said. "I can't play with these guys."

"What do you mean?" I asked, floored by this rather late-in-the-day demand. "They're playing beautifully on our songs."

"No they aren't," he replied. "I can't go onstage with them."

I couldn't exactly tell Jeff to fuck off and destroy the last ten months of working with him to develop the group, and as we were so close to the edge—in every sense of the word—I pleaded with him to at least keep Jared, who'd been with me since the beginning of Gods and Monsters in 1989, who loved Jeff's voice, and who saw this as the ultimate payoff for us after three years of trying to kick the group forward.

"OK, let's keep Jared for now. But we HAVE to audition a new drummer. There's a guy named Paul I met recently I think can do it for sure."

At this point we had less than a month before our showcase at St Ann's, and my back was up against the wall. I went against all my instincts and agreed to fire Tony to appease Jeff. It was not my finest moment, and I am not proud of it. Tony was and is an excellent player, and was also one of the sweetest people I've ever worked with, which counts for a lot in a business filled with pricks.

I went home and called Tony to give him the bad news. I told him that Jeff had given me no choice; that he'd put a gun to my head. Tony got really choked up and emotional. He really believed in the project, and he was sorry to be bounced out of it so unceremoniously.

"Watch your back," he told me. "You and Jared are next."

After that I then spent a couple of fruitless nights at Montana Studios auditioning drummers with Jeff and Jared. Jeff's friend Paul proved to be a lanky dreadlocked slacker kid Jeff had met at a supermarket somewhere in the East Village. Jeff had never heard him play before, but he liked his look and was "positive" Paul could do it.

"I'm taking the leap of faith here," he told me—just as I had the taken the leap of faith with Jeff at our demo session, but with much different results.

The guy showed up, shuffled over to the drum kit, and played some desultory basic patterns without any real finesse or conviction. Basically, he was what you might call a flubadub. Jeff got on the drums repeatedly to demonstrate what he wanted—and Jeff could really play the drums, as well as a host of other instruments—but Paul seemed flummoxed by even being there.

After flailing around a little bit longer, Paul gave Jeff a sheepish look and said, "I'm sorry, man." He then excused himself and left quickly.

"Damn, I was sure he could do it," Jeff told me. "I took the leap of faith with him!" He repeated it again and again before splitting.

Jared and I just looked at each other incredulously. No apologies, no remorse—we'd indulged Jeff's whim and it had proven a complete waste of our time.

I lined up a couple more drummers to audition over the next couple nights, including a studio guy named Alan Bezzozi, who was recommended to us by Janine Nichols, and who said we played "way too loud." Next!

Another contender was Steve Holley, who had once played with Elton John and Paul McCartney & Wings. He was OK, but he didn't really seem into our music, which probably wasn't 'pop' enough for his sensibilities.

Time was running out—and then Jeff called me with yet another ultimatum.

"Jared has to go," he said. "He just can't play this music."

I stood my ground and defended Jared's musicianship and overall vibe. He was a key man in the band to me—which is probably all the more reason why Jeff wanted to get rid of him. Maybe Jeff had caught Jared smiling sardonically at me when Paul came in to fart around on the drums.

Jeff spoke with a steely, ruthless tone in his voice, something I'd never quite heard from him before.

"If you still want to be a player here"—meaning in *his* band—"you have to fire Jared. Or I am not going to go through with this show."

Jesus!

This was a big power move on Jeff's part, fueled most likely by the Imago brain trust, by George Stein, by Jeff's buddies, by the ladies of St Ann's—all acting in concert and egging Jeff on.

Off with his head!

My experience on the New York music scene then and now has been that people generally love to pick apart any nascent creative situation and kill it in the cradle before it really has a chance to develop, mainly out of spite and boredom. There are no disinterested onlookers, especially if they have no real part to play in what you're doing. If they aren't involved or don't have a piece of it—watch out!

And if they do have a part in it, sometimes it's even worse.

Again, I reluctantly and shamefully went along with Jeff's bullshit, which I am not proud of. Perhaps I should have stood up to him in retrospect, but it was too late now. I just could not imagine backing out and canceling our St Ann's showcase, and I couldn't risk the chance or handle the embarrassment of Jeff backing out on me. The show had just been advertised in the *Village Voice* as a new iteration of Gods and Monsters, complete with Jack Vartoogian's photo of the two of us: me proudly standing over a seated Jeff, looking very much like his mentor.

I tried to appeal to him one last time.

"You're gonna have to call Jared, man," I said. "I just can't be the one to tell him. Are you absolutely sure you want to do this? He's fucking great and he's been with me from the get-go."

"He plays with a pick sometimes," Jeff replied. "It's not what I want. I'll call him."

Jared was furious. He'd invested a couple years playing with me in the band, and he was an ace player. Jeff's calling his abilities into question really cut to the quick. Plus he had been Jeff's biggest advocate when I suggested bringing him into the band as our singer. Jared rightly demanded a payoff for his time, and I agreed, dispensing pretty much what was left at this point of our dwindling Imago rehearsal funds.

□

Casting about for a rhythm section with only three weeks left to go, I scheduled a meeting with Jeff and the young son of a famous New York jazz saxophonist on the advice of my friend Jon Tiven.

The guy arrived with his bass and played for us a bit. I could see Jeff was impressed by his youthful good looks and musicianship, but I remained cool. Physically, this guy was handsome and personable, and he demonstrated himself to be quite an accomplished bassist. He asked Jeff if he knew 'Teen Town,' a famous Weather Report tune that featured a hyperactive bassline by Jaco Pastorius.

"Sure," Jeff replied causally, and then the two of them ripped into this furious fusion instrumental, with Jeff playing one of my electric guitars. Jeff mimed an exaggerated look of excitement while he was playing—a parody of his true feelings, which made me smile as I watched on—and then yelled out, "Oh, yeah—'TEEN TOWN'!"

This was the kind of empty but technically dazzling music Jeff had studied at the Guitar Center in Los Angeles, and of which he was pretty disdainful by now. Flushed from playing this testosterone-pumped jazz/rock tune, and proud that Jeff had followed his lead into playing it, the guy then casually made a remark about "fruits" while glancing in my direction—the kind of slur designed to get Jeff to bond with him over me in the future, should this kid be asked into our band project. I suppose the guy had me pegged as gay.

Jeff looked shocked at his crass remark—he was fiercely PC in that department—and soon told the guy he had to leave as we had someone else coming over to audition (which was not true).

After hating Jeff for firing Tony and Jared, I started to love him again after the way he dismissed this guy, which I saw as a vote of confidence.

"Jesus Christ—'Teen Town'," was all he said after the guy left. It was the antithesis of the music he wanted to play at this point. Plus he probably saw some potential competition down the line with the bass player's youthful good looks. The main thing that sealed the guy's fate, though, was the fact that he was also the son of a famous musician. We couldn't have two of these in our group!

❑

Shortly afterward, we had a meeting with Susan Feldman and Janine Nichols at St Ann's to discuss our upcoming show. I got there early.

"Have *you* heard 'Harem Man'?" Susan asked me in all sincerity.

"Of course," I replied testily. "I wrote the music." What an inane question. But it was nice that Jeff was circulating our work tapes to her, and that she still seemed excited by the project.

"You know I've hired the person who makes the giant puppets for the annual Village Halloween Parade for your show. We're going to have a couple huge ones onstage behind you guys when you play here."

Great, I thought, *just what we need*. We didn't have a rhythm section yet, but we did have some giant puppets.

Jeff walked in and shook my hand.

"It's GODS AND MONSTERS," Susan announced, a touch sarcastically.

Jeff shot her a withering look. Perhaps he had already decided to abandon the project; maybe he had already shared his doubts about the project with Susan when he had played her 'Harem Man.' Susan had told me he'd been hanging out a lot at St Ann's—almost living there—and she and Janine were certainly among Jeff's closest confidants. Janine had even lent him her old Telecaster to rehearse our songs on. (I had already lent him my 60s Guild 12-string acoustic—one of my prize possessions—for the same purpose.)

We didn't stay long, as there wasn't much to discuss, and by now I was filled with anxiety as to what the next plot twist might be. We were getting perilously close to the showcase, and we still didn't have our new line-up together, thanks to Jeff axing Tony and Jared, insisting we change horses in midstream.

Jeff rang a few days later. He said he'd finally found the ideal rhythm section for us in Anton Fier on drums and Tony Maimone on bass. Both were serious, respected players; they were both originally from Ohio and had great pedigrees.

I'd met Anton once before, standing outside the very hip Mudd Club at 6am directly after playing a show there with Captain Beefheart the night after John Lennon was shot. He had played with the cult indie band The Feelies, and I'd seen him kick ass at the Ritz with his own group, The Golden Palominos. He was a great player with formidable chops—John Bonham-esque.

Tony had played for years with the avant-garde rock band Pere Ubu, and I had jammed with him a couple of times for fun on the side while squabbling with Julia.

The two of them had just finished a tour with ex-Hüsker Dü front man Bob Mould, whom they'd apparently had some serious disagreements with. Nick Hill had recommended them to Jeff. I saw them as potential saviors for our upcoming showcase.

"Now it really is going to be a supergroup," Jeff said in an assured voice.

I agreed with him, although in my estimation Tony and Jared were just as strong players. But Fier and Maimone had bigger reputations, and I was pleased that Jeff sounded excited and positive again. I was also glad that he had had the sense to gravitate toward more experienced players over guys like Paul the slacker kid drummer.

Looking back on it now, I think the whole bloodbath with Tony and Jared had occurred because Jeff wanted to call the shots and bring in his own handpicked players. And maybe also Tony and Jared were "too black ... too strong," to quote Malcolm X, for Jeff's band aesthetic. Not to imply that Jeff was racist, of course ... merely that Jared and Tony's Black Rock Coalition connection and funk and jazz roots did not quite tally with the 'classic rock' image Jeff wanted to convey for the group

In any case, with the new recruits in place, we had a real shot again. I was still worried, as there were only ten days to go until the showcase, but these guys were pros, so they ought to be able to handle it. I began to get excited again.

We were finally back on track—or so I thought.

Chapter Seven

With Anton Fier and Tony Maimone onboard, on March 3 we started rehearsing in earnest, five-to-six hours a day, at Vinnie's Music, an uptown rehearsal space. We had exactly ten days to pull it together.

I'd given work cassettes of most of our songs to the two new guys in advance, and when they showed up I felt positive that they would be able to pull off the miracle of getting their heads around this complex music in time for our Friday the 13th show.

The songs in the set for the night included 'Grace,' 'Mojo Pin,' 'Distortion,' 'Malign Fiesta (No Soul),' 'Story Without Words,' 'Harem Man,' 'Cruel,' and 'She is Free,' plus the epic new song Jeff and I had just completed, 'No One Must Find You Here.'

There were also others that Jeff and I had decided to perform as a duo: 'In The Cantina' and 'Bluebird Blues.' Both had rubato-style shifting meters and semi-improvisational sections that would be difficult to teach smoothly to the guys, as good as they were—we had never codified their structures exactly, and we liked to improvise around them when we played them live—so we elected to simplify and perform them in duo versions.

In addition, we planned to perform some of our signature cover songs as a duo, including 'How Long Will It Take,' 'Hymne A L'Amour,' 'Sweet Thing,' and our latest addition, 'If I Had Wings (Dink's Song),' for which, during the final days of rehearsal, we decided to bring in Tony and Anton halfway through the song.

Jeff and I also elected to perform one solo number apiece. I chose my recent instrumental 'Dream Of A Russian Princess,' which I had tried unsuccessfully to get Jeff to write lyrics for, and Jeff went for his version of Mahalia Jackson's 'Satisfied Mind.'

Thus we had 17 numbers all together—a very hefty set, and probably much too much material for a label showcase, but as St Ann's was selling tickets for a show, we wanted to give the audience their money's worth. Especially as there was national press attention pending.

Back in February, I'd received a call from someone at *Rolling Stone* informing me that they wanted to feature Jeff and me in their forthcoming annual 'New Faces' feature, which each year spotlights new and up-and-coming artists. This was most likely the result of my old friend David Fricke giving a nudge to someone at the magazine. I'd been sending David tapes of our work in progress, and he was really excited by the results. (He remains one of my biggest advocates in the press.)

A couple of weeks before the showcase, on a chilly Saturday afternoon in February, Jeff and I took the subway out to Coney Island to meet the photographer Chris Buck, who shot a number of striking photos of us on the boardwalk, and more back in his studio. Jeff had cut his luxuriant locks ultra-short for the occasion. "Now I look like Vanilla Ice," he joked.

Some great pictures emerged from this session, several of which have been published over the years. My favorite is the one where I am falling backward, and Jeff is lovingly catching me in his arms. If Jeff had already decided to leave Gods and Monsters at this point, I doubt he would have gone through with this photo shoot. But perhaps he knew the media exposure would be good for him, even if he had already quit the band in his head.

Jeff made small talk during our cold walk on the boardwalk about the East Village music scene, which he now felt himself a part of, and spoke of having recently performed vocal gymnastics in one of John Zorn's COBRA live improvisational pieces, Rebecca Moore and her Fluxus connections seemingly having brought out the artsier side of

Jeff. But he didn't say much when I queried him about future gigs and other post-showcase plans.

"Who do you think we should approach, label-wise, if Imago passes on us after our showcase?" I'd ask. At best, Jeff would offer up terse, enigmatic one-liners—"let's just take this one step at a time"—intermingled with long, brooding silences.

This passive-aggressiveness frankly drove me up the wall. In constrast, I am a very blunt and plain-speaking person who usually blurts out whatever is on my mind to sympathetic—and occasionally not so sympathetic—ears. I find it therapeutic, actually. (The late great producer Phil Ramone once described me as a "compulsive truth-teller" in his regular column for *The Huffington Post*, where he cited me as one of his favorite artists.)

Back in rehearsal, the new rhythm section was meshing beautifully with Jeff and me, providing the muscular authority required to underpin our songs, and we all seemed to get along pretty well. We often joked together as we shared a cab back to our respective apartments. I recall the guys ribbing Jeff in a good-natured way about his high speaking-voice one day.

"Yes," he replied, in an exaggerated falsetto, "and it just keeps getting higher ... and higher."

By now, Jeff had moved out of Rebecca's apartment—my calendar shows he was staying with his friend Brooke as early as February 18. Why, I'm not sure, and I didn't want to pressure him to find out. Perhaps he just wanted to be alone to rehearse and refine his parts for the showcase. Many of our songs lacked finished lyrics at this point and had only skeletal, tentative vocal melodies. Meanwhile, Tony, Anton, and I were laying down pounding instrumental grooves in rehearsal, so Jeff had his work cut out for him.

Jeff had also started bringing Janine Nichols's Telecaster to rehearsal. This was something new, and initially I tried to discourage it. As good a guitarist as Jeff was—and he was excellent—I believed that the group and our music worked best with him handling the lead singer role and me the guitar parts. A couple of years later, Jeff cited this as a reason why he decided to leave the band, telling *Rolling Stone* that there was "some question as to whether I could play guitar in the band."

In fact, I'd relented on this point shortly after venting my misgivings about having two guitars live in the group to Tony in a cab ride home from rehearsal one night after we'd dropped off Jeff at where he was staying at in Midtown.

"Awwwww, you know the kid just loves that feeling of having that guitar hanging around his neck while he sings," Tony said.

In truth, Jeff did seem to use his guitar more as a prop at this point. The parts he developed for our songs were fairly inaudible to everyone in the band, no matter how I tried to adjust the volume levels in rehearsal to bring out a dual guitar attack. It is true that I have a preference, and a reputation, for playing loud, but this was ballsy rock'n'roll, not chamber music. Much as I loved bands like Humble Pie with their twin-guitar thrust, though, our music was already quite dense, with my contrapuntal fingerpicking covering a lot of sonic holes, so there wasn't a whole lot of room for a second guitar voice.

Still, once he insisted on it, I encouraged the development of Jeff's guitar playing in the band. As with his vocals, I trusted that he would come up with parts that would make sense within the overall scheme of our sound. He and I got together separately from the others at my apartment to work out some dual guitar parts and make good on Jeff's desire to play more onstage.

I have some cool double-guitar sketches of a new instrumental I had composed called 'Apismatisin',' which I wanted the band to tackle after the St Ann's showcase. (I sent a work tape of it to Fricke before the St Ann's show, and he loved it.)

Once the St Ann's show had been advertised in the *Village Voice*, all sorts of people started poking around and calling me up to check the status of the project. One of them was Marty Thau, the legendary record promo man and founder of Red Star Records, who had released the classic first album by Suicide and was now very curious about our label status. There were also various potential managers calling me with possible local gigs. I invited them all to the showcase.

On Sunday March 8, I was scheduled to perform live at Merkin Concert Hall uptown for John Schaefer's *New Sounds* show, a beacon of new music in New York and a staple of the city's WNYC FM radio station.

John had put me on his show as a solo performer several times before, but on this occasion he was broadcasting live from an elegant recital hall uptown, and the show was due to go out live on NPR. I asked the lanky, laidback, and erudite host whether I could bring along my new protégé for a few numbers, and he agreed.

In preparation for the event, I asked my neighbor Nina Winthrop, a choreographer and friend of Susan Feldman's who lived in a large loft nearby, if I could borrow one of her large throw rugs on which to set up my effects onstage—the idea being that I could whisk the rug, and my considerable arsenal of effects, onstage in one go, rather than have to laboriously assemble my rig in front of the audience, which would not have been possible, anyway, within the strict time constrains of a live broadcast. Nina agreed, and also invited Jeff and me over to her loft for a cocktail party she was throwing a few days before the broadcast.

I have an indelible image in my mind of Jeff sitting aloof and silent by himself that day, absorbed in playing with Nina's cats in an innocent, child-like way—totally ignoring the adult party going on in the large dining room next door. He seemed like his old, sweet self—the opposite of the ruthless partner I had come to dread dealing with. I hated pussyfooting around him.

Sunday dawned, and we arrived at Merkin Hall early to set up. We were sharing a bill that afternoon with electronic music pioneer Morton Subotnick, whose *Silver Apples Of The Moon* album I had grown up with, and his wife, the pre-eminent avant-garde vocalist Joan La Barbara.

The duo performed a 25-minute excerpt from one of Subotnick's new pieces entitled 'Jacob's Room,' after a Virginia Woolf novel, but with an added Holocaust-themed text. Joan then offered a virtuosic 30-minute solo performance entitled 'In The Dreamtime,' utilizing extensive electronic vocal processing.

Backstage, Jeff and I were somewhat nervous. Subotnick and La Barbara were the de facto headliners; who knew what the *New Sounds* audience would make of our new songs? While I paced around, Jeff, in his ubiquitous 'Christ on the cross' T-shirt, made a few cocky, ill-timed remarks to the older couple. They seemed visibly annoyed, and I found it all very embarrassing.

When Jeff wandered off, I attempted to repair the damage by trying to tell Subotnick what a fan I was of his work. He cut me off in mid-sentence, glared, and said, "Your friend's quite a comedian, isn't he?"

Jeff's sense of humor was an acquired taste. To his friends and fans, he could say or do no wrong; anything that came out of his mouth was hilarious, the punkier and more irreverent the better. But to people not attuned to his wavelength, he could come across as insensitive and boorish. (A few years later, his onstage imitation of Bob Dylan would reportedly enrage its subject.)

Finally, it was our turn to go on. I played a few solo numbers and then invited Jeff on to perform 'Grace,' 'Mojo Pin,' and 'How Long Will It Take.' He sang beautifully, as per usual. I then finished my set with a couple more solo numbers to an ovation from the full house, for which I called Jeff back out to take a bow.

◻

On Tuesday March 10, three days before the St Ann's showcase, the *New York Times* ran a review of the afternoon's concert by the classical critic Allan Kozinn. We got a really brilliant notice at the end:

Gary Lucas, a virtuosic and imaginative rock guitarist, closed the concert with a selection of fire-breathing solo performances and collaborations with Jeff Buckley, a singer with a strong, supple voice.

I was elated, and I believed this augured well for our band showcase three nights later. Kate Hyman, her assistant, and Susan Feldman had all been in the audience that afternoon, too, and they all seemed positive about our appearance.

At our band rehearsals, though, a discordant note had crept in.

I recall walking into the studio the night the *Times* article came out, before Jeff had arrived, expecting to be congratulated by Tony and Anton. But the two of them were strangely quiet. Tony had a big, shit-eating grin on his face, as if to say, "I know something that you don't know—and you're not gonna like it one bit when you find out what it is."

Jeff arrived and we played through most of our set. He didn't really look at me or talk to me. He looked like someone who had made a big decision but wasn't yet ready to share it. Nothing I said to try and buck him up seemed to work.

The run-through of our set was perfunctory at best on his part. He just seemed to be going through the motions. I put this down to him trying to save his voice for the big show, which is true up to a point— that's what singers do. Still, there was a chilly vibe to Jeff that made for a wan, dispiriting atmosphere in the rehearsal room. Reading between the lines, it was like he was thinking, *How I wish I didn't have to go through with this showcase.*

I called a break and the other guys drifted out to the kitchen area.

Trying to revive Jeff's spirits, I said brightly, "Hey man, what about adding 'Fool's Cap' to the show? Remember that great demo we recorded last fall? We could do it as a duo—it would be really easy to work up."

I'd always loved the song, and I was really proud of the version we'd recorded in my living room. But Jeff had never wanted to perform it live, perhaps as the lyrics not so subtly spelled out an ambitious agenda:

Although the door was open
There's nothing left for you now
But to hide your dreams away
Until they come into play

Jeff froze and shot me a disgusted, angry look.

"Right! And then I'll be wearing a Fool's Cap in public—just like a fucking organ grinder's monkey."

He was reading way too much into my suggestion. Despite our age difference, I had never looked at him or treated him as anything but an equal in our creative collaboration. Jeff could have renamed the song at any point, had he wanted to.

'Fool's Cap' was the title of my original guitar instrumental, written well before I had met Jeff, and came from how I viewed myself on a bad day for having foolishly given up my day job to pursue the ephemeral dream of making music for a living. I was the one wearing the Fool's Cap.

Jeff's vehement rejection of my suggestion gives a pretty clear window into how he had come to view his role in our project at that point. He obviously felt overshadowed and overpowered by me, despite the many attempts I tried to make along the way to make him feel comfortable within the band.

Still, Gods and Monsters had obviously started as my band—and that incontrovertible fact rankled him no end. But I never pulled rank on him. I co-wrote all of my songs with Jeff on a 50/50 basis, made him the front man, let him play guitar in the band (even though I had all the bases covered there, and it seemed superfluous), and even allowed him the luxury of firing our original rhythm section (my biggest and most costly mistake). Honestly, what more could I have done to satisfy Jeff outside of renaming us The Jeff Buckley Band featuring Gary Lucas?

But even that wouldn't have been enough. Jeff was itching to go solo, to be the main event. I cannot recall seeing a billing for him and his group in later years as anything other than 'Jeff Buckley.' That was his apparent destiny.

Jeff had the example of his famous father to live up to; a growing coterie of friends and fans whispering in his ear, telling him he was a star and that he should be performing solo; and a manager/lawyer who refused to let him sign a partnership contract with me, and who was instead waiting to set up a solo career once our development deal with Imago had lapsed.

Speaking of Imago, hadn't they already given me a resounding vote of no confidence by summoning Jeff to meet Terry Ellis without me? The writing was writ large on the schoolyard wall, which is pretty much what I think of the music business: a schoolyard filled with the same shallow and sadistic bullies that bedeviled my childhood. Yet I continued to believe in our project, and I was fired up anew by Allan Kozinn's positive review in the *Times*.

I am sure, though, that the review bothered Jeff. If he had already written off the whole collaboration with me in his mind at that point, this glowing review, on the cusp of our major showcase, probably caused him to doubt himself.

I said a prayer that night that our public performance only days away would turn around all the forces that seemed to be lining up against me, and would replace all the bad energy with only good vibes.

❑

On the afternoon of Thursday March 12 I'd arranged for Jeff and me to go on WNYU's *New Afternoon* show, a favorite hangout of mine since I started appearing there in the mid 80s. WNYU had been a good friend to my music and me over the years, and it was where I first met Jason Candler, a young NYU undergrad and a soulful, intelligent, and ever-so-smart sound engineer and computer whiz who also hosted a great blues show.

Jason was one of the first people to pick up on what I was doing with my electronic guitar sounds, and he subsequently arranged for me to score a student film, Peter Steinberg's *The Kite Flies Out Of Sight, or Be Positive Ketchup*, which won an award from the NYU Film School. Jason began sitting in with my band on sax in the late 90s, and has been a permanent member of Gods and Monsters since 1998.

Jason had helped get us invited to perform on this daily new music show, which he engineered that day. A tape exists of our performance. We do most of our duo repertoire, plus an up-tempo, charging version of 'Farewell Angelina,' where Jeff first tries out his Bob Dylan vocal impression.

"This is really folky, man," Jeff says as we launch into the song.

Later, before he blasts into his harp solo, we get a very Dylan-esque, elongated "O-kaaaaaayyy—want to take me back home, yes you waaaant!"

Later on in the show, Jeff joked about how he had developed "a pressure zit" on his face in anticipation of our showcase the next day. He also gave a shout-out to his friends in the hardcore band Murphy's Law, whom he had apparently played with in an earlier spell in New York, which came as a surprise to me. Jeff had never mentioned to me that he had lived in New York for a while, trying to make music, several years before the Tim Buckley show at St Ann's. I only learned about it after reading David Browne's *Dream Brother* some years later.

That night, I went to a loft party for Roulette, an avant-garde performance space in Soho, where I ran into Yale Evelev—the guy who had instigated the formation of Gods and Monsters by proposing I put a band together to play the Welcome Back To Brooklyn Festival in the summer of 1989. Yale was working freelance for Elektra Records at the time, and he'd brought with him to play on a video monitor at the party a compilation tape of Elektra's many historic and cutting-edge artists, including The Doors, Nico, and Iggy Pop.

On the tape was an old clip of Tim Buckley singing 'No Man Can Find The War' that had originally aired on Leonard Bernstein's CBS

TV special *The Age Of Rock* in 1967. Yale leaned around when Tim appeared onscreen, caught my eye in the darkness, and kissed his middle finger ostentatiously, shaking it at me in a rather rude gesture.

Yale had been one of my earliest advocates in music, but once Gods and Monsters became a vehicle for my avant-pop experimentation, he pretty much renounced his support for my work. He clearly didn't approve of my new venture with Jeff Buckley—despite not having heard a note of it, of course.

This problem has dogged me throughout my career. As I am a very quixotic and chameleonic artist, many folks have found it difficult to embrace every manifestation of what I have accomplished in music.

But that's their problem. I have never tailored my music to fit anyone's idea of what is hip, fashionable, or acceptable. I have always followed my own muse—and, first and foremost, my need to satisfy myself artistically.

Yale had me pegged from the beginning as a solo avant-garde guitarist, which is fine as far as that goes, but there was so much more for me to explore out there in the world of music. Working with Jeff was the most exciting project I had been involved with since my days with Captain Beefheart. So if Yale couldn't get behind it ... c'est la vie.

□

St Ann:

From the Hebrew 'Hannah,'
Meaning 'favor' or 'grace,'
Mother of the Virgin Mary,
Grandmother of Jesus Christ.

Friday the 13th of March 1992 dawned bright and clear.

I went down to the church early in the afternoon—only to be greeted by several grotesque giant puppets strung up on poles at the back of the pulpit where we were going to perform that evening. I wasn't cheered by their presence there at all—they looked pathetic and lifeless.

I spotted a sheaf of programs lying by the door that were to be given out at the show. One line caught my eye:

"Gods and Monsters are led by Gary Lucas, who pilots the group into the outlands."

First of all, at this point I very much viewed Gods and Monsters as a co-op group led by myself and Jeff. This program note—obviously St Ann's kiss-off to the project—seemed to be setting me up as the fall-guy driving this rickety, jerry-rigged, under-rehearsed band right off the rails and into the outlands.

There were experimental flourishes in the music, for sure, but Jeff and I were going for an accessible sound—a sound that, while at times challenging the notions of the standard-issue corporate rock we abhorred, would still be user-friendly.

I was setting up my side table of effects and my two amps when Anton and Tony arrived and began assembling their gear on the pulpit. Jeff showed up a little later, looking bedraggled and much the worse for wear.

"Sorry I'm late," he announced, in a high, reedy voice. "I was up all night ... and I have a nosebleed."

I don't know what Jeff had been up to, and I never did ask him.

He'd rented himself a Marshall stack from Vinnie's Music, which was set up on pulpit right. I was on the pulpit left. Tony stood near Jeff, with Anton behind us in the center. David Schnirman, a sweet but acerbic balding and bewhiskered soundman replete with ponytail, was setting up mics. His job was working the board and taking care of the sound onstage and in the house.

I'd worked with David before, including the show at Merkin Hall five days previously. He was the house guy for Arts At St Ann's. His soundboard was all the way in the back of the church, near the exit where we had all filed out onto the street to the strains of 'Moon River' at the Tim Buckley tribute almost a year before.

David and Anton got into a little tiff right off the bat over the lack of a drum riser. There was an obvious rub between these two. I pointedly ignored this, strapped on my electric, and began running through 'Mojo Pin' unamplified. When I looked up, I noticed Jeff studying my hands intently, trying to figure out how I played it. It seemed odd at the time, since this was one of the songs Jeff had elected not to play guitar on at all, preferring to concentrate on his singing. Later, it dawned on me that he was taking mental notes as to how to play this song solo, somewhere down the line.

The afternoon dragged on, as soundchecks often do—hurry up and wait. At one point I went out for a bite, and when I came back Jeff was sitting on Anton's stool, pounding the snare drum repeatedly and relentlessly:

Thwack! Thwack!! Thwack!!!

This went on for about five minutes. I knew Jeff was a good drummer, but this was hardly a demonstration of his skills. No, this was a manifestation of bloody single-minded rage.

THWACK! THWACK!! THWACK!!!

Jeff was in one of his moods, and I didn't want to go there. Finally, Schnirman had to rein him in.

"Come on already, Jeff," he said in an annoyed tone over the PA. "Let's move on."

The spell was broken. Jeff got up and walked off the pulpit and out of the church hall.

Shortly after this, Anton lit up the stub of a joint and the three of us surreptitiously shared a toke. Right then, out of nowhere, the Father of the church appeared from the back of the hall. Anton quickly snuffed out the smoldering joint, but the smoke hung thick in the air. The priest glared at us accusingly and sniffed the air. Clearly this wasn't incense. Then he silently walked out.

Later that afternoon, having gotten wind of our infraction, Susan and Janine bawled us out. We were told that we risked having the entire concert cancelled. We didn't smoke in there any more.

Dusk descended. The doors opened and the pews started to fill up with spectators and fans—there was a line stretching around the block outside the church. We were assembled backstage, not really talking to one another, until at 8pm Susan pushed us out into the church.

We climbed up onto the pulpit to healthy applause, and Jeff said in a low voice, "Hello St Ann's."

I spoke into my mic.

"Hello," I began. "First thing is, I want to dispel an impression people might get if they see the sign outside that said 'Gary Lucas' Gods and Monsters featuring Jeff Scott Buckley.' This sign was constructed about six months ago, and, uh, the band is very much now a kind of a co-op arrangement—and we've co-opted Tony Maimone and Anton Fier"—their names drawing big applause from the crowd—"to join us in this thing."

"This one's called 'Cruel,'" Jeff announced.

He hit a hit a fuzzed-out chord, I hit the fingerpicked intro, and away we go ...

Two and a half hours later, we came up for air, and received a prolonged standing ovation.

I won't do a total blow-by-blow account of the show here because I'd rather you hear it for yourself.

It is astonishing in its power overall—so much so that it scares me. We were on fire that night.

It is a tour de force showcasing the raw, unfettered, unrefined Jeff Buckley at his white-hot best, in my opinion.

A board tape exists in all its glory, taken from the master DAT tape David Schnirman gave me at the end of the show.

It has been bootlegged over the years from copies I made off the master, subsequently leaked by others, and if you seek it out hard enough you can probably find most of the performance online, albeit in a very lo-fi state. (I recently found most of the songs on YouTube, but with the song titles scrambled, no personnel information, and later photos of Jeff accompanying the music.)

There is nothing else in any of the voluminous audio and visual documentation of Jeff's entire career that compares to this tape for sheer rock bravado and daredevil risk-taking. Jeff was going for it that night—we all were. He rocks harder than you've ever heard him before on those tapes. The whole band is smoking throughout.

One day, an official release of this concert tape will emerge for the world to hear. And people will be forced to reevaluate the official narrative of Jeff's career:

"GODDAMNIT if this wasn't a fucking great rock band! Jeff sang his ASS off, and the band played their hearts out."

"Maybe Jeff should have stuck with this Gods and Monsters project and seen it through."

"He might still be alive today ..."

I've had many people tell me these things when they've heard the tape—it's that good.

In most accounts of Jeff's life, this concert and this incarnation in his career have been written off as a failed experiment that Jeff wanted best forgotten. I am sure he and his management wanted this episode to be quickly papered over so that Jeff could later emerge as his own man—fresh and bursting out of the forehead of Zeus and whatnot—when he had his official 'coming out' on Columbia Records two and a half years later.

But I can only tell you what Jeff told me repeatedly over the years, once in a long message he left on my answering machine: "It's my dream to go in the studio someday and properly record those songs." He knew just how good they were. And he was proud of them.

There are some awkward moments in the between-song patter, such as Jeff's unfunny imitation of Jim Morrison as a creaky disembodied voice on an old 78rpm record, but there are some touching ones, too. One in particular that stands out is Jeff's introduction to 'Grace':

> This is a song called 'Grace' ... and one day I was cleaning up my room ... and I was thinking that, uh ... my usual obsession with death and dying ... and, uh ... there can be a point where you really don't care, because there's someone ... there's someone ...

I cringed onstage when I heard Jeff refer to his "usual obsession with death and dying." It just seemed callous and juvenile—or, as Todd Rundgren put it, with the title of one of his albums, *The Ever Popular Tortured Artist Effect.*

What an inappropriate remark, I thought.

Now I am just made sad recalling it.

My friend the German photographer Andre Grossman videotaped a lot of the concert. Maybe this too will come out some day. A fragment was shown on the BBC as part of a piece about Jeff after his death. There was a lot of video taken of us back in the day, in fact, including Jeff's appearance with me at the CMJ in October '91. There are also photos from this concert taken by Carla Gahr,

208

daughter of my friend, the famous 60s music photographer David Gahr.

Despite all the energies unleashed that night—energies that burst continuously onstage over the two and a half hours like fireworks— Jeff never once made eye contact with me or the other guys in the band during the show. There was no group interplay, none of the camaraderie that is so much fun for an audience to see in bands who feel at ease with themselves onstage. No, Jeff stayed in his comfort zone throughout—or, rather, his discomfort zone.

I couldn't help but observe Jeff up close while I played. In fact, I kept looking in his direction, to try to catch his eye and get some interaction going. And while my efforts in that department came to naught, I noticed an anxious, conflicted, occasionally agonized expression on his face, as if to say, "I really wish I didn't have to be up here onstage—I'd rather be anywhere else but here. But I'm stuck, and I have to give it my best shot. I don't want to embarrass myself. I just have to get through this." Thankfully, you don't pick up on this hearing the tape.

One song I want to discuss in detail is 'No One Must Find You Here,' the last song we performed before leaving the stage en masse before coming back on for two encores.

For me, this 11-minute opus—with multiple movements and time signature changes—is right up there with 'Grace' and 'Mojo Pin.' Significantly, it contains a short snippet of instrumental music written solely by Jeff—the first music he ever contributed to our collaborations—a short, wistful waltz-time section that occurs six minutes and 45 seconds into the song.

He suggested adding it as a brief interlude a couple days before the show. I found it charming and integrated it into the song. (So much for me fighting his musical contributions—I welcomed them.)

Lyrically, this song is a heroic and elegiac lament, and a renunciation of everything the singer/protagonist has believed in and worked on in his life:

Take my shoes and bury them
With pen and paper and broken vows
In memory of the lover I will never be
Whose answers kill her into his arms
Ohhhhhhhhhh
Ohhhhhhhhhhhh
Every man and woman
Think of me when you're home

Wishing in a maelstrom of all your dreams and plans
Misty-eyes and shock of tears shaken
Wishing for an end somehow to cut off these demands
Waiting it for all your days taken

Take my eyes and bury them
You won't need them to see into the dark
I apologize to my woman
For all the hours of caress I gave
For the damage I've done
For all the waste I have made
I say Ohhhhhhhhhh
Ohhhhhhhhhhhhhhhh
Taken, breaking away
All this love
But never to see the light of day

This treasure will bring you down
To the bottom of the only sea
I'm the one who brought the axe down
I refuse to be set free

Bring me down
Oh bring me near

Well there ain't no way to stop this now
It's so close to home
And no one must find you here

Many of these lines have an ominous cast to them now, considering what went down so tragically in Memphis, five years later. Tears well up every time I listen to this track.

Jeff had a loose sheaf of lyrics on a music stand off to one side to which he referred occasionally. He threw all his lyrics up in the air, willy-nilly, at the very end of the song while he name-checked the band-members:

"Tony Maimone ... Anton Fier ... Gary Lucas ... Jeff—thank you St Ann's!"

Then we filed offstage to thunderous applause.

It was a nice, "fuck this shit" gesture, very punky—and I would have loved it, had I been a mere spectator in the audience. But my heart sank. Jeff's actions signaled to me his total disassociation from the project, despite our having just given a spectacular performance.

We re-ascended the pulpit and played two more songs for our encore, 'Bluebird Blues' and 'Mojo Pin,' and then filed off the stage to a standing ovation that lased several minutes.

There was a huge groaning board of catered food waiting for us in the backstage area, and we all tucked in to it without saying much to each other, aside from the usual pleasantries. ("Great show!") I thanked Tony and Anton profusely—they had pulled off a real miracle by learning some very complex music in ten days.

Many folks came back to congratulate us on the show, including Don Palmer from the New York State Council of the Arts.

"Young man, that was really something," he told Jeff. "You guys were great!"

Jeff smiled, but he wasn't giving much away to anyone.

Significantly, the Imago folks chose not to come backstage. After a few minutes, I went out into the rapidly clearing hall. Kate Hyman was putting on her coat and about to leave with her entourage when she saw me.

"Terrible sound in here," she said in a frosty voice. "It was so loud! I couldn't hear anything very well."

That was the nature of the church, with its high-vaulted ceiling. Sound just swirled around and around in a muddy maelstrom right up to the rafters and then disappeared into the ether. The rather small PA used in the church was clearly not adequate to capturing and defining our sound properly—especially with a heavy drummer like Anton pounding away, Tony pumping out his industrial-strength basslines, and my guitar cranked full throttle.

But we were a rock group, for chrissake. This was not jazz, nor was it chamber music. Yet Kate notwithstanding, enough people in there had ears to hear and love what we were laying down—as illustrated by the standing ovation at the end.

But from the censorious expression on her face, Kate had obviously already made up her mind about the project weeks earlier. My heart sank further.

"I did hear one song I liked a lot, though," she said. "I think it was called 'She Is Free.' I'll be in touch."

With that, she gave me a haughty smile and walked off into the night.

Hal Willner, who had been with her, stayed behind for a moment. He had been the prime instigator in having put me and Jeff to work together in the first place. Now he just looked embarrassed to be there.

"Why did she just walk off like that, Hal?" I asked. "What did *you* think? I mean, we got a standing ovation just now."

Hal knew Kate was going to pass on our project, and that she had her eye on Jeff alone as the prize to salvage from the wreckage, but, ever the diplomat, he didn't really have the heart to tell me this to my face.

"I don't know what she's thinking," he said, shaking his head, before awkwardly adding, "I enjoyed it, though."

Maybe he did. Maybe he was lying through his teeth. But it was nice of him to say it.

Next up was Danny Fields, with a supercilious Cheshire cat grin on his face. As a behind-the-scenes gossipmonger, he probably knew fully well what was going down with Jeff.

"Oh, Gary," he crooned, in a barely disguised gloat, rolling his eyes in mock sympathy. "You really gave it your *all*, didn't you?"

Jesus!

Susan Feldman had suggested Danny as a possible manager for Jeff and me, but we had dismissed the idea quickly. Perhaps this was his payback.

I hardened my heart—fuck these people!—and climbed back onto the stage to begin packing up my gear. Jeff came out from the backstage area and started doing the same. I tried to buck us both up.

"Jeff, you were amazing," I said. "The whole band was great—we fucking rocked! But it doesn't look like Imago are gonna go for this. Kate just kind of dismissed the whole thing to me just now."

Jeff didn't say anything.

"But I KNOW if we hang in there we'll get another major label interested in us for sure," I continued. "I'm positive about this." I was determined to forge ahead. Never say die!

Jeff remained silent. He looked drained by the show, and he obviously had a lot on his mind. His young actor friend Michael Tighe—to whom he had given a shout-out when introducing 'Satisfied Mind'—was waiting for him. And then sweet Rebecca Moore came over and complimented our performance, God bless her.

"You guys were great," she said. If she knew what was going down, she wasn't letting on.

"We'll talk," Jeff said.

I went home with my Caroline, who as a very observant casting director mentioned that Jeff hadn't looked at anyone in the band while we were performing. I told her about the non-reaction from Imago, and her face fell. She looked crestfallen.

"Oh dear," she said.

Caroline is a wonderful person who has put up with a lot from me over the years, and has stood by me loyally through one reversal of fortune after another in this crazy business.

And she had really believed in the dream of Jeff and me united.

Chapter Eight

The next day was Saturday.

I got up after sleeping late and straight away popped the board tape of the show into my DAT player. Suddenly, the muddy sound in the church was but a dim memory. Through my speakers, a roar of distinct and in-your-face music filled the room: Jeff's voice rang out loud and clear, and my guitar had a presence to it that was as sharp and distinct as a ringing bell. And while mixed a bit softer than Jeff and I in this two-track live tape, Tony and Anton were very much present.

'Cruel' was up first, and it rocked like a motherfucker.

"Oh my God," I called out to Caroline, who was still in the bedroom. "Listen to this!"

She came into the room and was struck immediately by the overwhelming power of the music. Jeff's supple voice handled every twist and turn, and suddenly his lyrics came into focus. As usual, I hadn't really absorbed them in the rehearsal, preferring to focus on getting the instrumental grooves tight, but suddenly his strength as a poetic lyricist was apparent, in spades, in song after song.

"He did it again!" I exclaimed. "Listen to these vocals ... the guy nailed it. This sounds incredible."

Caroline agreed.

"Fuck Imago," I continued. "For sure we'll get a deal with another label with this."

We both marveled at the power of the tape. The engineer, David Schnirman, had managed to catch, on the fly, a high-quality aural snapshot of a classic concert performance. We had all the evidence now that we needed to go forward.

Caroline and I started dancing around the room, grooving to 'Grace,' when suddenly the phone rang. It was Jeff.

"Yo Jeff!" I shouted happily into the phone over the din of the playback. "I'm listening back to last night's tape ... it sounds INCREDIBLE ... we'll get a deal no problem with this."

"That's why I wanted to call you," he replied, cutting me off in a tense voice. "I just ... I just don't want to continue with this."

"What? What did you say?"

I was stunned.

□

"I said I'm just not comfortable with this any more," Jeff added. "I don't want to make a record with you or this band. I just want to work on developing my voice more."

Sure.

I made Caroline turn down the music.

"So you mean you're just gonna CHUMP IT after all that work we've put into this?" I shot back, flabbergasted—'chumping it' being a favorite Beefheart expression.

Jeff didn't like that.

"No, I'm not the one here 'chumping it,'" he replied, his tone turning nasty now. He obviously had bigger plans beyond just working on developing his voice.

Oh man ... I didn't know what to say. I was absolutely crushed.

It went back and forth like this for a while, with my attempts to win him back with kind words about his performance and the future of the project alternating with flashes of anger at his betrayal. I felt sick, like he had just stabbed me in the front.

Eventually I just got tired of the back and forth.

"OK, that's it. I'm not gonna beg you to stay."

Maybe he would have liked that—but that's not my style.

I just hung up.

I felt nauseous. Because in one grim flash of insight, I knew that by walking out on me—after I'd had one previous major label deal blow up in my face the year before—Jeff had just condemned me to indie hell for the rest of my career.

My shot at grabbing the false gold ring of a major-label deal—which with the advent of the internet means less and less in hindsight, but which in 1992 was something desirable—and of having my music career accelerated by association of such a deal, had just missed by a mile.

And now I was falling.

❑

I stumbled through the rest of the weekend in a wretched state of shock and denial. All my plans had come crashing down. I felt like I had been abandoned by everyone except Caroline, who did her best to comfort me.

I called Susan Feldman, who had once been a confidant and co-conspirator in the project, for advice. She was pretty cold. I appealed to her about the reasons behind Jeff's betrayal, but she didn't want to hear about it.

Jeff was their golden boy, and by protesting loudly about the way he kicked me to the curb—an action they had helped grease the skids for by hooking him up with George Stein—I was making myself an inconvenient witness to his ruthlessness. Which was not at all in character to Jeff's cultivated golden boy image. When I kept moaning to her about Jeff's betrayal, she rather rudely cut me short.

I was damaged goods now.

I rang my lawyer Michael Ackerman in LA to tell him the bad news. We both had already experienced a mutual heartbreak when Jeff fired Michael's close friend, Jared Nickerson, from Gods and Monsters.

This latest reversal of our fortunes made him apoplectic.

217

"After all the hard work I did lining up this deal for you guys, he's gonna go and walk out on it now? Who does he think he is? Deals don't just grown on trees, you know! What an idiot!" Not sensing, of course, what Jeff and his management were lining up.

Ackerman then made the alarming prediction that Jeff was heading for an early demise. Maybe he was alluding to something that I didn't know about here. I'd smoked pot with Jeff on numerous occasions but never seen him take any other drugs. That doesn't mean he wasn't taking them—I just didn't see it. Perhaps that's what Michael had heard through the grapevine.

Apropos of this, I got another call a few weeks later from my friend Steve Paul, David Johansen's manager, who wanted to know whether I knew anything about Jeff being a hard-drug abuser.

I couldn't believe what I was hearing. I was shocked, and I vehemently denied any knowledge of such a thing. But even if what these guys were saying was not based on any concrete information, it's not hard to guess why they may have suspected it, as Jeff had certainly put the vibe out there in songs like 'Mojo Pin,' and those comments about "my usual thoughts of death and dying."

□

I got through the rest of the weekend somehow.

On Sunday night, looking for a sympathetic ear and someone who was close to Jeff, I reached out to Janine Nichols. She too was pretty cold to me on the phone. Did she know Jeff had just quit on me? She wasn't letting on, but of course she knew.

When I tried to talk out my frustration and heartache over Jeff, looking for some kind of sympathy and advice, she dismissed his treatment of me.

"Well he's only 24 years old—he's a boy," she said, "And you've worked together for—how long?" she added—like it was nothing, like all the hard work I'd put in was of no consequence.

Then she went in for the kill.

"And, after all, he *is* a Buckley."

I guess in her eyes, Jeff's age and pedigree as a descendant of so-called rock royalty gave him the preordained right to treat people ruthlessly.

I made myself even more vulnerable at this point by telling her that, as a double Gemini, I feared the worst was to come now that Mercury was about to go into retrograde. All sorts of things could go wrong during that three-week period, and I would appear to be going "backward in the heavens."

This must have sounded ridiculous to her.

She just laughed and hung up.

□

As predicted, things got even worse on Monday. A devastating review of Friday's show appeared in the *New York Times* under the byline of Peter Watrous—the paper's number two pop critic in every sense of the phrase.

I'd introduced Watrous to my former Yale classmate and friend, Jon Pareles, the *Times'* chief pop critic, at a Sonny Sharrock show at the Kitchen a couple of years earlier. My introduction resulted in Watrous being hired by Pareles shortly thereafter. They say no good turn goes unpunished!

In his review, Watrous praised Jeff as "surreally gifted," but had some mean-spirited reservations both about his onstage patter and the "B-team musical celebrities" (ouch!) in the band. But the most damning part of the review, which cut to the quick of my songwriting abilities, was this: "The group's songs, short on melody and barely arranged, with absolutely no dynamics, were plain rock, as gray as yesterday's potatoes."

Of course, if any fair-minded listener was to hear the board tape of the concert, they would instantly know this to be a crock of shit. Even a cursory listen to 'Mojo Pin' and 'Grace' would make plain to anyone with a passing knowledge of music—particularly rock music and its history—that these songs are rife with memorable melodies and are certainly not mere "plain rock." Time changes, key changes, mood changes, and dynamics abound. These songs have rightfully over the years been celebrated as art-rock anthems. And Jeff, who became the *Times'* critical darling a few years later, performed these songs constantly right up until the day he died.

Watrous was famous for his nasty reviews. His bosses probably paid him for them by the column inch. John Zorn spotted him in the audience at a show once and stopped his set to scream at him and insult him from the stage. Another musician friend of mine once slapped Watrous in the face in a movie theater after a particularly bad review.

People always say there is no such thing as bad publicity, but that is just not true. Some artists claim never to read their reviews, but it's hard not to look at them. If you are a sensitive person, as most artists are, the humiliation of a bad review lingers on inside after everyone else has forgotten it.

In a lifetime of mostly great reviews, Watrous gave me two poisonous ones that affected my career in a deplorable and destructive way. His panning of show I did as a duo with the guitarist Jean-Paul Bourelly at the Newport Jazz Festival in 1990 came at a time I was under contract with Julia at CBS, and it caused people at the label to question whether or not I was a viable artist worthy of their label.

And this latest review of our St Ann's show, which wiped out all the good vibes of Allan Kozinn's review the week earlier, more or less hammered the final nail into the coffin of my band project—not only with Jeff but also with Imago.

Kate Hyman later confirmed that when Terry Ellis got ahold of the *Times* review when they were both at the NARM record industry convention in New Orleans that week, he came running over to her waving the newspaper in her face.

"So," he asked, "why should we invest any more money in this?"

□

I was a wreck.

I spoke with Jeff a few times on the phone that week and did my best to tactfully patch things up and try to keep the project rolling. He was still adamant about quitting, but in a softer, more passive-aggressive way. We had one more band appearance scheduled for a week later on Sunday March 22 at the Knitting Factory, playing live on Nick Hill's *Music Faucet.*

If Jeff was really quitting, why didn't he just cancel out? Obviously, he wanted to further heighten his profile in New York, especially after that *Times* review. I asked him if he wanted to rehearse one more time at Vinnie's Music before the gig.

"Yeah, let's do it at *Vinnie's,*" he replied sarcastically, as if it was the dumbest idea in the world. He obviously had an agenda.

I rang Susan Feldman again to try to get some more information about what Jeff was up to. She was sympathetic and commiserating while simultaneously putting me down by trumpeting her wunderkind's abilities in a smug singsong voice.

"Jeff is *exploding* with ideas," she said, dangling a carrot, "and just maybe you can figure out a way to keep working with him."

She was still going on, too, about how it might have worked out if Jeff and I had fallen in love with each other. Of course, I knew Jeff was exploding with ideas the day I met him. I just didn't love his songs. Short of jumping on working up songs from his demo tape, I had tried my best to accommodate him throughout all our months together.

We met at Vinnie's on Friday night for what was to be our last band rehearsal together. Jeff showed up with my acoustic 12-string guitar in its case—the return of the loaner guitar I'd given him to work on our songs over the last few months. To my surprise, he actively started cranking up Janine's Telecaster to work on developing counter-lines against my guitar playing.

Perhaps the line in Watrous's review about the songs being "barely arranged" had rankled him a little bit. But considering Jeff had fired my rhythm section of choice and brought in Tony and Anton with only ten days to work on some very complicated music, the board tape reveals that our songs were thoroughly and spectacularly arranged.

Still, Jeff wanted to tinker some more on them. But if he hadn't developed his guitar lines to his own satisfaction the week before, that was his problem—he had certainly had time to think about this aspect of our performance in the run-up to the show. Again, I'd trusted him to hold up his end of the bargain instrumentally, as I did with Anton and Tony, so I did not dictate guitar parts to him.

Jeff's guitar was way down, volume-wise, not only on the St Ann's tape but also what he was cranking out live in the pulpit. He barely played through most of the songs, in fact, preferring to just let his guitar dangle from his neck as decoration while he concentrated on giving his all to singing.

Now, with the last hurrah in sight, he was determined to be heard more on guitar at our final show together. And he was.

Thanks to the efforts of Irene Trudel (who had recorded 'Farewell Angelina' a few months before) at the mixing desk, what went out live over WFMU that night and was captured on the board tape reveals more dynamic interplay between us and more of Jeff's skills on guitar. He's a lot louder onstage here than he was at St Ann's. He was asserting himself extra hard, trying to show the audience that *he* was the bandleader.

Fine—except for the fact that he was quitting.

□

There was one really ugly moment at this rehearsal.

Jeff had neglected to pay Tony and Anton for their time to date, for rehearsing and playing the St Ann's show, but he was the one holding the balance of the money Imago had given us. I'd already paid off Tony Lewis and Jared Nickerson, so I had no more funds from the label in my bank account.

Anton began loudly—and quite rightly—calling for his bread when he got there, and I was forced into the defensive posture—as the 'leader'—of telling him, "I don't have it ... Jeff has it."

Jeff remained silent until Anton finally lost it.

"Gary," he said, "if you don't pay us right now, I'm gonna pop you one."

"I've got it," Jeff said meekly. "Sorry! I'll get it to you ..."

When I got home from the rehearsal I unpacked my 12-string from its case. The pristine finish on the front of the guitar directly over the sound hole was marred—no, rutted—with multiple deep scratches. Jeff had frenzied out on my beautiful guitar repeatedly using a pick, with no regard for the wooden body of the instrument.

It was totally emblematic of the way Jeff had been treating me. I felt sick.

□

Saturday passed slowly, agonizingly. I felt for sure that this was the end of the band but I kept going back into denial about it. I was driving myself—and Caroline—crazy.

The following day I went over in a cab to the Knitting Factory with my gear in the fading twilight of late afternoon. It was freezing cold, and there were snowdrifts on the ground. I hauled my gear inside and met Jeff and the guys downstairs in the bar.

Carla Gahr was also there. She took a couple of photos of us outside the club and more later onstage. She chirped and zoomed around us hither and yon like a hummingbird on Ritalin, snapping away all the while. Jeff marveled at this. "She's mad," he said admiringly.

Also on the bill were "the three Peters"—Peter Stampfel from the legendary Holy Modal Rounders, Peter Case from the LA power pop band The Plimsouls, and Peter Blegvad from UK art-rockers Slapp

Happy. When they came in I said hello and I bonded right away with Stampfel, who later performed a wicked solo version of 'Goldfinger' on banjo. (A couple of years later, we would be performing live together at the same venue as The Du-Tels.)

The order for the night had Jeff and me opening the program as a duo, followed by the three Peters, with Gods and Monsters closing the night. Before Nick Hill's live show began at 9pm, a separate set took place in the club that was unconnected with *Music Faucet*: guitarist Marc Ribot and his band The Rootless Cosmopolitans playing a set of avant-noise jazz.

Jeff and I lingered at the door to listen for a minute, and then Jeff walked out. I followed him out into the corridor. "He sounds just like Zoot Horn," he whispered in a disparaging tone, referring to former Magic Band guitarist Zoot Horn Rollo.

The Rootless Cosmopolitans finished their set, packed up, and left. Then the WFMU crew moved in and set up their remote feed to the station. The place was filling up rapidly, and before long it was time to play.

Wiping away my anguish, I tried to keep a stiff upper lip, taking to the stage with Jeff in tow and letting Nick introduce us over the airwaves. We opened with my skipping solo-acoustic arrangement of Hoagy Carmichael's 'Cosmics,' with Jeff chiming in on finger cymbals on the beat, before launching into our rousing duo version of 'If I Had Wings.' We pulled out all the stops, and the crowd went nuts.

We went off, and then a bit later Jeff was called up for an interview with Nick. Then the three Peters came and went, and finally it was Gods and Monsters' turn. We opened with 'No One Must Find You Here,' but it sounded unfocused and diffuse, quite unlike the epic version we'd performed the week before. We did a manic version of 'Malign Fiesta (No Soul),' with Jeff throwing in "Hope I die before I get old" at the very end à la The Who's 'My Generation.' 'Cruel,' 'Distortion,' and 'Mojo Pin' followed, and then we finished with 'Grace.'

Jeff was a lot more vocal than usual, and he played his guitar harder and louder than he had the week before. He strutted his stuff aggressively and made his usual bad wisecracks. There were some good moments, but these were not the incandescent versions of St Ann's. There was a white heat emanating from deep within the music we made the week before that was absent from this performance. Perhaps it was the small room, with its boxy sound; we were too reined in and constrained by the small stage. There was never a moment where anything really took off.

The evening ended with Jeff and I coming back as a duo for 'Hymne A L'Amour.' This was the one really transcendental moment of the show: for those five minutes: we truly soared. But then Jeff broke the spell with a grand announcement to the crowd of scene-makers, friends, and WFMU supporters: "This is our last show—the band is breaking up!" As it if was *his* band.

He then put on a Ringo voice to add, "Let's kick Gary out of the band and steal all his good ideas!"

It was horrible. Unforgivable. *What an asshole*, I thought. *I started this band, and we will bloody well continue, with or without Jeff.*

But I held my tongue. It was a very mean-spirited thing to say, but also very revealing—very Oedipal. Over the years, I've had a number of people analyze our relationship in those terms: Jeff projecting all of his anger on me as the father figure he had to slay.

□

The lights went up, and Jeff disappeared into the crowd without so much as a goodbye. I packed up and thanked the band profusely. They seemed a little bewildered, with a look of "this is it, after all the hard work we put into learning this shit?" on their faces ... but I'm sure they knew what was coming.

I got a lift home that night from my old school friend Mark Plakias. He lived in our building with his wife and kids, and he was one of the hippest people I knew—one of the first major Beefheart and Zappa fans at Yale, and an amateur jazz pianist.

"Man, you guys were great," he said. "What the heck was Jeff going on about—are you really breaking up?"

I poured my heart out to Mark that night. Riding down Houston Street for what seemed like the millionth time of my life, the song 'I'm Not Satisfied' from The Mothers Of Invention's *Freak Out* kept playing in my head.

Some years later, I was asked how I felt about Jeff's betrayal for a BBC documentary. "I was crushed" was how I simply put it. Devastated.

All the symptoms of a classic depression took hold in my daily, and my nocturnal life. I couldn't sleep well, and I had a series of terrifying dreams where a grinning Jeff mocked my every step. In retaliation, I fed him ground glass in a milkshake before waking with a start.

I found it hard to get out of bed in the morning, and I stopped caring about my appearance. I wore the same clothes day after day, and I stopped shaving regularly.

I brooded about my seemingly hopeless situation every waking moment, and in my dreams, too. I talked incessantly about my unhappiness to my wife and friends.

I was fucked.

And there was nothing I could do about it.

□

A week or so later, Jeff called and said we should meet to talk things over. Just hearing from him, I felt elated once again. I was still in denial. That was the power he had over me then—I was hooked.

Still I was guarded, because of all that had happened recently, but perhaps he wanted to keep the relationship going with me?

We met at a West Village landmark known formally as Café Spaghetto (but more commonly as Home Cooking) at the corner of Bleecker and Carmine Street. Jeff seemed low-key and not nearly as snotty as he had been on the phone. We talked in vague generalities for a while, and then the subject turned to our recent shows. Right away Jeff got down to specifics.

"When we played at St Ann's the other night I noticed you were standing right up in the front with me," he said pointedly.

"Yeah," I replied, "so what?"

"Well, when Mick and Keith play—Keith always stands behind Mick."

Jesus—so that *was* his problem. But I was flattered, I suppose, that he saw us in terms of Mick and Keith.

"Jeff," I said firmly, "I started this group. I've led Gods and Monsters for three years now—and for two years before I ever met you. And I am not going to stand in the back of a group I started and play behind you as your back-up guitarist."

There was not much more to say to each other after that.

Jeff paid the bill—the first and last time I ever saw him do that. I guess he felt guilty for all the damage he had done to my dreams— dreams I had so naively had thought of as *our* dreams. And then we went our separate ways.

In retrospect, Jeff's statement about our relative positions onstage may well have been a trial balloon he was floating to see if might be able to bend me to his will and get me to agree to stand behind him in the future, should we ever resume working together in a band. It seems so petty, but it goes with the territory. I'd heard on good authority that Mick Jagger tried to lay down the law to Jeff Beck about the very same issue when he was contemplating having Beck join him on his maiden solo tour. But I was having none of it. Having had the pleasure of seeing Led Zeppelin play live, for instance, I thought Jeff's notion of relative stage positions was a crock of shit. Jimmy Page was always right up front in Robert Plant's face, playing to him and off of him. And it worked beautifully.

I thought the whole motive behind rising up to be—that is, empowering Jeff to come to New York to be the lead singer in my band—was to encourage us both to rock out together. To be our badass selves. That's what his girlfriend Joan Wasser later asserted were Jeff's posthumous wishes for all of his friends at the wake held a week after he drowned in 1997. Not for me to be put in my subordinate 'place' in some future stage configuration.

You may say I was acting too proud here. That I should have grasped the vague and fairly insubstantial olive branch he was kind of holding out for me here if I had really wanted to be a 'player.' That if I had played my cards right, he probably would have invited me into his eventual band. But I could not and would not back down on this point.

I was proud of my abilities and what I had accomplished to date, with and without Jeff, and I do not like to play a subordinate role unless I have willingly entered into such an arrangement from the get-go (such as when I've been asked to play on sessions for Chris Cornell and Bryan Ferry). There was no real guarantee of any future work or collaboration with Jeff. He was just sounding me out to see how tractable and amenable to his wishes I might be in the future— to see how far he could push me.

There was only one way I was prepared to move forward with Jeff—as an equal. But based on the band he subsequently did put together, Jeff didn't want an outstanding musical partner onstage with him at all.

Nope, he wanted to be the adored star of the Jeff Buckley Show, and therefore hired younger and more malleable guys without any real musical profile or face, who he could control and place wherever he wanted them to stand onstage.

Which was way off in the back.

By then, I knew myself pretty well. I knew what I was and was not capable of putting up with—and I knew I could never put up with that. Nevertheless, it did not make me feel any better about the present situation.

Be that as it may, I kept inviting Jeff onstage with me for the bunch of solo gigs I had lined up for the spring in the forlorn hope he would change his mind and resume working with me full throttle.

On Sunday April 5, I had a solo show at Roulette, the prestigious avant-garde loft in Tribeca with great acoustics and all wood paneling, run by the trombonist and curator Jim Staley.

I brought Jeff on to do our usual duo numbers. There are clips from this show floating around on YouTube, plus the version of 'Grace' that appears on our *Songs To No One* album. Jeff introduced the song that night by blowing a plaintive snatch of 'Old Susannah' on his harmonica.

It was a good night for our music, but there was a somber, hushed atmosphere in the room, perhaps something to do with Roulette being one of the sanctum sanctorums of the avant-garde in the city. At the end, Jeff called out my name over and over to the crowd to sustained applause, which was appreciated, but it saddened me, too, and hardly lessened the sting of him leaving.

My show at the Knitting Factory on Saturday April 18—the second night of Passover—was originally scheduled to be a Gods and Monsters engagement. But with Jeff adamant that he didn't want to appear with the band any more, it became a solo show, which I cheekily advertised as 'Gary Lucas's Passover Satyr.' I greeted folks at the door by handing out free matzo, with the option of a schmear of butter.

One of the Passover Seder rituals is to open the front door of your house after dinner to allow the angel Elijah to waft inside. I remember telling the crowd, "We're waiting for Elijah to enter at the door. That must be him now!"

I then opened the door at the side of the stage, which led to a darkened hallway, and Jeff strode in, looking like The Joker from *Batman* without his makeup.

"You're not Elijah," I said, in mock disappointment.

"I'm going to pass over you," he replied.

And so it went.

Nonetheless, it was a good show. Sometimes the personal friction between us helped strike sparks onstage.

But I wished it had not been that way at all.

□

Shortly after the Knitting Factory show, Kate Hyman finally called Jeff and me to her office to resolve our unfinished business with Imago. I had last set eyes on her at the end of our St Ann's showcase, which she had curtly dismissed.

Since then, I'd heard through the grapevine that she'd left town in a fever a week later and gotten married in the Graceland chapel in Las Vegas. How rock'n'roll! (She had the marriage annulled a few weeks later.)

Now that our Imago development deal was about to expire, however, Kate was intent on separating the two of us once and for all—as if she needed any help here—and she was determined to keep Jeff in the fold, hoping to sign him to Imago.

The two of them were waiting for me in her office. Jeff seemed to know what was about to go down, but he later feigned total ignorance.

"Basically, I just want to work with you," she said, pointing a finger at Jeff. "I don't want to work with you," she added, pointing her finger at little old me. It was just one more humiliation in a season full of them.

"Didn't you hear the tape of our show?" I asked.

I brandished a cassette of the St Ann's board tape, which I'd brought there with me—the Holy Grail, as far as I was concerned, that validated the band, the project, and our collaboration.

"I don't have to hear it," she snapped. "I was there."

(In a recent interview with *Uncut* magazine, Kate said was she was angry with me after observing me "leaping in front of Jeff" during the St Ann's show. This is totally untrue, and I have to laugh, as I have never leaped in front of anyone onstage in my life, tethered as I am, rather umbilically, to my effects pedals and table. Video clips of the show bear this out. Nope, no leaping here!)

"The sound sucked in the church," I replied. "This tape captures all of our songs really well. You can hear everything clearly. Listen to it, please—the audience gives us a long standing ovation at the end. Remember?"

"What do they matter?" Jeff interjected loftily. "They're just consumers."

Jesus. With friends like these ...

I am still rankled by this absurd remark and Jeff's apparent contempt for the folks who supported us there that day.

Meanwhile, 'Old Pal' Irwin Chusid was regularly spinning tracks from the board tape on his WFMU show and getting a great response from listeners. As much as Jeff disdained the tape of the show in our meeting with Kate, he was not fighting to take it off the air, as he knew it was helping to enhance his reputation in New York.

I remember hearing Irwin play 'Cruel' one afternoon, and at the end announce reverentially, "Gary Lucas—the guitar ... Jeff Buckley—THE VOICE!" It was so smarmy that it made me cringe. It still does.

Now, however, Kate refused to even accept a cassette of the show from me. She looked angry and rattled. No doubt she feared Jeff was slipping out of her grasp, and that he was perhaps already being courted by another label, now that George Stein was in the picture.

Suddenly, Kate threw a carrot in my direction by hinting at keeping me involved as a writer for the project, as she knew Jeff could use my help in that department. She kept casting longing looks at Jeff, no doubt hoping to win him over, but Jeff had his poker face on as usual, and wasn't giving anything away. Outside of that one remark dismissing the board tape, I don't recall him saying anything much at all during the meeting.

And that was it. I picked myself up with as much gravitas as I could muster and left with Jeff. We walked down many long blocks of 8th Avenue together.

"Did you know that was coming?" I asked as soon as we got out of the building, disgusted at the way he hadn't offered one word of defense on my behalf (or the project's). He'd just sat there and let Hyman's scorn rain down on me, even putting the boot in himself with his dismissive remark about "consumers." It was not the first time he'd done this to me.

"No," he said, and quickly changed the subject.

I didn't believe him. I was sure he and Kate had been in touch since the show, but I dropped it. I was still witlessly trying to be nice to him, hoping to get him to continue working with me. But as Caroline had warned me a few days before, "Don't ever count on Jeff. Just when you need him the most, he won't be there for you at all." Feminine intuition. She knew this guy well.

I started going off on major labels, thinking that if Jeff changed his mind, maybe we could land a deal with his beloved 4AD Records or another indie.

"Do you think Beefheart would have been able to get a major label deal today?" Jeff asked, out of the blue. Signing with a major was obviously on his mind. Kate Hyman wanted to continue working with him, and for that she would need to offer him a full-scale solo contract with Imago once our development deal lapsed.

"I doubt it," I replied. "Don was signed at a time when record company people actually took chances. Now they just want something safe and slick and synthetic that they can package and market easily. Don would never get a major label deal today."

Jeff stayed quiet, but my answer seemed to bother him. He obviously wanted to be regarded in the tradition of an uncompromising maverick, like Beefheart. But if he was really that kind of artist, why were mainstream labels like Imago—and, though I didn't know it yet, Columbia—courting him for a solo deal? In his heart of hearts, I think Jeff feared that maybe they just regarded him as a pretty boy with a beautiful voice, and I am sure this suspicion caused him some anxiety.

□

Thursday April 23. A midnight show at CBGB's, a club I had played many times as a solo performer. I have this written in my 1992 agenda as a Gods and Monsters show, then scratched it out. I'd retained the date as a solo show after Jeff walked from the band, and had invited Jeff to sit in with me again.

From Jeff's perspective, what did he have to lose by performing with me at this point? He would be gaining more valuable exposure, and he'd be honing his craft at the same time.

I showed up at the club around 11pm with my normal rig—two large coffin-style flight cases containing my J-45 acoustic and National steel guitar, a smaller flight case for my '64 Strat, and my Monster case filled with effects pedals.

Thurston Moore from Sonic Youth was there checking out the band before me. I knew him slightly, and after saying hello he made a crack about my cases. "We usually carry two or three of our guitars in one of those things." Whatever. I invited him to stay for my show, telling him that Jeff Buckley was on the way over to sing with me. He didn't bat an eyelid, but swooped the scene hurriedly while I was still setting up.

There was no sign of Jeff, but that was fine with me. Solo is always my preferred mode. Then, toward the end of my set, I saw Jeff arrive, looking disheveled and out of breath, as if he had run all the way to the venue.

I called him up onstage and we launched into our reggae cover, 'How Long Will It Take.' All was forgotten, and we were making music together again. That was what counted the most. You can hear our rousing performance of the song from this show on *Songs To No One*.

We were grooving soulfully. The great CBGB's sound system was pumping out our message of love, and their in-house recording setup captured the moment beautifully. After that, we stormed through our typical duo set and climbed down from the high wooden stage together around 1am.

Much to my surprise, coming offstage I spied my old friend and bassist Jared Nickerson standing near the front of the oddly shaped room. He had a stony look on his face. I hadn't noticed him come in, and he hadn't been on my guest list. I gave him a warm embrace, and then a sheepish Jeff, who was no doubt amazed to see Jared there after engineering his firing from the band, stepped forward to greet him.

"Jared!" he said. "Thanks for coming ... no hard feelings, man."

Jeff stretched out his hand. Jared glared at him and icily refused to shake. It was like a mirror image of Jeff and David Kahne up at Black Rock the year before.

"I'm not going to shake hands with you, Jeff Buckley," Jared said haughtily. "Because I don't respect you. I'm used to playing with men. And you're not a man."

Jeff looked shocked! He was speechless.

"You told me I couldn't play that music correctly," Jared went on in an indignant, angry rush of words. "You didn't like the way I played the bass, and you threw me out of the band because I used a pick on one number. Well fuck you! I was at the St Ann's show—I went there just to see what my replacement could do better than me. And you know what? Tony Maimone used a pick on the same damn number that you got on my case for. So where do you come off bullshitting me with that bullshit for? I worked my ass off for you!"

Jeff looked completely bummed out. He mumbled an apology, said goodbye, and got out of CBGB's as fast as he could.

"Didn't really give me that much satisfaction saying that to him, Gary," Jared told me, "but I had to say it. Shit! It needed to be said. I was there at that show, man. I saw the whole thing go down."

Jared shook his head in disgust.

"I understand, man," I replied. "I'm really sorry, Jared, about what happened with Jeff. You know how I feel about you, man. He put a gun to my head."

"That's OK," he replied. "I don't blame you."

We parted as friends. In truth, I was delighted that Jared had stood up to Jeff like that. It was something I'd never really been able to do, for fear of losing him as a partner, and Jeff, knowing that I loved him and was scared of losing him, seemed to use that against me.

In my observation, most people were not willing, once they fell under Jeff's spell, to try and tell him anything—much less lay down the law with him. He had the ability to make grown men tiptoe and kowtow around him. (The people who were to later sign him and throw pots of money at him, for instance, were all sold on the notion that Jeff absolutely knew what he was doing.)

A few months after this confrontation at CBGB's, Jared was asked to join UK post-modern rocker Matt Johnson in his band The The. It was a sign that, despite all the insanity in the trenches of this business of music, good musicians sometimes do manage to hang on and survive—sometimes they even flourish.

☐

Saturday May 2. I'd agreed to do an 'out-store' performance right on the street directly outside Rebel Rebel, the hip indie record store on Bleecker Street.

I'd been asked to do this at the behest of the owner, an Israeli-born record freak named Ofer, who was a fan of Jeff's and wanted me to try and get him to show up to sing with me, but as there was no PA I'd told him this was unlikely. Instead, I executed a guerilla-style operation with a tiny Gallien-Krueger amp and a single pedal—and still managed to raise a ruckus before the police came by and asked me to shut it down.

While I was wailing on my guitar out in the sreet, out of the corner of my eye I saw Peter Wright, the rather short English label manager of Mute Records America, peeking around the corner of a building two doors away—perhaps hoping to get a gander at Jeff in secret, in case there were any rival record execs about. A buzz had started, now that our Imago deal had lapsed, and presumably the pukkah Wright was trying to determine what the Jeff Buckley hoopla was all about.

Peter's surreptitious but ultimately fruitless attempt at

intelligence-gathering reminded me of Kate Hyman hiding behind the door of her Imago office before Jeff and I went in to meet with her the first time—just another taste of the childish and clumsy tactics that are the stock in trade of record company weasels everywhere.

Of course, I'd dropped by Mute's offices and left a cassette of our demos the previous fall, but Wright had never responded. Now he was trying to play catch-up.

That night, Jeff and I had a duo gig at Tramps on 24th Street, where I'd had my record-release party (with Jeff as special guest) the previous fall. We were opening for The Jazz Butcher, an English indie band, and our show had been listed in the *Village Voice* as being by 'Jeff Buckley and Gary Lucas'—the first time Jeff's name had preceded mine in an ad.

"That's the way our names should always be listed," Jeff said, taunting me smugly, when I arrived to set up.

Jeff was shooting pool by himself in the front window of the club. He reminded me of a manic, hopped-up version of Paul Newman's 'Fast' Eddie Felson character in *The Hustler*.

"This is *you*," he said before leaning over the table and ostentatiously running his cue back and forth between his fingers, ostensibly concentrating on setting up his next shot. Then he violently shoved the cue hard against the cue ball, ramming another ball into a side pocket. Ouch!

I guess he was still smarting from the tongue-lashing Jared had given him at CBGB's the week before. He probably thought I had set him up (not true), so now he was taking his revenge.

Plus, as I was soon to learn, Jeff was flush with triumph because the following week he was to begin appearing solo at a small club in the East Village called Sin-é … and he was about to perform onstage before his new major label A&R champion, none other than my old friend and occasional nemesis Steve Berkowitz, the former Columbia product manager now running the Legacy re-issues program and doing occasional A&R there.

Berkowitz walked into the club a few minutes before we went onstage, and gave me his customary greeting: "Jah Luke!" He then huddled with his new protégé while we waited to hit the stage.

As I've mentioned, I'd had some unpleasant run-ins with Berkowitz in the past when I worked at CBS. This was the guy who'd also basically laughed in my face when I'd played him my demos with Julia. Now I knew where Jeff had come up with that expensive Mahalia Jackson boxed set—the one he'd showily displayed to Jared, Tony, and me right before he brought the axe down on those guys. It was from this set that he'd drawn his version of 'Satisfied Mind,' and it came from Berkowitz. Say it ain't so, Jeff!

Later, it dawned on me that by meeting with Berkowitz while he and I were both under contract with Imago, Jeff had technically violated our agreement with the label—except, as I later learned, on reading *Dream Brother*, Jeff had never signed the agreement. Imago had given us an advance in good faith based on my signature alone.

No wonder Kate Hyman had looked so rattled at our last meeting. She was sure Jeff was going to fly the coop the moment our development deal elapsed. Had Jeff signed the contract, Imago would have had first option on a solo record deal with him as long as it matched any rival offer.

Even so, to take the money from Imago and then meet rival A&R executives was in violation of the spirit of our development deal.

But fuck it. This kind of ruthless, unethical behavior goes on constantly in the music business, with or without contracts. "You can't afford to sue us." You got it right there, buddy.

Had I known Jeff was meeting with Berkowitz (which I now suspect) while we were under contract to Imago, I might have admonished him about it, but I obviously couldn't have stopped him from doing it. People are gonna do what they're gonna do.

That said, it sure was a bummer to see the whole scheme fall into place before me at Tramps the way it did at that precise moment.

We get offered a development deal on the basis of the demos I arranged to be recorded, but really Jeff wants to be signed as a solo artist. He lets it be known to nearly everyone within earshot that he doesn't really want to be working on this project with me, but is stuck with me for the duration. He needs me as a stepping stone, as no one is interested in his own demos.

Then in a power move he fires key members of my group ten days before our big label showcase to further weaken the project and to insure its certain failure. Miraculously, the guys he brings in at the 11th hour manage to get their heads round our music well enough to win us a standing ovation at our big showcase.

Jeff turns his back on the project and publicly quits the band a week later, claiming he "just wants to develop his singing in the clubs", while waiting for the Imago deal to lapse.

He agrees however to continue singing with me while preparing for his solo coming out at Sine so as to further hone his chops and build his fan base in NYC, while his manager lines up offers for him.

And now here he is at Tramps, performing with me before his new Columbia Records champion. Columbia Records—the very label that had tossed me out on the street from my own deal so coldly the year before.

I felt like I was trapped in a nightmare from which I could not awake.

□

I went onstage first and sat in a chair hovering over my effects pedals. Jeff waited a beat and then bounded out onstage in classic rock star mode, waving his arms in triumph as if he was onstage at the Hollywood Bowl.

"HELLOOOOOOOOO NEW YORK!"

I guess he was trying to demonstrate his rock-star potential to Berkowitz.

I don't remember much else about what would prove to be our last duo set together, but I'm sure it went fine. I do remember that

Berkowitz came over while I was packing up my gear, and in typical jive-ass fashion he made a disparaging remark about my digital delay pedals.

"Oh, I see you're using a *machine* to play," he said, like he was describing a toilet seat.

I explained what the pedal was—how it allowed me to play counterpoint to my own guitar lines.

"Yeah," Jeff said dismissively, putting the boot in once again. "It's just a *machine*," he added, the implication being that it was a cheap prop to mask my inability to play the guitar. (Years later, Jeff would release the song 'Tongue' as a B-side, essentially using the same 'machine' to loop his guitar line over and over to no real discernible effect.)

And that, as they say, was that—for the time being anyway.

I went home to lick my wounds and ponder my next moves, "deep in dark despair," as The Yardbirds' 'Heart Full Of Soul' would have it.

Jeff stopped returning my phone calls after that show and shortly began his run of solo appearances at Sin-é in the East Village. The buzz was on. He had long lines of people waiting to see him perform, with presidents of major labels dropping by in their limos to check him out.

I heard about all this through the grapevine. I didn't want to be anywhere near the place. I wanted nothing to do with it, and to be as far away as possible from this grotesque carnival and coronation.

Disgusted by the whole phony circus, I played The Fall's 'Music Scene' over and over again:

I'll be part of the music scene
Envy of the choosy set
Part of the music scare

Danny Fields later told me that Clive Davis, the head of Arista, and Seymour Stein, the president of Sire, had both been by Sin-é to check Jeff out. Both were keen on signing him, but both had noticed a distinct lack of original material. In fact, Jeff's sets at this time were wall-to-wall covers—Edith Piaf, Nusrat Fateh Ali Khan; all his faves, you name it. I think the only original he may have played back then was 'Mojo Pin,' which appeared on his first Columbia EP, *Live At Sin-é.*

"He doesn't really have many songs," I told Danny.

"That doesn't matter to Clive," he quickly replied. "He'll provide him with the best songs money can buy."

That was Clive's MO. His forte was signing a big voice like Whitney Houston and farming out the actual songwriting to the usual hit-meisters.

"I don't think Jeff will stand for that," I said, "as much as he wants to make it."

I was right. Jeff had the example of his father to live up to, and his father had many, many classics to his name by the time of his death: 'Song To The Siren,' 'Morning Glory,' 'Once I Was,' 'Strange Feelin',' and so on. Jeff had a lot of catching up to do.

☐

Meanwhile, I was preoccupied, naturally, with trying to make a living, now that one major-label deal and then a possible second one had blown up in my face, all in the same year. Just as Caroline had predicted, my erstwhile friend and collaborator was nowhere to be found.

My friend Peter Feldman, the cousin of Susan Feldman, came to my rescue for a minute by recommending me for session work at the New York City jingle house JSM Music. Had I played my cards right, I might even have been hired onto the staff, as the owner took a shine to my playing and my composing. Which would have been nice, as there was money to be made in jingles.

But I hated it. I felt like a bigger whore now than when I had worked at CBS. They basically just wanted sound-alikes from me.

For instance, the agency rep at a jingle session would ask, "Can you sound like The Edge on this one?"

"I don't know what that sounds like," I'd shoot back. "I don't really know their stuff. Besides, I don't copy anyone."

No, you'd have to specifically want Gary Lucas playing on your session, and all my sounds, which were not easy for anyone to duplicate. But all the jingle house wanted was generic rock guitar of the day: speed-metal, Joe Satriani-style tapping, and so on. But I couldn't (or wouldn't) play like that … so I didn't last very long there.

I got a taste of the money to be made in jingles when I was eventually cut in on a writing credit for something or other and the royalty checks started coming. But it wasn't enough really to hold my attention, especially as part of the hustle entailed being on call at the jingle house basically 24/7, and hanging with the other studio guys.

Loner that I am, I really didn't want to be part of any fraternity that would have me for a member, to quote Groucho Marx. I never felt like one of the boys and I have never been a 'studio cat.' I am a concert and recording artist, a songwriter and a composer. I will do the occasional session, but only for artists I like. I am not a gun for hire.

The guys at the jingle house looked down at my performing and recording aspirations as mere fantasy. Here, they thought, was where the *real* musicians work and play and hang out together. All the rest was transient to them. I, on the other hand, loved touring, and wanted to try to accelerate that part of my career.

And so the jingle house rescinded the offer of a staff guitarist job pretty quickly, once it became clear that I wasn't quite so tractable a player as had first been assumed.

My favorite memory of the absurdity of the whole jingle hustle was working with the alternative singer Syd Straw on a jingle for Cotton Inc. It was a re-tooling of the famous 'Touch The Feel Of Cotton— The Fabric Of Our Lives' jingle written by Zack Smith (one half of 80s band Scandal) and sung by Aaron Neville.

241

Syd and I cut a credible re-working of this well-known jingle to great approval from the house account executive. But then of course we needed to get the go-ahead from the ad agency and the reps from Cotton Inc, and this is where we ran into trouble.

The day before the Cotton Inc people were due to show up, I was told to be sure to wear simple cotton jeans and a cotton shirt to the meeting. Jesus! The next day, the agency folks listened to our track over and over again without saying anything.

Syd then excused herself and went off to the ladies room.

"As long as I am in charge of this account," one of the old biddies from Cotton Inc announced as soon as Syd left the room, "that girl will NEVER be the voice of Cotton!"

There really wasn't much there for me—they didn't understand my writing or playing at all—and soon I was back on the street. I supported myself, as I had done for several years at that point, through gigging as much as possible, mainly in Europe, and advances on record contracts.

I also did the odd session for artist friends such as Kip Hanrahan, for whom I recorded a few tracks that spring for his Paul Haines music and poetry compilation *Darn It!* And I occasionally scored soundtracks for television and films, and even assembled a reggae compilation for CBS, which my notes tell me was mastered with my participation on May 15 that spring.

It felt odd to be back working temporarily in the belly of the beast, but I still had a few friends inside CBS Records (which had recently been bought by Sony and was now known as Sony Music). They were trying to help me get through a very difficult period and thus threw me a gig or two whenever they could. Folks like Gary Pacheco, who worked in their reissues department, and who had always championed my talent.

I couldn't wait to get back to playing overseas, though. New York just felt so damn claustrophobic. I felt as if everyone was laughing at me behind my back.

I recall a gig on June 6 at the BimHuis in Amsterdam, one of my favorite places to play, where I'd recorded much of my first solo album, *Skeleton At The Feast*. I finished my set, before only a handful of people, with an acoustic instrumental version of 'No One Must Find You Here.' I played my heart out in a fever, mourning the loss of my friend and collaborator, and the seeming destruction of all of my best-laid plans and dreams.

The next night, I went on a canal ride in the small boat owned by my good friend Joep Ver. We sailed from his artist's squat in an old mustard factory up and down the canals that ring this most beautiful city.

The boat cruise with Joep—and the sublime views of Amsterdam from his boat—used to be one of the biggest pleasures of my touring life. This time, I was stone miserable throughout. I couldn't shake the feeling of having been betrayed by Jeff.

We anchored near one of Joep's favorite bars and went in. The giant video screen was showing U2 performing live in Rio before an audience of thousands. There was The Edge kicking out his guitar jams in a style I had no interest in emulating.

While Joep drank himself silly, I sat there nursing a fresh orange juice and smoked joint after joint after joint, feeling beaten, betrayed, and damned. Feeling the most alienated and miserable I have ever felt in my life.

It all seemed so pointless. So futile.

Chapter Nine

But I rallied eventually.

I was down, but I wasn't out. I am a very determined person—a workaholic—and there is nothing like throwing yourself into good old-fashioned work to lift you out of the slough of despond. Stay in the game!

First order of business was putting out a follow-up to *Skeleton At The Feast*. I felt it was time to accentuate the other side of what I had been up to over the last several years: namely, making avant-garde rock with Gods and Monsters (in various configurations, of course).

Enemy Records' Mike Knuth was receptive to the idea. He had signed me in the first place because of the strength of my instrumental 'King Strong,' which had been floating around for almost four years among underground collectors.

He wanted this track on the album—in fact, he wanted it so bad that he offered to publish it. I remember sitting in the White Horse Tavern with him looking at a sheaf of documents with my name misspelled as 'Lukas' on them. Signing the papers would bind this song to him forever. My misspelled name was a bad omen, so I politely declined, and instead set up my own publishing company, Brillianteen Music.

The songs I'd recorded in England with Rolo McGinty in the late 80s had convinced Rick Chertoff that I knew what I was doing as a songwriter and recording artist, and had helped to get me signed to Columbia Records, so they too were definitely going on the album. But the question of whether or not to involve Jeff on the album was hanging in the air.

Knuth wanted nothing to do with this idea. He had simply never liked Jeff's performances with me, which I never quite understood.

I debated for a minute whether or not to try and include Jeff on the album. He hadn't yet signed to Sony at this point, and he might well have been into the idea, to help pave the way on an indie level for his future anointment, when he eventually surfaced on a major.

And then I thought: fuck it! My career didn't start with Jeff, and it isn't gonna end with him. Plus the guy has been a total jerk to me … and now he isn't returning my calls. Who needs the further humiliation of chasing after him to try and get him on this album?

Not me, I can assure you. And that was that.

I assembled the album over a few months from the cache of existing tracks I'd been sitting on for a while. I also recorded a few new ones, and re-jiggered a few older ones, such as 'Poison Tree,' the first song I'd ever written. I had a two-track master of it as played by Gods and Monsters mk2, with Julia Heyward on vocals.

That spring I fortuitously ran into the wonderfully brilliant Mary Margaret O'Hara at a session for Kip Hanrahan's *Darn It!* album with Paul Haines. I played Mary the song; she dug it and loved the idea of singing with me. We shared a lot in common, in terms of stylistic approach—she hadn't been called the female Beefheart for nothing.

And at the tail end of one of Kit's sessions at RPM Studios, I put the track up and got a fantastic vocal out of Mary, setting her spooky, enchanted voice—which actually shared a lot of similarities with Jeff's vocal at the end of our 'Grace' demo—against my acoustic death-letter blues, which Paul described as "that taut rope sound." I liked that description.

Gods and Monsters was released that fall, complete with a classic Anton Corbijn photo of me turned upside down so it appeared as though I was walking on water. (In fact, he had photographed me skirting the edge of a giant puddle.) It received major accolades in the press, including a four-star review in *Rolling Stone* by the late Robert Palmer, the erudite Southern blues scholar and musician who was an early champion of my work. Palmer had also been the chief pop critic of the *New York Times* at one point, and I'll never forget the way my spirits lifted after reading his review. It seemed to totally validate my music and vision, and in the Holy Bible of Rock to boot. And it came from a much more knowledgeable writer, and a much higher authority, than the benighted jerk at the *Times* who had abused my good name several times already with his nasty and injurious reviews.

Around the same time, an editor at the *Village Voice*, the venerable alternative New York City weekly, called me out of the blue and asked me to pose for a rooftop shot with the French expat photographer Michel del Sol. In August, one of the resulting photographs ran in the centerfold of the *Voice* to coincide with a solo show I was giving in town.

I remember running into Jeff's friend Michael Tighe by chance on the street the day after the *Voice* came out. He'd obviously seen the photo, which seems to have conferred newfound legitimacy on me as an artist.

"Hey Gary, I saw your picture in the *Voice*—looking good."

"How's Jeff?" I asked.

"He's great," Michael replied. "Man, we've been listening together to those songs you wrote with him ... really cool!"

Jeff had obviously played him a cassette of the St Ann's show. It cheered me up to learn that despite all of Jeff's posturing to try and distance himself from our project, he knew just how good those songs and performances really were—and was proud enough of the recordings to share them with people he cared about. And Michael was one of his closest friends.

☐

Things began to accelerate again that fall.

In September, I was invited by avant-garde saxophonist and composer John Zorn to perform my live score to the 1920 film *The*

Golem with my childhood friend and collaborator Walter Horn at Zorn's Festival of Radical Jewish Culture in Munich.

While waiting for my luggage to come down the chute at Munich Airport, I ran into Lou Reed, who was also performing at this festival. He was extremely friendly to me—perhaps because I had cited his playing on The Velvet Underground's 'I Heard Her Call My Name' as my favorite guitar solo in a *Musician* magazine article that fall—and he came to watch me perform during the festival.

"I could listen to you play for hours, Gary!" he later told me.

We became friends, and I spent time jamming with Lou at his apartment uptown when we got back. He let me test out a guitar a famous luthier had given him, complete with a floating whammy bar, and in my eagerness to put it through its paces I ripped the whammy bar clear out of its socket.

"You're an animal, Gary," said Lou—high praise indeed, coming from the *Rock 'N Roll Animal* himself.

I had also put Gods and Monsters back together again. I wasn't going to let Jeff have the last word: "The band is breaking up" my ass!

As Tony Lewis was out on the road with Arto Lindsay's Ambitious Lovers, and Jared Nickerson had been scooped up by The The, I regrouped with Oren Bloedow, a nimble bass player, and Jonathan Kane, a fantastic drummer, formerly of Swans. Jonathan had an incendiary touch and sounded like a combination Keith Moon and Fred Below, plus he was a super-nice guy. He would hang in there with me through thick and thin for the next ten years plus.

We commenced a US tour on November 3 1992—the night Bill Clinton was first elected President. We hit the road around midnight and drove all night to Detroit for the first show. The next night we played at Prince's club, the 7th Street Entry, in Minneapolis, and sold out the place, thanks to a major feature on us in the local paper. At the end of the gig, the club DJ got on the mic and said, "Gods and Monsters, you rocked our world!"

Life was sweet again, for a minute. One minute I'm freaking out that my singer has flown the coop almost to the day *Rolling Stone* comes out with that 'New Faces' feature where we are pictured in a photo as partners. Next minute I'm being cheered as a hero by a packed club out in the hinterlands of America with only a bassist and drummer for support. Look Ma, no singer!

I could go on and provide a blow-by-blow of all my activities from this point on, but I'll leave that for another day, and another tome.

Meanwhile, back to Jeff.

I had deliberately kept myself aloof and above the fray concerning his progress. I heard reports about his gigs in town, and once about how he had asked from the stage during a gig whether or not I was in the house, adding that I probably didn't have enough money to gain admission to the club. How tacky. But I had obviously affected him, and continued to do so, whether by being there or not being there— and I guess he was disappointed that I wasn't actively pursuing him.

Eventually, I heard that he'd signed to Columbia via Berkowitz for a staggering sum of money—a million-dollar deal, in effect, and one that supposedly gave him total creative freedom, with no cap on his album budget. Yes, Columbia: the same label that had given me the heave-ho the year before. The irony wasn't lost on me.

In the meantime, I soldiered on and put out one acclaimed album after another. Of course, none of the fly-by-night companies that issued them had any platform to speak of to launch them and promote them, so they largely fell on deaf ears. Most of these indie labels bit the dust shortly after issuing my albums, so the records mainly disappeared from the marketplace as physical goods after a few years.

But with the advent of the digital revolution, and with the rights to most of my albums eventually reverting to me, most of them are now available online. I am extremely proud of them all—they are my children. They all received stellar reviews worldwide, and they were all recorded on a shoestring. You don't need mega-budgets to get the truth on tape.

I remember recording in Murray Weinstock's cluttered loft studio Love Notes Music—he had long since moved out of Krypton, where we recorded the 'Grace' and 'Mojo Pin' demos—and literally stepping over piles of dog shit on my way into the booth to record a guitar overdub.

For a millisecond, I envied Jeff with his lavish Sony budget. But I knew the results I was getting would be harder and truer than those derived from months spent farting around in a luxurious studio with a major label's meter running. There's nothing like a lack of resources to concentrate the creative mind.

□

On February 10 1993, my new lineup of Gods and Monsters played a gig at a club called the Grand, formerly the Cat Club, on East 13th Street. It was shortly before we were due to fly to the Netherlands to play a festival at the Paradiso, my favorite club in Europe. I remember eyeballing the fixtures in this newly refurbished rock club—all swanky Italian marble—and making a crack about "mafia marble," which was overheard by the club owner—and which earned me a very hard stare. We rocked hard, and we received an ovation at the end.

Afterward, a tall, good-looking kid came forward from the crowd while I was packing up and introduced himself as Mick Grondhal. He said he was a big fan of my music and playing, and that he was now playing with Jeff in a trio.

This was news to me. I had heard about Jeff's solo concerts in town and that he was putting a group together, but I didn't know how far along he was.

I shook Mick's hand and wished him the best, and told him to say hi to Jeff. I liked the look of this guy. He had a kind, sensitive face; he was a bit shy but seemed like an extremely nice person.

At this point, though, I had written off ever hearing from Jeff again. Not only had he cut me out of his life after he started playing at Sin-é, but he had done the same to lots of people who'd helped him when he was first starting out in New York—people like Debbie Schwartz, who had flogged his *Babylon Dungeon Sessions* tape all over town.

The pattern grew worse the bigger he got. Meeting this sweet, seemingly innocent boy a few years earlier, who would ever have predicted that he would become so ruthless?

In any case, my band went off to play that Dutch festival, and then the following month we did a lengthy three-week tour of six European countries, which went very well indeed. Back in New York, I kept alternating solo gigs with band gigs in town, and I began playing a lot at a new club known as the Fez under Time Cafe, where Jeff was also starting to play regularly with his trio.

On Tuesday August 17, I was surprised, to put it mildly, to receive a call from Jeff out of the blue. It was the first I had heard from him directly for about a year.

"Hello?"

"Gary?" he said in a soft, meek voice. "This is Jeff."

There was a long pause. I think he was afraid I might hang up on him.

"Hi, Jeff," I said finally, in a noncommittal tone. Secretly I was happy to hear from him, but I didn't want to show it. "How are you?"

"I'm well, I'm OK," he replied. "You've probably heard I was signed by Columbia."

"Yes I heard ... congratulations."

"Yeah, well—thanks. Anyway—ah, the thing is ..."

He paused to collect himself, and then in a fast tumble of words, he said:

"Remember those great songs we used to perform together, 'Grace' and 'Mojo Pin'?"

"Of course."

"Well, I want to record them on the album I'm going to make for Columbia up in Woodstock, at Bearsville Studios next month ... and I want you to play on them."

This was good news.

"Sure," I said, "I'd be delighted to, Jeff."

This was obviously easy for me to agree to. My spirits lifted, and I started to feel warm about Jeff all over again.

It must have finally dawned on somebody up at Sony that their prize acquisition had written very few songs of his own. He had dazzled everyone at Sin-é for sure with his electric live presence, but he had been signed on the strength of his voice and good looks and charisma—not on his material. He lacked songs of his own—or good ones, at any rate—and the label had finally woken up to the fact that Jeff couldn't make a record of covers only.

Someone in authority at Sony, having just thrown down many hundreds of thousands of dollars to sign Jeff without it occurring to them that he had no real original repertoire, must have by necessity given a second look to the work we two had done together.

And somebody up there had decided that our original demos for 'Mojo Pin' and 'Grace'—which I had paid for in blood, sweat, and tears—were worthy candidates to be re-recorded for Jeff's debut. They were top-shelf material, in fact—so top-shelf that they would end up opening Jeff's one and only official studio album.

Jeff and I chatted a bit more, and I mentioned that I knew Bearsville well, having produced an album up there with Peter Gordon nine years earlier.

"Cool," he replied. "I've got Andy Wallace lined up to produce the album—you know him, he did Nirvana's *Nevermind* album. It's going to be amazing."

He said he'd be in touch.

I hung up the phone, smiled, and called Caroline to tell her the news. Jeff's sun was shining again for me—briefly, at least.

Caroline and I were both really happy about this turn of events. Finally, some vindication for the songs Jeff and I wrote together—as well as a possible payoff down the line for all the hard work and time I'd put in—and for all the slights and humiliations I'd endured at his hand. I saw this as a great chance for us to reconcile.

□

Jeff called again a few days later to set up a rehearsal with his new band at Context in the East Village on Saturday August 28. Andy Wallace came along to monitor the sessions. He was an affable, balding older guy with a wispy beard who looked like a traditional jazz fan—the least likely candidate to have produced Nirvana I could have imagined.

When I arrived, Jeff was busy in the front office, strumming some jazzy chords on an acoustic guitar and writing down music furiously on a notepad with music staffs.

"Hey man, give me a second," he said, "I'm working on a new song." The song in question was 'Lover, You Should Have Come Over.' Whether he was actually in the throes of songwriting I don't know—it seemed a bit too melodramatic a display to me, as if designed to impress.

Still, I was happy to see him.

We went into a studio room, and there I met Jeff's drummer Matt Johnson, a sharp-faced wiry guy, and the aforementioned Mick Grondahl, who smiled broadly when I walked in. I was introduced to Andy, and then I got out my Strat. Jeff strapped on his Tele, and we started playing the two songs pretty much as we always had.

There was no change at that point in my basic arrangement until we got to the end of 'Mojo Pin.' When I went to leap into the thrash coda, Jeff said, "No, let's end it there." I guess he was self-editing himself—I had composed this hardcore section to catch his ear back in the day, and it was just not going to fit on his major-label debut.

Mick and Matt gingerly went through all the stops and starts of the songs, with Jeff and I drilling them whenever the music drifted off base. Andy pronounced himself happy and promptly split.

As soon as Andy left the room, Jeff said, "THIS is what we REALLY want to play," and asked me to kick off 'No One Must Find You Here,' the epic that had closed our Friday the 13th showcase.

I retuned my Strat and launched into my fingerpicked intro as Jeff began wailing ecstatically. The other two guys had probably never heard the song before. They kicked in as best they could, but the music soon devolved into an aimless, muddy psychedelic jam that went on and on.

It was painful for me to hear this music so desecrated. Jeff and the others seemed blissed out by it, so I wisely decided not to rock the boat by saying anything, but as a unit they were not very tight— amateurish, even—at this point. But it was still early days for them, and they would later prove to be exceptional players.

□

A few days later, Jeff and I worked out a deal whereby I would be paid $1,500 plus travel expenses to record the two songs with him and his band up in Woodstock—not too shabby for those days.

In the late morning of Tuesday September 28, I took the train from Penn Station up to Rhinebeck. My old friends Dennis and Lois gave me a lift to the station, and at the other end I was met by a young guy of Asian descent who introduced himself as Murali Coryell. I asked him if his dad was the great jazz guitarist Larry Coryell, which he shyly confirmed, confiding in me that he also played the guitar.

After the 20-minute drive, we arrived at Bearsville Studios, a rustic compound set back in the woods off the winding highway that snakes through Woodstock. It was a large rambling complex with several different cabins attached on the property. The main building contained various smaller mixing rooms and a large Studio A with a loft area and a barn-like vaulted ceiling. There was also a state-of-the-art control room that nonetheless hadn't changed all that much since I was last there in the 80s.

We drove up a winding road through the leafy glade that surrounds the complex and parked outside the main building. Murali helped me drag my bags and guitars inside and then split.

Andy Wallace and the band were lounging around in the commissary area outside the studio control room. There was a pinball machine, a coffee maker, and a fridge, with framed gold and platinum albums hanging on the pine walls—all the usual accouterments of the major recording studio.

Jeff sat in the center of it all, wearing a spiffy new 40s-style patterned jacket with zip—a departure from his usual T-shirts, and presumably just one of the spoils of his Columbia deal. The guys seemed happy to see me, and Jeff got up to give me a hug.

"Hey man, great to see you," I said, hugging him back. "It's so weird to be back in this studio—driving up here from the train station was such a trip."

I mentioned that my driver was Larry Coryell's son. Jeff shot me an annoyed look and quickly changed the subject—no mention of any other sons of famous fathers here!

After drinking some coffee, I was ushered in to Studio A by Andy Wallace and began setting up my pedal effects, taking off the bubble wrap I kept them in and connecting them together. Wallace looked askance—horrified is more like it—at the tangle of wires and the beat-up pedals, which had seen a lot of action over the past few years.

"Let's get ourselves organized here," he remarked, pointedly and a touch patronizingly. I don't think he had quite figured out yet where all my pedals and clutter fit into the big picture sonically, but he knew that I had written the guitar parts to these songs, and I was a friend of Jeff, so ...

"You know, Jeff is so organized," he went on, gratuitously, "and so efficient."

Unlike you, you weirdo guitar player.

There was more:

"I think he's quite the most gifted individual I've probably ever met—don't you agree?"

This may all have been true, to him, but did I need to have it rubbed in my face at this point? Laying it on with a trowel, daring me to contradict him, as if I was a nobody who was lucky to be there.

"Oh yes, he certainly is," I replied, nodding my head with as much sincerity as I could muster, Eddie Haskell style. I wasn't about to get into an argument with him over the relative merits of "the precious one" (Caroline's pet name for Jeff). I knew my collaborator's strengths and weaknesses pretty well by then.

Wallace was a good engineer, and an accomplished, hands-on mixer, but also somewhat of an anal, buttoned-down martinet. Then again, I suppose you'd have to be, to be both an engineer and a producer. That said, I was never quite sure why exactly Jeff had hired him to produce this album. Beyond the hip Nirvana credentials, he didn't seem like Jeff's type of guy—and certainly not the type of guy I would hire to produce my major label debut, if I had my druthers.

Speaking of being 'organized,' I am pretty much the opposite of that in the studio. I tend to let it all hang out and erupt rather than manicuring parts to death, which is why I have never enjoyed being in studios very much (or producing albums for other folks for that matter). I am more about capturing the moment, spontaneity, mystic inspiration, and the energies thrown off in combustible situations— preferably live. The major label approach, of course, is to freeze-dry and tweak every sound on an album to try and make it scientifically palatable for mass consumption—and it is much worse in that regard today than it was 20 years ago.

There was a Roland JC-120 amp already set up in the studio, which is of course the amp I used at home, and also the amp I used for live gigs in New York. I saw a Marshall lying around, too, and I mentioned to Jeff and Andy that I had just used one extensively on an album I had recorded a few weeks earlier in Chicago with The Killer Shrews (my group with Jon Langford of The Mekons and Tony Maimone). I asked if I might plug into that.

"No," Jeff said, "I want the exact same sound as you had in your apartment when we worked together."

Wallace started getting sounds up on his board, and while he was preoccupied I took Jeff aside.

"Listen," I said, "I've been thinking ... why don't you also record 'She Is Free' on this album? It's a stone hit."

"Umm, not this time," Jeff replied uneasily, looking off in the distance. He'd obviously been going back and forth with Wallace and Berkowitz over the repertoire for the album.

Well, I tried!

Tracking for 'Mojo Pin' was first on the recording agenda. Matt and Mick laid down their parts together, with me playing the same fingerpicked lines from the original demo, which were later doubled with Jeff playing the same lines on his Telecaster. I was impressed with Matt's fluid and jazzy drumming on this track. He really adds a swinging dimension to the song, opening it up and letting it breathe. Overall, I would vote him the session's Most Valuable Player, but Mick was certainly no slouch, and after endless takes recording the backing track in sections, he came up with a re-harmonization of the bassline that had us all cheering.

The bolero section was tough to nail down as a band en masse. The rhythm section had trouble getting the dah-dah-dah dah! Dah-dah-dah dah! accents right. I tried to demonstrate how it should go to them by scat singing the percussion parts, and right then it dawned on me that it was the same rhythm Lord Richard Buckley had chanted to impersonate a locomotive in his famous routine 'The Train.' Boppity bop! Boppity bop!

"Man," I laughed, "this sounds just like Lord Buckley's 'The Train.'"

"What?" Jeff replied. "What did you say?" He was all ears after hearing the Buckley name.

I explained how Lord Buckley, a white 50s comedian, put on a black hipster voice as part of his act. Jeff had never heard of him but seemed enthralled by my stories and the fact that he shared a last name with this relatively obscure American genius. It seemed serendipitous to what we were laying down in the studio.

"Sounds like Beavis & Butthead to me," Mick chimed in,

mimicking the MTV cartoon bad boys' sinister maniacal laughter to the rhythm of the 'Mojo Pin' bolero:

"Heh-heh-heh heh! Heh-heh-heh heh! Heh-heh-heh heh! Heh-heh-heh heh!"

They all laughed, and all of a sudden I realized I was the odd man out here.

Of course, Jeff loved cartoons. In the period right after he quit Gods and Monsters, he taped a short playlet of his own devising called *The Adventures Of Spinach The Cat* and put it on the answering machine at Rebecca Moore's place. When you tried to call, you had to suffer through this five-minute opus before you could leave a message. What a joker!

The three other musicians kept taking mysterious trips to the loo throughout the afternoon and the next day. Ah … rock'n'roll. Again I was odd-man-out, beyond sharing spliffs with them at night.

Matt came back from one of these trips all fired up and talking about the drum pattern he was going to play under the bolero section. I liked his spirit, his cool:

"The way I see it, we've built up some real tension here," he said, "and now I am gonna have to pay it off here in a big-ass way."

That line has stuck with me all these years. Matt really understood what I was going for in the original instrumental, and his drumming is outstanding on the final track.

☐

We finally got the basic track down, and Andy called a break for the night. I was bunking in my own room in one of the guest cabins that abutted the studio, where Mick and Matt also had rooms. Jeff had an entire building to himself behind the studio—what Andy referred to as "The Writer's Cottage."

The four of us sans Wallace all hung out together that night, smoking joints and giggling over a VHS tape of weird B-movie horror clips. Jeff left after a while to go back to his Writer's Cottage.

The next morning, I got up very early and took a stroll on the grounds. I was looking for Jeff. I wanted to talk to him about the music we were recording. I found his cottage, walked up to the front of it, and peered through the picture window to see if he was home.

Jeff was hunched over a table with a piece of paper before him and a pencil in his hand. He had a brooding, agonized look on his face.

He felt my presence at the window and glanced up with a shocked expression, and our eyes met for a second.

It was as if I'd caught him in the throes of an act too embarrassing, too naked to be shared. I chose not to go in there.

I quickly averted my gaze and returned to the band quarters. Now I understood why this was The Writer's Cottage, and why Jeff was sweating in there.

He was still trying to write songs for his album, and the meter was running on a very expensive studio.

□

Jeff went into Bearsville on September 20 and left on October 30. Six weeks is an extremely long time to record an album in such an expensive studio—especially when you are still writing it.

A former big-name record producer told me recently that I lead a life of "privilege" because I tour all over the world constantly.

"Privilege?" I replied. "I work my ass off to do this."

It's my job.

Now, Jeff was certainly working his ass off up there, but talk about privilege—how many artists get the chance and the luxury of being booked into a top-flight studio for their debut album by a major label without having all the songs written?

How many artists would ever get an open-ended budget to record for as long as it took to 'get it right'?

I know of only one. And really, as good and as promising as Jeff was, what kind of mass hypnosis had descended on the theoretically shrewd sharpies running Sony Music to possibly justify this endless funding from the get-go of an untried and untested new artist?

Hence Jeff's haunted expression when I caught him in an unguarded moment. It was the look of a guy who was way, way under pressure.

Jeff now had to make good on all the trust invested in him and money thrown at him—to pay it off in a big-ass way.

There but for the Grace of God ...

◻

Later, in the studio, it was back to business.

My early morning glimpse of Jeff at work was never mentioned. It was just too personal. I could commiserate with him on one level—but not that much.

We tackled 'Grace' next, and here I intervened to stick up for my original arrangement. I had brought a cassette with me of our original demo for Andy Wallace's edification.

I wanted him to hear all of my guitar parts, and in particular an arpeggio part played under the lines

And the rain is falling
And I believe my time has come

that had not survived the rehearsal. I wanted it in the final recording. I was trying to stand up for the integrity of my original vision of the track.

"Andy," I said, "would you please listen to this tape of the original demo?"

Jeff looked daggers at me, as if to say: How dare you try to continue to put your stamp on this song? But he let it go.

To his credit, Andy put up the cassette and we listened together. When it came to the part I was referring to, I flagged it up for him, and he liked what he heard. He had me record it as a single staccato line played with a flat pick instead of fingerpicking it.

I didn't care—it was a great part, and I was pleased to see it stay in there. Shades of Jared and the great flat-picking contretemps.

In the lunch break, one of Columbia's marketing flunkies, a girl who was the new product manager of their latest Great White Hope, the Boston band Stompbox, showed up to banter with Jeff and the guys. She was apparently the advance scout/spy for Berkowitz, who never once bothered to show his face while I was there. She made a tacky remark about my having a "bad hair day." In truth, I never cut or combed it much in this period.

That evening, I witnessed Jeff record an intense vocal for his song 'Eternal Life.' We sat there with Andy in the studio control room as Jeff nailed it. He sang superbly as usual—but it still did not convince me that Sony knew what it was doing by investing so heavily and lavishly in him. This was a song dating back to the *Babylon Dungeon* sessions, and it hadn't totally impressed me when he played it to me back in 1991.

On my third and final day at Bearsville, I spent most of the morning into mid-afternoon adding my ambient space guitar and also some lead guitar overdubs to 'Mojo Pin' and 'Grace.' Jeff deliberately stayed away from the studio and let Andy do his thing.

We got a lot down that day. There's the looped drone that opens 'Mojo Pin' and the entire *Grace* album, to which I added whammy bar harmonics on top, plus the futuristic backward, sped-up guitar loops that occur throughout the song, and the E-bowed passage that comes in on the line "Drop down we two to serve and pray for love." It gets very raga-like there.

For 'Grace,' I created a host of eerie sounds and new parts on my guitar, beginning with the violin-like clock chimes in the intro—bing bong, bing bong—that then rise a step higher over my fingerpicked arpeggio. It really works well in this particular passage, connoting as it does the passing of time.

The same violin sound, achieved with my volume pedal and a delay pedal, limn the vocal in the first verse as well. It sounds like a violin, but it is my guitar. On the last word of "Afraid to die" I produced a sighing, ghostly harmonic bend.

More spectral guitar occurs on the line "Walking to the bright lights in sorrow." You hear a swooning, descending glissando, like the sound of a world collapsing, which is my glass bottleneck on my Strat run through a pitch shifter and a delay pedal.

The spiky, tinkling sounds that follow "Oh my love" are me hammering-on up the neck of my guitar through another pitch-shifter setting. And at "I believe my time has come," the flat-picked arpeggio noted earlier comes in. The swooping seagull sounds that ensue, the high pitched violin-like sound that wells up in the instrumental breaks, and the wordless chorale section—that is all my guitar.

At the end of the line "And forget with this kiss," my wah-wah'd, fuzzed-out guitar erupts under Jeff's vocal and rides the song out with guttural bluesy wails and shrieks. Finally, the phasing effect that comes in on the line "It goes so slow" is me playing the rhythm-guitar chords through a flanger. There are also lots of feedback-laden whammy-bar stabs in this section.

It was a really fun and creative day. Andy Wallace gave me my psychedelic head here, encouraging me to improvise and try different things out throughout the song. He then picked out what he thought worked best after I'd gone.

I think Jeff deliberately stayed in the other room, away from this particular session, because he didn't want to affect the outcome with his presence—but also because he was a tad envious at what I could do with a guitar once I was unleashed. As I've mentioned, my playing tended to overpower him. I never did this deliberately, it was just in the nature of my playing, but it seemed to make him uneasy.

One of the main reasons our group wouldn't have survived very long was his inability to reconcile himself with another person onstage who could operate at his level of musicianship—unlike classic guitarist/singer duos such as Jimmy Page and Robert Plant, or Jeff Beck and Rod Stewart, fantastic equals who would goad and inspire one another to new heights while performing. Nope, in Jeff's cosmogony, I had to be subordinate.

Still, he knew I could provide the wild card, the X-factor, on guitar, and he wanted this particular spice on his album. And thus I was brought in to perform on it—not just for old time's sake.

He truly appreciated it, too. When I opened the *Grace* album for the first time in the fall of 1994, I saw that I had received a special thanks from Jeff for "magical guitarness," which made me very happy.

□

After I'd laid down my final guitar touches, I went back to the commissary area. Jeff was intently playing pinball while the others watched him and egged him on. He saw me come in and broke away from the machine to begin miming his version of a pinball-machine addict in the throes of his obsession.

He rolled his eyes and worked invisible flippers with his hands, then fell back into the arms of his laughing bandmates, who held him up under his arms and walked him around the room in the way you would a drunken friend.

All the while, in a strangulated comic voice, Jeff was saying, "I can't help it! Let me at it! I want to play! I WANT TO PLAY!" As if he needed a fix.

At the time, I laughed along with everyone else at Jeff's wacky sense of humor. I don't find this incident so funny any more.

□

It was time to leave. I packed up my Monster case and took my overnight bag from the cabin. Jeff helped me drag it all it out to the parking lot. We waited together for the taxi that would take me to Rhinebeck station. It was a crisp fall evening up in sleepy old Woodstock, and the sun was setting.

"I really enjoyed these three days," I said. "Thank you, Jeff."

"No problem," he replied. "You sounded great. Thank YOU!"

"Jeff," I continued, almost coyly, "I have a question for you. There are some other artists out there who have asked me to collaborate with them recently. What do you think ... should I?"

I guess I was trying to sound him out to see how much he really valued my work—and whether I could get him to write some new songs with me. I had recently worked with the singer Joan Osborne on songs for her yet-to-be-released album *Relish*, and I'd been hanging out with both Nick Cave and his band The Bad Seeds and also my favorite band from the 80s, The Fall, when they were in New York.

The Fall's guitarist, Craig Scanlon, was angling to get me in the band. I had a problem though: both Nick Cave and Mark E. Smith and their respective bands loved to hang out together and drink socially. Being a virtual teetotaler, and basically a loner, I could never really make the hang with them.

When I visited Cave once after his concert at the Town Hall NYC, he invited me to go with his boys to a karaoke bar, which I politely declined. Same with The Fall—when I met them, Smith kept buying me pints and tried to get me to shoot pool with them in some dive bar. But I am just not one of the lads.

Not that I expected Jeff to put me on a retainer for my exclusive services, of course, but I did want to keep writing songs with him, because of how combustible we were as collaborators.

"If I were you," he said, "I would try and collaborate with as many people as possible."

This has proven to be really excellent advice over the years—as long as it's with someone whose work I respect.

Then he hugged himself and put on an airy voice, similar to the 'enchanted elves' voices he channeled at the end of our 'Grace' demo:

"I'm a butterfly!"

And went skipping and twirling butterfly-like around and around the parking lot before heading back into the studio.

Chapter Ten

I came home from Bearsville and told Caroline how well it had gone, but also how shocked I was to find that Jeff was still trying to write material for the album while ensconced in such an expensive studio. I then kind of forgot about it all and got on with my life—the normal hustle.

Every day I was hunting for more gigs, more publicity, practicing, writing new material, collaborating, recording. That was—and still is—my life.

On Veteran's Day, November 11, I returned from yet another Knitting Factory tour of Europe, this one known as the JAM, or Jewish Avant-Garde Music tour, where I performed my soundtrack to *The Golem*. The next day, Mick Grondahl rang me out of the blue and asked if he could come over to my apartment and hang.

"But of course," I replied—I always liked this guy.

We spent a couple hours schmoozing and reminiscing about the sessions in Bearsville. Mick told me that Jeff was agonizing over the mixes, still trying to formulate the repertoire for the album, and that he was going head-to-head with Columbia over it.

Mick told me again how much he loved my playing, and how he'd enjoyed seeing me lead Gods and Monsters sans Jeff at the Grand. And then he zinged me.

"Gary, I really want you to be in this group with us."

I was flattered and touched. What a sweet, big-hearted guy Mick was. But I couldn't say yes.

"Thanks Mick," I said. "I appreciate your support, I really do, but if I was ever even going to consider this, it's got to come from Jeff. Unless I hear from him, forget about it. I'm not chasing after him."

Mick looked disappointed but said he understood completely. We parted as friends. I always found him to be a total gentleman, with a very sympathetic ear. He is really a genuinely nice person.

Our conversation took place right at the time Jeff was starting to bring his best friend, Michael Tighe, into the band as second guitarist for their live gigs. Perhaps Mick felt squeezed out by Tighe coming into the band and would have preferred an ally in there he could trust. Groups are rife with factional politics—it comes and goes with the territory.

But after our last duo gig at Tramps, I never again chased after Jeff to play with him. Why should I? I had learned the hard way that it never paid to pursue him for anything. The more you chased after Jeff, the more elusive and bloody-minded he became.

I also didn't really want to be in Jeff's band. I had my pride, and Gods and Monsters was still a going concern. We didn't have major-label backing, of course, but I really wasn't that desperate, and I didn't want to be derailed by the whims of someone else, someone I didn't trust.

For the same reason, I turned down Joan Osborne's manager when he proposed I join her band after recording 'Spider Web' and 'Help Me' for her *Relish* album. I thought about it briefly, but there was quite a catch: in order to become a group member, I had to promise to put my own solo career on hold for a minimum of two years, and not release my own albums in that time, instead devoting my energies 100 percent to Joan.

This I could not agree to. I couldn't understand how releasing my own work while playing with Joan would harm her profile, record sales, or touring business. Surely it would only enhance it?

Meanwhile, I think Jeff was annoyed that I wasn't avidly pursuing him for a spot in his band. Word got back to me that on December 18, at the CBGB's Gallery on the Bowery (a converted performance space right next to the famous punk club), Jeff had asked from the stage:

"Is Gary Lucas in the house?"

No response.

"Because I forgot to put him on the list. "

Laughter from the crowd.

"Will somebody give him five bucks from me? And his wife? Because I really fucked up ... he probably came to the door and said, oh I'm not on the list—fuck it."

The implication was that I had been chasing after him but was too impoverished to pay the measly entrance fee for his gig. Just so mean ...

The thought of pursuing Jeff for anything was something I considered to be a waste of time. It was beneath me, frankly. Once bitten, twice shy.

It was nice to play on his album, and I was happy that he was recording our songs, but I wanted to spare myself any further humiliation. I am not a masochist.

In late November, Columbia released the *Live At Sin-é* EP to start prepping folks for the fully fledged studio album release to come. The album opened with a solo version of 'Mojo Pin,' which was nice, but it was a little too stripped-down for my tastes. I was greatly anticipating the studio version, but I had another ten months to wait.

□

After the Bearsville sessions, I stuck to my previous policy of staying away from Jeff and his gigs with rare exception. In the two times I did venture out to see him play I found him perfunctory, bordering on dismissive of me backstage. He never ever came to see me play.

On February 26 1994, my friend Irene Trudel, the WFMU DJ who had recorded several live sessions with me and Jeff, threw a party in her apartment in Hoboken to which she had invited a bunch of her radio colleagues, including 'Old Pal' Irwin Chusid and also her new beau, my old friend Peter Keepnews, the *New York Times* writer. Irene and Peter had met for the first time almost a year ago on the subway en route to a shoot for the video for my song 'Skin The Rabbit.'

After hanging at Irene's for a while, against my better judgment I was talked into going to Maxwell's, an indie rock club down the road in Hoboken, to see Jeff perform with his new lineup.

The sound was muddy, and the band seemed very tentative. In all fairness, Michael Tighe did not seem to be adding very much in the way of guitar playing to the overall proceedings. The music was OK, but it was not a standout performance.

I went up to say hello after their set. Jeff was friendly but distant, focusing mainly on chatting up the Sony reps and WFMU contingent who had come to see him perform. Decidedly frosty, though, was George Stein, who looked really annoyed to see me there, especially after seeing many fans in the club come up to greet me warmly and say hello. He glowered at Caroline and me like we were insects who had crawled into the vicinity of his star.

I remember my wife using those very terms to describe Stein's overt hostility at the gig. Later, when we got home, she shuddered at the memory of this encounter and couldn't understand why he acted the way he did, or why Jeff was so cool to both of us.

She seemed really hurt by this. For me, it was just par for the course. I tried to explain to her that now that Jeff had no further use for me for the time being, he didn't see much percentage in being nice to me.

If Stein and Jeff were annoyed with me at this point, I would say that it was mainly because they knew I would never ever roll over and embrace the official Sony/Buckley narrative concerning the demise of Gods and Monsters with Jeff—namely that it was, in their eyes, a "failed experiment."

Instead, I had vociferously gone on record to friends, critics, and anyone who cared to hear my version of events as to the validity of the project, with the Friday the 13th St Ann's tape as Exhibit A—and also as to the shabby way I had been treated by Jeff, despite being invited to play on his album.

However, there was no reason whatsoever for Stein to display any anger toward Caroline. That was unforgivable.

In early summer, *Rolling Stone* ran a 'Random Notes' item about the imminent release of *Grace*. I was prominently name-checked as a key collaborator on the album, most likely thanks to David Fricke. I reckon that upset someone in the Buckley camp, because when *Grace* was finally rolled out in late August 1994 in the USA, my name was absent from the promo cassette every music writer was sent to base their advance reviews on.

This was the beginning of my 'disappearing' from the official historical narrative of the album by the Columbia publicity and marketing departments, possibly with the approval of Jeff himself.

Jim Bessman wrote an advance review and feature article for the July 16 edition of *Billboard*, quoting Berkowitz extensively and name-checking pretty much everyone who had worked on the album—including Karl Berger, the free-jazz composer living in Woodstock who wrote the string arrangements. My name was conspicuously absent from the article, which was seen by all and sundry in the music industry.

This rankled me, and rightly so. Credit is everything. And 'Mojo Pin' and 'Grace,' which began as my solo guitar instrumentals, are the first two songs on the album.

In fact, the very first thing one hears is my guitar playing the distinctive "woooooh" motif that opens 'Mojo Pin'—but you would never know that if I didn't inform you of it myself.

I am duly credited as the co-writer of those songs in the publishing credits in the booklet that comes with *Grace*. And, as I've mentioned, Jeff does give me "special thanks" there, too. But it seems you had to get hold of the actual physical CD to discover this information.

Why would the Sony brain trust seemingly absent me from the

album's marketing and publicity campaigns? God forbid any reviewers might learn that somebody other than Jeff had something to do with those two opening songs. For years, many people have wrongfully assumed that those two anthems are built on Jeff's guitar riffs.

Thankfully, a few writers out there who knew the score about our working together did mention me favorably in their reviews. In his *Spin* review, Byron Coley praised Jeff's self-confidence on the album while noting that some of it "may come from the grounding his material is given by the extraordinary guitarist Gary Lucas, with whom he works on some tunes here." In *The Big Takeover*, Rebecca Turner wrote, "The best tracks are the ones he co-wrote with Gary Lucas." But my name was nowhere to be found in the majority of reviews.

This dovetails with Jeff's determination to present himself as a sui generis artist—hence his trashing of his father's music in interviews. In his desire to avoid invidious comparisons with his talented father, and to be taken for his own artist, Jeff disparaged Tim and his achievements during several key interviews around the release of *Grace*. He vehemently denied any traces of Tim's influence on him. But this was ultimately a red herring—listeners can hear for themselves how much Jeff was influenced vocally by Tim Buckley. It was in his DNA.

I also recall an interview where Jeff shot his mouth off to the press in his "bad-boy with integrity" punk mode, warning his fans not to watch MTV: "It'll rot your brain!" Yet a year or so later, there he was as a guest on *120 Minutes* with his ever-faithful sidekick Michael Tighe.

I guess it finally dawned on Jeff, as he succumbed to Columbia's marketing department, that he needed to play the industry game a little bit more in order to notch up his sales stats. Columbia Records had promised him the moon: we will give you a million-dollar advance for a three-album deal, and you will be allowed to build your career slowly at your own pace with no pressure from us, your Medici-like patrons. We of course view you as a long-term artist-development story. That's what we're all about—we, the largest record company in the world, are masters at this—and we're not going for the quick hit, we're going to build you as an underground phenomenon, initially, and just continue to develop you for as long as it takes.

Sure!

As Columbia Records recording artists Pink Floyd so eloquently put it: Welcome to the machine.

The irony is that Jeff could have had a slow-building career, had he elected to sign with an indie label. There were plenty that would have jumped at the chance to sign him, including Big Cat, which released *Live At Sin-é* in Britain at Jeff's behest after Sony UK passed on it.

But Jeff wanted to have his cake and eat it too. He wanted to sign with the biggest and coldest major in the known universe—and yet still remain an underground cult sensation. The two phenomena are mutually exclusive.

All that horseshit fed to Jeff about guaranteeing him a slow build to "take the time for whatever it takes to get it right" was just that—horseshit. Let's face it, in the main, the people running major record labels are cold businessmen who expect a big return on their investment—the quicker the better. That's just the way it is. Some things will never change, as the song goes.

□

Upon hearing *Grace* for the first time, I had very conflicted feelings. I was thrilled to hear my two songs come on initially in their final mix form, especially with the strings added on 'Grace,' and also the wordless chorale section, which was new to me, but I was saddened also that they'd opted for very tame mixes—not just on my songs but on the album as a whole.

A footnote here: Jeff sent rough mixes of both songs to me a few months earlier, and to my ears they are far superior to the final mixes of both songs that appeared on *Grace*. They have a raw and wild energy about them. My guitars are not so buried in these mixes. The sound field and the overall vibe is much more intense. The energy level is ratcheted up exponentially. Plus you can really hear me "really wailing," as Leonard Bernstein first put it.

This obviously proved too much for the powers that be at CBS. They had a certain investment in the "Jeff as guitar hero" marketing angle, and thus my guitars were mixed way down.

I realize critics and fans have praised *Grace* to the skies over the years, but in my opinion there's a fundamental visceral excitement lacking on the overall record. It sounds like it was mixed over a long period of time by a committee second-guessing every note of it every step of the way—which in a sense it was. There was a whole lot of second-guessing—the mixing and re-recording dragged on for months—and a whole lot of playing it safe.

I've come to love this album over time, but back then I found it a bit disappointing. It never really caught fire, in my opinion, in the way I would have liked to have heard it. It was as if all the innate rock energy—guitar-wise particularly—had been bled out of it. That includes Jeff's playing as well as my own contributions, which were mixed way low on our two songs.

Jeff was absolutely a great guitarist, but you would hardly remark on this aspect of his talent listening to the album. The whole thing sounded too damn 'tasteful' for my money, both sound-wise and energy-wise, for all the money lavished on it.

I know this will strike many readers here as heresy—my wife included—but honestly this is what I felt at the time.

Grace grew on me over the years, but I cringed when I first heard some of it, just as Jeff had cringed on hearing some of his father's songs. 'So Real,' for instance, seemed very juvenile to me, as I've said already. I guess Jeff thought including it would get the little girls all moist and dewy—and he was probably right there. Still, I cannot deny that many fans bonded with this track—different strokes for different folks, I guess.

There also seemed to me to be an embarrassing emphasis on cover versions versus original material: three covers in total, on an album containing only ten tracks, of which four were co-written. There are only three 100 percent Jeff Buckley-penned originals on *Grace*: 'Eternal Life' and 'Last Goodbye,' which both date back to Jeff's *Babylon Dungeon Sessions* tape, and 'Lover, You Should Have Come Over,' which I apparently witnessed in gestation.

For all the time and money Columbia Records had invested in Jeff, he didn't seem to have been very prolific. Either that, or the original songs Jeff turned in for consideration were deemed not commercial enough for inclusion by Berkowitz and company.

There were some songs on *Grace* that undeniably moved me, though. 'Last Goodbye' to me works very well indeed. Jeff's guitar riff is undeniable catchy. Nice slide-playing also. His moody vocal meshes well with the band, and the Indo-European 'weeping strings' give the song an almost Bollywood flavor. The whole song is epic, and deservedly number three on the album.

And Jeff's vocals on Benjamin Britten's 'Corpus Christi Carol' give me chills today—so ethereal and ghostly. The song is so otherworldly as written, anyway—good choice for a cover! Britten is one of my favorite composers, and I had no idea Jeff was hip to him— and thus was pleasantly surprised to find this on the album when it finally arrived.

□

Shortly after the release of *Grace*, Enemy Records put out a new studio album of mine entitled *Bad Boys Of The Arctic*. Recorded on a shoestring, with no real platform to promote and publicize it, it died the death, per usual, despite receiving some rave reviews, including four stars in *Stereo Review*.

I was very proud of the record, and I wished Jeff had gone more in this kind of adventurous musical direction for his debut album. I loved what we'd done with 'Grace' and 'Mojo Pin' and the other songs we'd written together. I just didn't get some of his choices of material.

Ironically, this time around Enemy's Michael Knuth begged me to include a Jeff Buckley track on my album, as he knew that it would help boost sales. This I refused to even consider. I knew that both Jeff and Columbia would oppose lending me a track so as not to muddy the waters of his maiden effort. Plus I had already received one too many slights from Jeff and those around him, particularly after the Maxwell's show.

Being excluded from the official Columbia Records publicity campaign for *Grace* hurt me, too. As well as my name being missing from many key reviews and articles about Jeff, no footage of me was taken for the electronic press kit, which went out to press all over the world and contained clips of Jeff and his band working in the studio in Bearsville. I would have given Jeff the biggest of props, given the chance. But all this just confirmed my resolve to keep going it alone and not seek any further contact with Jeff regarding possible collaboration or cooperation.

This 'disappearing' of me from the official Sony narrative concerning my role in the making of the *Grace* album—and Jeff's career in general—continued well after Jeff had passed away. Several deluxe boxed editions of this album have been released since then, with bonus tracks, new photos, extensive liner notes by Bill Flanagan, and a DVD about the making of the album.

There is not a single mention of me in the liner notes, nor a photo of me in the booklet, nor footage of me in the accompanying DVD.

I am still listed as the co-writer and co-publisher of the two opening songs, at least, and Jeff still gives me special thanks for my "magical guitarness"—all part of the original album credits. That they couldn't take away from me.

□

Not everyone was buying what Jeff was selling. His devilish choir-boy image—the tortured and doomed romantic agonist I loved in our songs together—seemed more of a 'chick thing,' as they say, than something that was automatically embraced by the rock masses. It left many male rock fans cold, particularly in the USA.

Not everyone in the rock press got behind the album. The reviews of *Grace* were decidedly mixed in the USA, with *Rolling Stone* for instance giving it only three stars out of five. Later, an editor at *Alternative Press* told me that when one of Jeff's music videos came on in a hotel room during the South by Southwest festival that year, the TV monitor received a shower of empty beer cans from the jaded critics in attendance.

Still, I always said loving things on the rare occasions I was asked to speak about Jeff, tempered sometimes with a truthful account from my perspective of what had gone down between us.

"I've always believed in him," I told Matt Diehl in his *Rolling Stone* profile of Jeff from October of that year. "If they make him Elvis Presley, fine—he can handle it."

In a *New York* magazine profile of Jeff, I mentioned how he had been bugged by my standing at the front of the stage with him, and his admonishment about how "Keith always stands behind Mick."

Shortly thereafter I got a long, cheerful message from Jeff on my answering machine to the effect of how thrilled he was with the way everything had been going for him—that I should take pride in playing a big part in his meteoric rise—and that it was his dream to someday go in and properly record all the songs we had written together.

But not now, of course, as he was "so busy."

I wasn't holding my breath for this, having learned the hard way never to let Jeff raise my expectations, but it was nice to get this message nonetheless.

□

Jeff toured all over the USA, Europe, and even Japan—wherever Sony had offices and could provide a platform to promote sales of *Grace*. They worked him relentlessly.

I followed his progress from afar as best I could. I was also touring as much as possible, all over the world and with various projects. Not on so grand a level, of course, but touring hard nonetheless.

I worked mainly solo, as I found that to try and operate a band without tour support is almost a surefire way to go bust, certainly without any real promotion behind your albums. It was hard to get traction, barnstorming around Europe by the seat of my pants. But I went out there year after year after year, building my base one fan at a time.

I traveled sometimes with a driver and sometimes on trains and planes, yo-yoing from gig to gig and country to country without a multinational machine supporting my appearances. But I loved the life of touring, and I loved playing for people and blowing their minds with my playing. And I knew that this was what I had to do in order to keep working and building my name and reputation—to establish myself as a player, and to remain a player.

I am still out there as much as possible today. That's my life.

□

I followed the fortunes of *Grace*, of course. Sales of which were not spectacular out of the box, given the money spent on it and all the publicity hoopla declaring the ascension of a major new Sony star and heartthrob. (In 1995, Jeff was declared one of *People* magazine's '50 Most Beautiful People In The World.')

I wasn't really surprised by the slow sales for the album, given the mutual contradiction of Jeff's aspiring to underground cult status and at the same time not really playing the company game, of his signing to Columbia and delivering an album with no obvious mainstream 'hit' on it.

Grace was beloved by many, including musicians such as Bono and

Jimmy Page—who brandished it on the cover of *Q* magazine as one of his favorite albums of 1994, but it performed well below par in the US marketplace.

Grace went as high as 147 on the *Billboard* 200 after some radio and video play for 'Last Goodbye,' but it never rose any higher. Of course, industry wisdom dictates that an album has to get into the Top 50 to begin selling in significant numbers.

Overseas, the picture was somewhat rosier. France and Australia in particular took to Jeff in a big way. He was viewed as a superstar in France, where they worship dead rock stars such as Jeff's father, and where Jeff performed at the prestigious Olympia Theatre in Paris. The album went gold in both countries and later platinum in Australia.

It obviously made a worldwide impact, but it did not live up to the unreasonable expectations held for it by Sony, which must have hurt Jeff. After his death, it started selling, and today it is said to have sold around two million copies worldwide. There is nothing like death as the ultimate career move, as they say.

Grace went on to make many best-of lists, including *Mojo*'s 'Best Rock Album Of The 90s,' and *Rolling Stone*'s '500 Greatest Albums Of All Time'—all very nice, but not much consolation to the deceased.

□

On June 2 1995, Caroline and I went to see Jeff play at Roseland uptown, where he and his band were opening for Atlantic's hot new signing, Juliana Hatfield.

Caroline had worked on casting a video for Hatfield and had wangled tickets, plus backstage passes and an invite to the show's after-party at Le Bar Bat. And as Jeff was opening, I broke my own rule of avoiding his shows, bit the bullet, and decided to go there early with Caroline to see him play.

The first thing that struck me in the Roseland lobby was a big merchandising table manned by Columbia staffers armed with Jeff

Buckley posters, postcards, and T-shirts, all emblazoned with the words 'Mystery White Boy Tour' and all sporting a little cartoon skull drawing by Jeff.

I was eerily reminded of our early days playing together when I frequently wore black scarves decorated with skulls, which you can spot me wearing on the back of the *Songs To No One* album. And I was also reminded of my album *Skeleton At The Feast*, which I brought with me to the church on the night of the St Ann's Tim Buckley tribute.

Seeing Jeff on a big stage with his band for the first time—and the last time, as it turned out—was very revealing. Jeff stood all the way over to the left at the very lip of the stage. There was a huge crowd of fans, mainly female, clustered in front of him throughout the show. He seemed oblivious to them, lost in his own world, often singing with his eyes shut.

Matt Johnson was set up with his drums far in the back on a riser stage center, and Michael Tighe and Mick Grondahl were huddled close to each other all the way to the back of stage left.

Jeff never once looked at his guys during the show, which was all too familiar to me. It appeared as if he'd instructed Mick and Michael never to smile or glance outwardly in the direction of the audience. These two shuffled around at the back, playing their instruments with their heads down—literally shoegazing. That's how Jeff wanted it—he had to be the focal point throughout.

"You know, I would never have been happy playing in this band," I said to Caroline.

Jeff was dressed in a sequined jacket that screamed 'star.' It looked very Hollywood to me, a far cry from his torn T-shirts of old. He had a roadie whose job seemed to consist of lighting cigarettes for Jeff and bringing him various guitars during the show.

Jeff began his set playing Janine Nichols's Telecaster, and then he switched to a black Les Paul after about four songs. In the changeover, his sequined jacket got entangled in the strap of his guitar, and he and the roadie spent an embarrassingly long time trying to tug it free.

My God, I thought, *what a perfect visual metaphor for all the showbiz bullshit Jeff's caught up in now.*

They opened the show with 'Dream Brother,' which struck me then as basically a rewrite of The Doors' 'The End'—same lugubrious tempo and doomy modal guitar. They also played a rather tame version of the MC5's 'Kick Out The Jams' that seemed like an incongruous bid for street cred. What really got the crowd going was Leonard Cohen's 'Hallelujah,' which in death has become the song with which Jeff is most identified. His coterie of mainly female fans seemed mostly to want to hear the soulful ballads.

We went backstage and Jeff seemed surprised to see us. He was friendly in his usual perfunctory way to me but only seemed to really come alive for Caroline. At the after-party, his manager scowled at us—like, what the fuck are you doing here? We only stayed a few moments.

□

I started to hear rumors of Jeff's alleged heroin usage later that year. As mentioned, this had first cropped up after the St Ann's massacre in a phone call from Steve Paul.

I had dismissed the notion then, believing Jeff was too smart to allow himself to be seduced by the very drug that had brought his father down. But in the fall of '95, I was visited by my old friend Fred Perry, whom I'd met back in Syracuse. His brother Richard Perry had produced Captain Beefheart's first album and many others since, including The Pointer Sisters and Rod Stewart.

Fred had literally inducted me into the world of Captain Beefheart. When I first ran into him on Marshall Street, near Syracuse University, he was carrying an acoustic guitar with him on which was written, in red magic marker, 'Captain Beefheart & His Magic Band.' That was the first time I had even heard mention of Beefheart.

A British rock freak, Fred had been a great cultural catalyst, singlehandedly turning the greater New York area on to Pink Floyd and Jimi Hendrix by bringing English import copies of their English albums up to the legendary New York DJ Scott Muni back in early 1967 to play on his WNEW show.

Fred and I had recently renewed our friendship some 25 years after we first met, and we had a lot of things to catch up on. He had some information about the mysterious death of my high school best friend Tom Karp, a brilliant but troubled soul who had washed up fully clothed underneath the Golden Gate Bridge in San Francisco in the spring of 1974, shortly before I was due to graduate from Yale.

Fred confirmed what I'd long suspected: that it was most likely suicide. Tom had grown increasingly distant from me after dropping out of first high school and then the Unitarian Church-run Free School of Syracuse to become a low-level pot and acid dealer. I still loved him anyway.

According to Fred, Tom had come out to San Francisco for a visit in 1974 and crashed at Fred's apartment. One night, having taken LSD with a group of people at Fred's, he had experienced a profoundly bad trip. He left suddenly in the early hours of the morning with an ashen, stricken look on his face. According to Fred, someone had said something that put Tom on the worst bummer of his life. Later that day, Tom's body washed up at the foot of the San Francisco Bay Bridge.

Hearing this was a big shock. I had had no idea. Tom's mother told me she had suspected foul play, but there was no evidence of that. But Fred also had some more recent shocking news.

"I ran into your former singer in a club the other night I was playing drums at," he said. "He was totally high on heroin."

"*Jeff?*" I said, astonished. I couldn't believe it.

"Yeah, I jammed on drums with him. He was totally trashed. It was pretty obvious."

This news rocked me to my core.

After Jeff died, this aspect of his seemingly golden career became fairly well known in the rock world, and among his fans, and there is much testimony in the various biographies about it. It had been common knowledge to his contemporaries in the East Village for some time. But it shows you just how far apart we were by then that this was the first I was hearing of it. (I was definitely not of that East Village music scene.)

Of course. This was Jeff's prerogative. It just made me really, really sad, and also alarmed.

Heroin had become very chic in New York again. It went in and out of fashion, no matter how many people died from it, or got hepatitis C from dirty needles. It still retained a romantic aura among musicians—a hangover from the beatnik era and the age of Charlie Parker.

It still does have this aura, I guess—but never for me.

Jeff was obsessed with his father's death. He had titled one of our songs 'Mojo Pin' and mimed shooting up when I asked for an explication of this term. I'd heard he'd even mimed shooting up onstage in Paris once while introducing this song, acting out his father's OD in a comical way. I didn't find this funny at all.

I have known many heroin users and former users in and out of the music business, and I refuse to sit in judgment on them. People deal with their problems in all sorts of ways. What people choose to put into their own bodies is their own business, as long as it doesn't personally harm me or those near to me. I am a libertarian in that respect.

As a non-user, though, I just feel awkward around users. They are for the most part in their own private universe, and it takes a big effort sometimes to communicate with them—much less relate to or rely on them or trust them. They are certainly prone to lying about their usage.

In Jeff's case, however, knowing him as I did—and loving him still through all the heartaches I'd been through with him—I thought it was a damn shame to hear this, and a total misdirection of his talents.

Even if he was only using heroin occasionally, this could easily turn into a negative spiral downward. He'd been given everything an artist dreams of receiving on a silver platter with his initials embossed in gold—and it still wasn't enough.

I'd seen this movie before—and so had Jeff, obviously. Maybe he just couldn't help himself, which made this doubly tragic. You could chalk it up to all the pressure he was under, which God knows was ratcheted up by securing a major label deal. This may have caused him to turn to the very thing that had killed his father.

Perhaps it had started out recreationally and then, as with so many casual users, escalated into a deadly habit. Perhaps it was a genetic predisposition handed down from his father.

To paraphrase Jeff on my chronic marijuana habit at the time: What a human waste. Hadn't any of these East Village hipsters surrounding Jeff learned anything at all after years of cautionary tales about celebrity junkie musicians and their untimely deaths?

I started hearing more and more about Jeff's drug use from all sorts of folks, including a casting agent neighbor who lived downstairs from us and had been keen to put Jeff in a film but had decided against it because the word on the street was that he had a major habit and was flaky and unreliable.

Many years later, Jeff's former drummer filled me on this period, describing Jeff as being "very decadent with the drugs." He described a 17-hour flight to Australia with Jeff and his band for their last tour: Jeff, dope-sick in first class, puking his guts out and suffering withdrawal symptoms, the stench carrying all the way back to where the band were sitting in economy.

□

Meanwhile, the royalties from co-writing 'Grace' and 'Mojo Pin' had started to come in, which was nice. They were surpassed though by my royalties from co-writing Joan Osborne's 'Spider Web,' from her triple-platinum *Relish* album, even though I shared the credit for that song with four other folks.

As with Jeff I had contributed the main guitar motif and harmonic chord structure for the entire song, but the guy who came up with the drum beat and the guy who came up with the standard-issue blues vocal line got an equal cut, which seemed unfair, but I swallowed it.

Even with splitting the writing credits that way, the royalties at this point were about four times as much as what the songs I co-wrote with Jeff were bringing in. Eventually, Joan sold three million copies of her *Relish* album.

□

Jeff was still in my heart and in my mind—especially after learning about his alleged drug use. But I made no attempt to contact him or go see him perform after Roseland. I really didn't know what I could do to help him, and for sure he wouldn't have wanted to hear or take my advice on that or any subject.

Once in this period, Caroline and I ran into Jeff coming out of a Sonic Youth show at Roseland. I'd been invited along personally by Thurston Moore. The opening act was a band called Helium, led by Jeff's friend Mary Timony.

"What are you guys dong here?" he demanded when we collided out in the street. "I was just in there to see Helium … No! No! Don't go in there!" he shouted, to our puzzlement. I really don't know why. Maybe there was a rub between him and Sonic Youth. We went on in anyway.

□

About a year before he died, Jeff rang me quite unexpectedly. I was surprised to hear from him as usual. We exchanged pleasantries, and then he got abruptly to the point.

"Remember those great songs we used to write together, and how we used to write them? You used to send me complete instrumentals."

"Of course I remember, Jeff."

A long pause, then:

"Well I was wondering ... do you have any music you've written you can send me? I'm getting ready to record my second album ... and wanted to know if you had any music that might work for me here."

He obviously needed some songs.

I was flattered.

"As a matter of fact I do," I said. "There's one I wrote not too long ago that I think would really suit your voice ... I mean I could really hear you sing this. I could hear your voice on it in my mind."

"Please send it to me," he said, which I did.

It was a piece I had titled 'Dream Of The Wild Horses,' after a short French film I had seen in the 60s of a white horse and a black horse running and cavorting in slow motion on a long sandy beach with the spray and foam of the ocean whipping around them. This image, and this music, reminded me so much of Jeff and me.

I sent Jeff the song, and he rang me again shortly after receiving it.

"I got your music," he said. "It's beautiful. Do you have any more?"

I sent him three more songs: two new instrumentals, one entitled 'A Wandering Minstrel Eye' and the other 'Land's End.' The third instrumental was an older piece I had given Julia back in the days of Gods and Monsters mk2, which had become our song 'Body On The Bayou.'

And then I didn't hear from Jeff again—typically.

Breaking my own rule about never chasing after a diva, I tried calling Jeff several times, leaving messages on his machine asking whether or not he liked the music I'd sent him. No response.

This really angered me. I thought it was the height of rudeness not to return calls, especially not to return the calls of a collaborator, and one you have solicited for music. Not very nice.

Whether or not Jeff planned to do anything with it, I certainly felt I was entitled to know one way or the other, as soon as possible. There were other singers out there I could give it to.

I ran into Mick Grondahl a few months later at the Fez, where I'd been appearing myself fairly regularly, at a showcase for Elysian Fields, Oren Bloedow's new band with his girlfriend Jennifer Charles. Both were friends of Jeff.

After their show, I told Mick how Jeff had done a runner on me once again.

"Boy, that sucks," he said. "I'll tell him to call you ... he should call you."

I always liked this guy, but still I never heard back from Jeff.

□

On February 4 1997, the Knitting Factory held a private party for close friends and artists who had played there regularly over the years—people who had helped establish the Knitting Factory 'brand'—to celebrate the venue's tenth anniversary.

As one of the people who had helped put the club on the map, I received a special invitation. I looked forward to the night, especially as Jeff was listed on the invitation as one of the special guest performers scheduled to play a solo set. I was eager to confront him there.

Since its earliest days as a walkup storefront on Houston Street, the Knitting Factory had moved to more expansive digs further downtown on Leonard Street. Michael Dorf had acquired and constructed a three-tiered space with three bars, three performance stages, offices, and a recording studio.

I went to this party alone, as Caroline was busy. I recall being greeted by a doorman, who said he didn't know who I was, and having to produce my special invite. I was annoyed that I hadn't been asked to perform—especially as Jeff had only performed there for the first time under my auspices at the CMJ in 1991. But I held my tongue.

I still had a good relationship with Michael Dorf at that time. He'd offered me my solo debut there in 1988, and had toured me several times in Europe. And I loved his club.

When I came into the venue for the big tenth anniversary party, the front bar was already full of downtown hipsters and Sony Music employees there for Jeff's set.

I pushed into the main performance space and caught a glimpse of Jeff finishing his soundcheck. He saw me, turned, and ran offstage as fast as he could. He obviously had heard how angry I was with him.

I went back outside into the hall near the ticket booth and started greeting old friends and comrades in arms, some of who had survived the Knitting Factory's grueling European tours along with me.

Right then, Jeff came out into the space trailed by his manager, who gave me the usual evil eye.

Up close, Jeff looked dreadful, frankly—bloated and puffy. It grieved me to see this. The former pretty boy was a boy no longer. He looked like he'd been through the wringer—which he probably had. I had never seen him look like this before.

He also looked very, very high.

I stared at him aghast, and suddenly his eyes narrowed into slits. He glared at me intensely for a moment, seething with rage, as if he had a demon within him who didn't like being caught out.

The evidence before me sadly seemed to confirm that all the stories I'd heard were probably true. My heart broke here.

Suddenly, Jeff relaxed, shrugged, and smiled at me. The storm within him had passed for the moment, and he put on that soft 'Jeff' voice.

"Hey man, I'm really sorry ... I fucked up. I know, I know, I should have got back to you about those songs. I'm sorry, Gary."

What could I say? My heart went out to him, as usual. He was in trouble, and I could see it.

"That's OK, Jeff," I replied. "I was concerned!"

I put my arm around Jeff's shoulder.

George Stein glared even more balefully than before and then walked off icily to go and schmooze some Sony people, who were streaming in through the front door. I had an intimate moment with Jeff right here in the middle of this chaos.

"So how's it going?" I asked, fearing the worst.

"You really want to know?"

Jeff drew me closer to him and then trained the saddest eyes I'd ever seen on me.

"You have no idea of how horribly *fucked* everything is for me right now. It's all shit. It's all shit," he repeated.

"What do you mean?"

"Between my label," he began, slowly, "my management ... and my band ... it's all shit."

My heart went out to him.

"Man, I'm sorry to hear that, Jeff. Really."

And I was.

I wasn't gloating. I obviously still had feelings for my former protégé. He wasn't a kid any more, and he now seemed close to going off the rails.

I didn't know what to say, so I turned to the business at hand.

"So, are you going to use that music I sent you?"

"I don't know. I'm not sure ..."

That was Jeff, always vague, always playing things close to the vest until the 11th hour.

"I have to go get ready for my set," he said.

Jeff turned and walked slowly up the stairs of the Knitting Factory to the door leading to the second floor balcony. From there he could enter his dressing room without going through the crowd now pouring into the main space to hear him perform.

When he reached the top of the stairs, he turned and gave me the most tragic, pitiable look I'd ever seen from him, which I registered as *Help me, please, I'm spiraling out of control ...*

□

A few minutes later, everyone in the lobby was herded into the main space, as the festivities proper were about to begin.

In the packed audience I saw Lou Reed and his girlfriend, the performance artist Laurie Anderson; Patti Smith's guitarist Lenny Kaye, a good guy and later a good friend; Tom Verlaine, Television's guitarist and leader; and Nick Hill from WFMU, who greeted me warmly and moved over to stand with me. We stood in the back right against the wall and waited for Jeff to come.

Nick, one of Jeff's earliest and most faithful friends in the city, had come up to Bearsville after I'd departed the *Grace* sessions in the hope of signing Jeff to an agreement after Jeff had casually asked "how'd you like to manage me?" over the phone. Jeff gave him the slip for a few days, and when they did finally sit down to talk he never once brought up the management idea.

Another time, Jeff had called Nick and told him, "I want to record five singles right now with you producing, and put them out on an indie label as soon as possible"—which Nick got all fired-up to do, but of course this too went nowhere, as Sony would never have allowed it to happen.

Nick just shrugged it off good-naturedly as being pure Jeff, just another one of his whims.

Once Jeff had hooked up with Sony, he cut himself off from many of his earliest friends and supporters in New York—including many of the old WFMU crew. So Nick had a much more cynical view of Jeff at this point, and had never once gone to see him play with his band.

Jeff came out with his Telecaster, plugged in, and began singing 'Lover, You Should Have Come Over' in a very low-key and desultory fashion. He followed this with several new, unrecognizable songs sung in a drawled voice. They didn't much rouse the crowd.

The *New York Post* music critic Dan Aquilante was standing nearby. He began whispering loudly to his buddy next to him in a voice I couldn't help but overhear. "So boring!" he exclaimed, noting that *Grace* hadn't done as well as Sony had wanted, and how the label was way in the hole on it.

In truth, Jeff was putting the crowd to sleep. Even Nick Hill started rolling his eyes when Jeff announced, "This is called 'Song 21' ... it has no title."

Jeff then launched into a lugubrious mid-tempo song with no discernible melody or hooks, reading the words off a music stand rather than having bothered to memorize them. (The song came out posthumously as 'Jewel Box.')

Then came another slow and lachrymose new song, 'Morning Theft.' Nick turned to me and whispered, "It's pretty obvious isn't it that Tim Buckley is Jeff Buckley's biggest influence."

We both smiled at that, well aware of the lengths Jeff had taken to put a distance between himself and his father in the press.

Gisburg, the pretty Austrian woman who had been one of the interns at the Tim Buckley tribute concert six years earlier (and was now a composer, singer, and recording artist in her own right), sidled up to me and said sarcastically, "Bah! Jeff's trying so hard to look *iconic* up there!"

She tried to pull me away from the performance.

"Come on, let's go downstairs and check out the other music."

There were several other acts playing downstairs at the Tap Bar. But I shook my head and stood my ground. I wanted to hear all these new songs Jeff was preparing for his next album.

Gisburg ambled off and disappeared.

Suddenly, Jeff made an announcement from the stage.

"I got an idea, actually ... well, if Gary Lucas isn't too mad at me, would he like to play a song?"

I was stunned. I really hadn't expected this.

"Go for it!" I heard someone behind me say. I pushed forward through the crowd and made my way up to the stage.

"We'll get on it ... we'll rev it up," Jeff continued. "Gary Lucas, ladies and gentlemen!"

The crowd whooped. Jeff un-strapped his Telecaster and handed it to me.

"So, what are we going to play?" I whispered. I really had no idea.

"'Grace,' of course," he said calmly, as if it was the most natural thing in the world.

I detuned the low E-string of his Telecaster to D, adjusted his guitar amp to get my level and sound, and launched into the opening riff as if on remote control.

Suddenly we were grooving and swaying together as one. All of my pain and resentment vanished in that moment, and we were totally rocking. We weren't really looking at each other, but we didn't need to. It didn't matter. We were totally in sync again.

A wave of bittersweet emotion surged through me as I listened to Jeff sing so beautifully.

There's a moon asking to stay
Long enough for the clouds to fly me away

Damn! I thought to myself. *I still love this guy. We have a telepathy and rapport between us that is so strong. It's undeniable.*

I stuck to my original arrangement on guitar—the only version I knew how to play—jettisoning the wordless choral section Jeff added in the middle of the album version. Jeff followed me unhesitatingly. He didn't miss a beat. He was soaring vocally, adding some stunning new vocal improvisations in his high falsetto.

He started tapping on an empty glass in time to the beat for a few bars midway through, while the ending had us both in over-the-top mode: me strumming furiously on the final discord, Jeff wailing at the top of his range.

The crowd went nuts. We hugged each other, and I left the stage feeling so elated. I was happy everyone there had witnessed this triumphant moment—particularly the Sony people.

When I waded back into the crowd, a fan came up to me and breathlessly told me, "That was fantastic. I've been waiting YEARS to see you guys play together again."

Lenny Kaye came over and shook my hand.

"You really rocked, man!"

I went to the back of the room and hung with Nick Hill, and we stayed to hear Jeff's final three songs. Our spontaneous duo performance elicited the biggest hand of the night of Jeff's entire set. It had an undeniable energy that lifted the bandstand.

☐

Afterward, I went upstairs to the dressing room to shake Jeff's hand.

"Thank you, man," I said. "That really meant a lot to me."

Jeff gave me a limpid handshake. He seemed relaxed now, completely the opposite of the tense and miserable Jeff I had spoken to before his set.

"You're welcome," he said.

"Sorry I didn't play that chorale section."

"That's OK, you always go back to the original version in a situation like that."

He seemed happy to see me.

"So what's next for you?" I asked.

"I'm leaving soon for Memphis to start recording with Tom Verlaine." He motioned behind me.

I turned, and there, hulking in the back of the dressing room, was the tall, gangly guitarist. I'd always like Television and Verlaine's playing, but he seemed like an odd choice of producer. He had no track record in that role, and was known to be diffident, if not difficult, with a lot of people.

His former manager, Steve Ralbovsky, an old friend from CBS and a shrewd A&R man, later told me that he thought it was a big mistake. "I can totally picture the two of them trying to work together in a studio," he said. "No way is that going to work. I know exactly what it will be like—and I wouldn't want to be around that."

Back in the dressing room, Jeff invited me to come see him soon in a new East Village club called Arlene's Grocery, run by the guy who had started Sin-é. But I elected to keep my distance as usual. Once bitten, twice shy. It was great to have been invited to play with him again at this anniversary show, but I still wasn't going to begin chasing after him.

Plus the way he looked and what he'd said to me downstairs before the show had scared me. Much as I loved Jeff still, what exactly could I do to help him? Attempt an intervention? To quote Lou Reed: "You can't tell anyone anything anyway." Quite rightly. Jeff was 31 years old at that point. He wasn't a kid you could scold.

I walked away from the Knitting Factory that night thinking: I still really love this guy. And whether or not he uses my music on his next album, I know we'll be collaborating again.

I felt certain of this.

We both knew just how great our collaboration was. But I was worried for him. He seemed a shadow of his former self, before the show and for the most part during the show, except when he'd caught fire singing 'Grace,' which had brought down the house.

I discussed this with Caroline when I got home, and we decided I should just play it cool and wait for Jeff to make the next move. If he needed me in any way, musically or otherwise, I'd be there for him.

□

I went off a few days later on a 22-city European tour that took me to Germany, Austria, the Netherlands, Belgium, Switzerland, and the Czech Republic. I never sat still waiting for the phone to ring, and I always kept gigging as much as possible, while also developing and recording new work as much as possible.

I had a gig in Washington DC with *The Golem* when I got back home, opening the new Jewish Community Center, and then I played two shows with the film at the new Knitting Factory space. I then gigged with my new Du-Tels duo with Peter Stampfel, and gave a master class up at Yale.

I brought Gods and Monsters into the Mercury Lounge a few weeks later, and then took part solo in Michael Dorf's annual Seder at the Knitting Factory, where the traditional service also featured avant-garde musical turns from invited musicians. I essayed the role of Elijah that night—shades of me ribbing Jeff at my Passover Satyr several years earlier—and played 'Ghosts' on my National steel guitar—the first track I ever recorded under my name at the Knitting Factory, and for the Knitting Factory label, all those years ago.

Looking back over my calendars in preparation for writing this book, I am struck by how often I was gigging in town and everywhere else I could in the world, with one project or another. Nothing has changed in that regard. It's my job.

❑

On Saturday April 26 1997, I performed a solo show at the Mercury Lounge. No sooner had I walked offstage after my set than Steve Berkowitz, whom I hadn't noticed in the crowd while I was performing, came forward out of the shadows to greet me. I was affable but wary.

"Jah Luke!" he began. "How goes it? You really rocked with Jeff at that Knitting Factory anniversary show."

I thanked him and he went on.

"You may be getting a call to go down to Memphis to work with Jeff. He's having trouble recording his new album ... in fact, he just fired Tom Verlaine, and sent his band back to New York. He's down there now by himself trying to write new songs. You know what I think of your work together—'Grace' was a beautiful thing."

It was nice to get the vote of confidence from him.

Berkowitz then proceeded to give me a long account of the tortuous path he'd been on over the last two years, trying to get Jeff to come up with material for an acceptable follow-up album. It was a litany of sending Jeff and his band to a cottage in Sag Harbor in the Hamptons, pairing him with this producer and that, and so on. It was a history of corporate money being spent on failed attempts to spark Jeff's writing. Which was sad.

With the cost of recording *Grace* in a very expensive studio, and then dithering over the mixes for another six months, plus the cost of tour support Columbia had kicked in for the band to travel in tour buses and stay in expensive hotels while on the road, the album's disappointing sales had dimmed the label's hopes for quick recoupment.

Add to this all the marketing expenses that went in to making posters and ads and expensive tchotchkes, not to mention all attendant publicity and promotional costs, and the company was obviously still way in the red.

Now the pressure was on for Jeff—and by extension Berkowitz— to come up with a hard-hitting and memorable second album that would be the ultimate pay-off to justify all that expensive coddling under the name of 'artist development.' But Jeff was not coming up with the goods, in the label's eyes, in terms of accessible songs, which must have hurt deeply. He never was that prolific a songwriter. This sounded like classic writer's block to me.

I told Berkowitz I was there if Jeff needed me. Of course I'd be there. I still loved the guy, despite everything, and I believed I could help kick-start him out of his creative torpor, given half a chance.

I also queried Berkowitz about Jeff's alleged heroin use, and mentioned that I thought Jeff was looking pretty bad at that last show.

Berkowitz's face flushed and his eyes hardened. He looked furious with me for bringing this up, and then excused himself. He obviously didn't want to go down that road. But as Jeff's collaborator-in-waiting, I felt I had a right to ask.

□

After this encounter, I went back on the road for a while, but naturally I was still hoping to hear from Jeff. Playing with him onstage again had reenergized me as to the possibilities for future collaboration. I mulled over the possibility of reaching out to him directly, but as he seemed to run in the opposite direction every time I did that, I thought I'd better just play it cool. I considered reaching out to someone like Mick Grondahl, but I jettisoned this idea, too, as I felt awkward to ask him to be a go-between.

If Jeff wanted me there to work with him, I reasoned, I would hear from him directly, or from Berkowitz. I busied myself with preparations for a new solo acoustic album, *Evangeline*, which was due to come out in mid June on a new indie label, Paradigm. I played a few gigs around town, at the Cooler and the Fez, and I waited to hear from Jeff.

Late on the afternoon of Friday May 30—Memorial Day—the phone finally rang in my apartment.

But it wasn't Jeff.

□

"Gary, Mike Shore here."

On the line was my old friend Michael Shore, a former music critic and big Captain Beefheart supporter, who had moved over to MTV News as a staff writer and news-gatherer.

"I hate to disturb you, but I thought you should know. Gary, have you heard the news? Jeff Buckley's been missing down in Memphis since yesterday."

"WHAT?" I gasped.

Mike went on to tell me all he knew.

Apparently Jeff had gone swimming in the Mississippi River the night before, with all his clothes on, including his heavy boots. The story was that he and his roadie had been on the way to the airport to meet his band, who were flying in from New York again to start recording with him afresh.

It was a hot night, and Jeff had apparently decided to stop suddenly en route to the airport, insisting on a swim in the Wolf River, a treacherous tributary of the Mississippi. Swimming was strictly forbidden there, but Jeff had swum there before, evidently, so he jumped in anyway, fully clothed.

The roadie watched Jeff swim around and around from the safety of the dock, where he had lugged their large boom box. Suddenly a passing boat kicked up a wake that threatened to engulf the dock. The roadie turned his back on Jeff for a second to rescue their boom box from being swept away.

When he turned back, Jeff had disappeared, seemingly dragged under the waves by the current. But they hadn't found his body yet.

"Oh man," I said. "I don't believe this."

"We're waiting for more reports to come in. I'll call you back and keep you in the loop. Sorry to have such bad news for you."

I hung up and staggered away from the phone, choking back tears. I shrieked, "Noooooooooooo ..."

I have never reacted to anything so viscerally in my life.

I feared the worst here.

I didn't know what else to think that might explain why Jeff would tempt fate like that by swimming in a deadly no-swim area. It was the only explanation that made any sense to me, given the state Jeff was in the last time I'd seen him.

The idea of Jeff on a whim taking a swim in a danger zone with all his clothes on, on the way to meet his band at the airport, just sounded crazy. It didn't quite add up.

When I'd last seen him, I witnessed some very manic mood swings: from the blackest of depressed states before the show, to the assertive and fiery vocal daredevil of old when we performed 'Grace,' to breezy and relaxed in the dressing room afterward.

Add to this Berkowitz's tales of Jeff abruptly firing his producer, shipping his band back to New York, and staying on in Memphis to try and write new songs for his album ... it sounded like someone in a mess of trouble.

"Fucking up."

That's what I thought then.

To me, Jeff's death is still a mystery.

☐

There is an unreleased song allegedly by Jeff that surfaced a few years ago on the internet that chills me to the bone every time I hear it. It's called 'River Of Dope.'

> *The door's no longer open for my name on their breath*
> *So long I've waited for the coming of death*
> *Will I be united with my innocence gone*
> *Will I burn to cinders as the river rolls on*
> *Hmmmm ... river, we sleep in your mud*
> *You give us poison when we drink your blood*
>
> *Look in my eyes and you'll see*
> *That I flow with the river, and I'm a slave to his song*
> *And I will drown forever where so many have gone*
> *Goodbye you people who have abandoned your hope*
> *Parade in early morning to the river of dope*
> *Hmmm, yeah the river of dope*

□

That night, after receiving the shocking news from my friend at MTV, I woke with a start in the early morning hours with a horrible realization.

I had recently put the finishing touches on my new album, *Evangeline*, which was due to be released in mid June by Paradigm. I had given the art director an old book, a family heirloom handed down to me, to help him select some appropriate cover art. It was a rare British edition from the 20s of Edgar Allan Poe's eldritch classic *Tales Of Mystery & Imagination*, with Aubrey Beardsley-like illustrations by the English artist Harry Clarke.

Against my wishes, the cover designer had chosen one of the elegant and weird black-and-white plates illustrating the story 'A Descent Into The Maelstrom,' the tale of a man who nearly drowns after being sucked down into a giant whirlpool.

Clarke's stark illustration depicted a terrified figure clutching a barrel for dear life, going around and around in a swirling riptide, being sucked down into the vortex of a giant waterspout.

I had objected to using that particular illustration for my album cover, as I thought it had nothing to do with the title. But I was overruled by the label's head of marketing, who felt it would make an exciting graphic for the cover.

The album had just gone into production that very week. Now it was too late to change it.

I realized to my horror—at 3am, the Hour of the Wolf—that my new album cover might be misconstrued as depicting Jeff's drowning. I was shaken by the possibility that people might see the cover when the album came out and think I was making a cruel and ironic statement concerning Jeff's demise.

No matter how it might be interpreted, though, the cover seemed to me a ghostly premonition of Jeff's death. It was as if I had been given a series of clues all along, throughout my tempestuous relationship with Jeff, foreshadowing how the whole thing would end up.

And this cover was the final clue.

□

All that weekend I was in denial.

I was in tears frequently, and then I would clamp down on my sobbing and go to the opposite hard-boiled extreme.

Jeff's a joker, I thought. *He probably just got fed up with all the pressure on him and did a runner somewhere. He's hiding out now, but he'll surface soon, once he clears his head.*

I was sure of it.

Jeff's body—nearly unrecognizable, except for his pierced navel—washed up a few days later in Memphis Harbor, at the foot of Beale Street.

The home of the blues.

□

I cried every day for a month.

My thoughts would drift to Jeff and all my love for him, despite our many ups and downs over the years. I would just break down and sob uncontrollably. I was haunted by his memory, and all our good times together.

I could feel his presence all around me. I so regretted that I had never really had a chance to say goodbye to him, or tell him how much I loved him.

But I think he knew that.

His inviting me to play onstage with him at the Knitting Factory for what turned out to be our last performance together was a way for him to reconcile with me and say that back to me in so many words. I was especially sad that the best collaborator I ever had—and possibly will ever have—was gone for good.

I was saddened and frustrated, too, to think of all the great songs we still had left to write together. And I was angry that Jeff had exited the earth so prematurely.

It was like a light going out.

□

I played a tribute for Jeff—more like a wake—a week after he died, at St Mark's Church on the Bowery, organized by Nick Hill. His old friend Penny Arcade acted as MC and introduced me as the guy who first discovered Jeff and nurtured his talent—the one who really got him started in New York. I was touched by this.

I played 'Dream Of The Wild Horses' and dedicated it to Jeff through a teary mist in my eyes. I explained how I had written it and given it to Jeff, but how he had been unable to complete it due to his sudden death. I choked up at the end of the song. Lenny Kaye followed me with Patti Smith's 'Ghost Dance,' but I couldn't concentrate on that very well. I was so overwhelmed emotionally.

I remember Joan Wasser, Jeff's last girlfriend, getting up to admonish the crowd in an anguished voice:

"We're all upset here. But just keep on keeping on, and just be your badass selves. Jeff would have wanted you to—he would have told you if he could have been here—JUST BE YOUR BADASS SELVES!"

It was a cry of defiant rage at all the pious sentiment that had welled up in the hard-bitten, close-knit East Village community upon the death of Jeff Buckley.

I had never been introduced to Joan, but I had seen her perform several years before at Wetlands with The Dam Builders. I watched her shriek into a microphone at the top of her lungs while furiously sawing an electric violin at the pain level.

I was disturbed by this then. Now I liked that girl all the more.

❑

I traveled to Palermo later that summer for a concert with Gods and Monsters, then to Paris to collaborate with my old friend, the French singing star Elli Medeiros. I had met Elli in the 80s on my honeymoon, and she'd recently contacted me with an invitation to collaborate with her. She had delightedly discovered my name among the credits of the *Grace* album.

I remember looking out the window of her apartment near the cemetery Pere Lachaise as the sun set over the streets of Paris. It seemed like Jeff was smiling down on me. I could feel him in the night air there.

Everywhere I went that summer I felt Jeff's presence surrounding me. In the waves lapping the beach near Palermo ... in the skies of Paris ... in the humid summer night air as I lay in Eli's guest room trying to go to sleep that evening.

Immanence.

❑

One night shortly after I came home, I had a dream about Jeff—that he was still alive.

In the dream, Jeff and his band were hiding out inside the hollow base of a huge oak tree standing in the middle of a dark secluded forest.

Jeff had successfully pulled off a disappearing act. The world all thought him dead. But here he was, living in a kind of tree house, except it was on ground level—a huge room carved out inside the tree.

In the dream, Jeff is hunched over with his back turned to me, the invisible observer, listening to a radio.

Suddenly, 'Grace' comes on the radio and fills the room.

When it finishes playing, an announcer comes on:

"That was the late, great Jeff Buckley, with his classic rock anthem 'Grace'—we miss you dearly, Jeff."

And Jeff and his band start laughing …

Epilogue

The book you are reading was originally published in September 2012 by Arcana, a large music-book publisher based in Rome.

In the aftermath of playing a tribute to Jeff Buckley for the Italian Fan Club in Rimini in November 2010, I was shown an article in the Italian music press about Jeff which mentioned me, and which got many facts wrong about our relationship and history.

It was suggested I write a letter of reply to the magazine, but I despaired of that as, in my experience, all too often such letters go unnoticed—if not unpublished. One of the main fan-club organizers then asked if instead I would be up for writing a book about working with Jeff, which I thought was a good idea, and which led me to Arcana and the first publication of my book last year, translated into Italian.

The reviews in Italy were excellent for the most part, and the response from Italian fans—many of them musicians—was gratifying. (You can read some of their comments on my website.)

For this first English edition by Jawbone Press, I wanted to add some further updates—and to underscore how I continue to strive constantly in my career to keep the spirit alive that I felt so keenly between Jeff and I when we first created our songs together.

Well before the *Grace* album came out in 1994, I was performing both 'Rise Up To Be' and 'And You Will' publicly in their original solo versions, and I was telling audiences with every chance I got about how excited I was working with Jeff on music soon to be unleashed upon the world in the form of 'Grace' and 'Mojo Pin.'

Since that time, I don't think a single Gary Lucas solo

performance or Gods and Monsters concert has gone by anywhere in the world where I have not warmly recalled onstage our friendship and honored my memories of Jeff by playing versions of our songs. And I have many times invited singers from all over the world to join me in paying loving tribute to Jeff.

□

As I write this on St Patrick's Day 2013, I would like to mention a couple of significant events that have occurred in the last year, before and after the publication of my book in Italy, that reaffirm my commitment to keeping the flame alive and burning.

One is the new film *Greetings From Tim Buckley*, which focuses on Jeff's early days in New York and his relationship with the specter of his father. Directed by Dan Algrant and starring Penn Badgley as Jeff, it was released this spring in cinemas worldwide.

I was a consultant on this film, and contributed my guitar playing to the soundtrack. In fact, my hands are visible playing the guitar in many shots in the film, as the Tony Award-winning actor Frank Wood, who portrays me in the film, is not a guitarist.

However, in my opinion, Frank did an excellent job playing 'Gary Lucas.' He studied clips of me on YouTube to prepare for the role, and we spoke at length before the shoot about what it was like to work and interact with Jeff. He is an extremely nice guy, and I think he really caught the nuances in my complex interactions with Jeff—particularly in the scene of us first performing together in my apartment, which features the two of us first bantering together and sounding each other out—and then Penn (as Jeff) wordlessly crooning over my 'Rise Up To Be' music.

The script, by Dan Algrant, Emma Sheanshang, and David Brendel, is moving and compelling, and really captures the flavor of Jeff's early days in New York City. That is why I so wholeheartedly threw myself into supporting this film. There were several other Jeff Buckley biopics announced as being in production around the same time, and I actually saw several of these scripts, courtesy of my wife, Caroline, who is a casting director. None came close to imparting what to me is the essence of Jeff Buckley—until I read this one.

This brings me to Penn Badgley. His embodiment of Jeff—the way he so gracefully inhabits Jeff's persona in the film—was so close to the Jeff I recall as to literally give me chills when I finally saw his performance onscreen in an early cut of the film. I was totally knocked out by Penn's playful and serious approach to portraying my friend, and I found his insights and abilities in bringing Jeff to life on the screen nothing short of miraculous.

Not only was Penn the same age, 24, when he made the film as Jeff was when I began working with him back in the day, but, like Jeff, he was also a Scorpio, and he really caught Jeff's steely, burning-eyed determination. As far as his musical gifts go, Penn's soaring vocal approach, accomplished guitar playing, and overall feel for our songs impressed me greatly, and I heard strong echoes there of my long lost partner. Penn turned out to be a thoughtful and sensitive guy who seemed unaffected—almost embarrassed—by his mega-success as the star of the hit television show *Gossip Girl*.

Well before shooting began, I visited Penn in his new East Village rental apartment, bringing my guitars along with me. He had just moved into this old building in the midsummer of 2011, and he had invited me over to work on some of the songs we would be performing together—or, rather, that Penn and Frank Wood would be performing together—in the film.

Penn greeting me warmly, and when I went to remove my guitars from their cases, he casually told me something that floored me. His new apartment was right over the apartment of his new neighbor: Jeff's friend, performance artist Penny Arcade.

Penn told me that according to Penny, Jeff had spent what would prove to be his last night in New York crashing on the sofa in Penny's apartment directly below us, before flying off to Memphis to begin recording songs with his band for what was to be his follow-up to

Grace. It was yet one more eerie coincidence in a chain of eerie coincidences that seem to haunt the story and legacy of Jeff Buckley.

Penn and I both took this for a very good sign. And as we started playing together that summer afternoon, and I witnessed Penn sing and play the guitar for the first time, I got a very similar frisson—an almost déjà vu-like vibe—which strongly reminded me of when Jeff first came round to my West Village apartment to work on 'The King's Chain' in the spring of 1991.

Penn was that good—that strong. And playing with him was inspiring. It was as if the spirit of Jeff was alive still and hovering in that old East Village building, and had wafted up to Penn's apartment to bestow blessings on our coming together.

The film shoot required me to stand-in for myself in some scenes, in full 'Gary Lucas' clobber to match Frank Wood's 'Gary Lucas' getup. And if you look closely, you can seem me visible for a few seconds in a couple of shots in the film's epic re-creation of the famous St Ann's Tim Buckley tribute concert, which as you will recall was also called *Greetings From Tim Buckley*.

To find myself back once again in that musty old church to perform in this scene was one of the weirdest experiences I've ever had in my life, frankly, and not easy for me emotionally. So many conflicted and bittersweet moments I'd lived through in that church came flooding back that day—not only memories of the original tribute concert, but also recollections of the fateful Friday the 13th Gods and Monsters showcase nearly a year later. At times I felt turbulent waters roiling my equanimity, particularly when certain bits of filmed business at hand did not correspond precisely with the proceedings as I recalled them.

But that is the nature of films based on actual historical events. There will always be liberties taken in the service of getting the story across. I fought as best I could with the directors and producers to keep it real compared to what went down back then. I won some and I lost some.

One of the most sympathetic to my concerns was Fred Zollo, the maverick New York-based producer of many projects I have admired, including the film *Mississippi Burning* and the Tony Award-winning Broadway musical *Once*.

With his sparkling eye and charming wit, Fred was actually the prime mover in coming up with the idea for this film in the first place, many years ago, and he eventually brought Dan Algrant and his partner Emma Sheanshang onboard with their friend David Brendel—who in another odd coincidence turned out to be the guy who had immediately replaced me at CBS Records as a copywriter when I took my leave there for the world of music in 1990. He inherited my office and desk—and claimed to have found an un-smoked spliff in one of the drawers!

What matters most in the lasting analysis of any film based on historical events is the overwhelming impression one is left with—does it ring true or not? All in all, I am more than satisfied with the job the film does in communicating the essential story of Jeff in those early New York City days.

To me, the film rocks—and it rocks hard. It is intimate, allusive, and poetic—not a typical 'biopic' at all. So I am not going to nitpick and go through each scene to correct various factual inaccuracies. Please see the film for yourself, and you can then check my book out to note any discrepancies if you so choose.

One admirable thing the filmmakers did to give an air of authenticity to the tale was to take pains to include some of the people who were around at the time, particularly in the penultimate St Ann's concert sequence. These include one of the original Arts At St Ann's organizers, Janine Nichols, who is glimpsed in the crowd in a cameo, and several of the actual musicians who performed there that night, such as myself and cellist Hank Roberts.

My old friend Hal Willner, the producer/impresario who had got the ball rolling with the Tim Buckley tribute back in 1991, showed up on the day of the St Ann's concert shoot during rehearsals to give a thumbs-up to the filming. Ultimately, though, it is Penn's performance that carries the film—he really comes close to channeling the spirit of Jeff in all his complicated, messy, and immaculate glory.

What I found disconcerting, but I am sure added to Penn's powerful performance onscreen, was that once filming began, he dived into the role and stayed in character throughout the shoot. Sometimes I would try to talk with him off the set while he was still in make-up, and he would just sit there and fix me with his big, brooding Scorpio eyes and not say anything at all, just not respond.

It was so much like Jeff in his "playing it close to the vest" moments that it really freaked me out. I just couldn't believe it. Penn had somehow intuited this side of Jeff by digging deep within himself. It wasn't something he could have picked up from studying any clip.

I joined him and the director and producers for the world premiere of the film at the Toronto Film Festival on September 9 2012. The audience, packed with film devotees and Jeff Buckley fans who had journeyed from far away to catch the film, embraced it at the end, and it received a glowing review in the *Hollywood Reporter*.

I talked to some of Jeff's fans afterward in the theater lobby and out on the street, and they told me how much our songs still meant to them. I was so gratified to hear this, and so happy to be able to continue to breathe life into our music.

I had done so earlier in the month, in fact. Directly before the film's world premiere, I had made my performing debut in Sardinia at the Santa Arresi Jazz Festival, where naturally I played 'Rise Up To Be.'

Right after that, on September 2, I was the featured soloist in a gala concert at the Paradiso in Amsterdam, with the famed 60-piece Metropole Orchestra, entitled *The Music Of Jeff Buckley And Gary Lucas*.

As I've mentioned, the Paradiso is one of favorite places to perform, and Jeff himself played there in July 1995. This orchestral concert of the Buckley–Lucas Songbook was the inspiration of my old friend Co de Kloet, a Dutch producer and broadcaster well known in Holland as the go-to guy for anything Zappa/Beefheart. I first met Co on tour with

Don Van Vliet in the Netherlands in 1980, and he had accompanied us to the Van Gogh Museum the day after our Paradiso show.

Co commissioned me to compose a score for national Dutch radio several years ago to accompany the last lengthy phone interview he'd conducted with Van Vliet. It was christened 'I Have A Cat,' and we have performed it together live at Zappanale in Germany and in Amsterdam.

After producing many concerts over the years with the Metropole Orchestra with special guests such as Todd Rundgren, Brian Eno, and Steve Vai, Co had the vision of re-imagining all of the Buckley–Lucas songs with orchestral accompaniment.

Determined to do this, and with the magnificent Metropole Orchestra at his disposal, he booked a night at the Paradiso featuring me performing my original guitar parts to these monumental songs of ours, underpinned by the Metropole's sensitive and lush orchestral accompaniment, and with several guest vocalists to re-interpret them afresh.

My first choice as vocalist was the great Italian singer Alessio Franchini, a massive Jeff Buckley fan and a very nice guy who hails from Livorno. I had performed with Alessio several times in the past, and I knew he could pull it off. Our first encounter was at a Hard Rock Café tribute in Paris mounted a few years ago by one of France's biggest Jeff Buckley supporters, Danielle Schuppert. I heard Alessio sing then, and was impressed with his range, dedication to the songs, and overall sincerity.

Alessio journeyed to New York a couple of years later especially to perform with me in a multi-artist tribute to Jeff Buckley that I curated on March 18 2011 at the Knitting Factory club, now relocated to Williamsburg, Brooklyn. Also flying in to perform with me that evening was Portuguese vocalist Diana Silveira, who loved our music and made the journey all the way from Lisbon—and also Cuba's biggest Jeff Buckley fan, singer-songwriter Haydée Milanés, who flew in from Havana to perform that evening.

I often prefer to have female vocalists perform these songs with me, because many male vocalists find it difficult to surmount the indelible imprint of Jeff's voice and give our songs a new twist—plus there is all that tricky business of multi-octave vocal leaps to negotiate.

Outside of Alessio, in my experience many male vocalists do not possess the lung capacity and the range to tackle these songs effectively. Whereas most male vocalists seem imprisoned by the weight of the "tablature as handed down by Jeff," a female voice is often more likely capable of surmounting the difficult vocal parts to these songs—and spinning them into stunning new shapes.

With Alessio, though, this was never a problem. He had grown up on Jeff, and he told me had fallen asleep listening to *Grace* on headphones innumerable times in his youth. He could scale the walls of these songs effortlessly and so sensitively, and also he could bring something all his own to the proceedings.

Co drafted in some talented young Dutch voices from the Amsterdam Musik Conservatorium, in consultation with the Head of the Pop Music Department, Jack Pisters. One in particular was the outstanding female singer Jolene Grunberg, who brought her magisterial presence to bear on 'Story Without Words,' and also blues mama Yori Swart, who whooped and hollered her way through 'Bluebird Blues' like a banshee, while her partner Okke Punt played some gutbucket electric blues harp. The leather-lunged Dutch singer Benjamin Van Der Plas completed the lineup, and he really drove home our song 'Cruel.'

Various young arrangers affiliated with the Metropole Orchestra living in far-flung locations were brought in to work up charts to showcase the very wide palette of the Metropole Orchestra, who have been called the number-one large fusion ensemble in Europe.

Mostly, I gave the arrangers their heads. As mentioned, I normally like to allow musical associates and interpreters to bring their own gifts to bear in collaboration. But I did go over the charts closely in the run-up to the show and was compelled to correct some wrong notes here and there. In one instance—an overwrought attempt at 'Harem Man'—I found the arrangement to be so far from the original as to render its contours unrecognizable. What Jeff and I had originally intended to be a Zeppellin-like dirty blues-rocker was now a whimsical film-noir soundtrack. I didn't get the point of it, and I could not play to it, so we chucked it out. Instead, Yori Swart, Okke Punt, and I performed the song as a stomping blues in the show, as originally intended—and it brought the house down.

In the main, though, I found the orchestral arrangements exceedingly well thought-out, especially those by Gerd Hermann Ortler and Tom Trapp. They lent a large-scale grandeur to the dimensions of our songs, re-casting them with an almost Wagnerian heft in many places, as well as adding lots of modern dissonance and Gil Evans-type touches that were in line with my own musical preferences.

On the night of the show, after four days of intensive rehearsals in Hilversum with the Metropole, the Paradiso was packed to the rafters. The whole thing went like a dream, and the orchestra rocked their collective asses off. Our conductor, Steve Sidwell, brought his fine English sensibility to bear in the service of the songs, and he was a beaming Buddha-like presence at the podium throughout.

One memorable moment in a concert of highlights was performing a sinuous raga-like duel with the Metropole's electric violin virtuoso Herman Van Haaren—just one of the many talented solists in the mighty Metropole Orchestra—at the beginning and end of 'No One Must Find You Here.'

I could see the orchestra bonding with our music during the rehearsals. They were intrigued by these songs. Their hypnotic aura, quirky stops and starts, and bittersweet emotional pull sucked them in relentlessly so that, on the night of our concert, they gave everything they had.

And our singers naturally shone and sparkled like diamonds, particularly Alessio Franchini, whose 'Mojo Pin' was one of the most transcendental moments in the concert—so much so that we repeated it at the end, as we'd run out of repertoire to play, and the crowd was shouting for more.

Jeff would have been proud of that I am sure. He had wide-ranging tastes in music, enjoying and soaking in everything from Bad Brains to Beefheart to Benjamin Britten. Judging by his deployment of orchestra on the *Grace* album, I know he would have loved to hear our songs rendered on such a vast and beautiful scale.

We got a standing ovation at the end. I say "we" as I felt Jeff's presence on the stage there beside me that night—as surely as the other performers—as we played our songs.

□

In closing these pages, I want to stress one more time that despite our differences during the course of our tempestuous working relationship, our coming together and creating together as one, our falling out with each other, and then our drawing close together once more near the end of Jeff's tragically short life, not a day goes by that I don't think of Jeff … and I feel blessed for having been able to collaborate with him so closely.

To have created songs with Jeff that continue to this day to lift people up and inspire them is a fantastic thing indeed. To inspire other people—to empower them to realize their fullest human potential—is still to me the greatest thing you can do with your life. And I am still out there doing it as much as possible in music, and invoking the name of Jeff Buckley in nearly every show I do.

Rise Up To Be.

I look back lovingly on my bittersweet time with Jeff Buckley.

Gary Lucas
New York City
St Patrick's Day 2013

INDEX

Unless otherwise stated, words in *italics* are album titles; words in 'quotes' are song titles. Numbers in **bold** refer to illustrations.

ACKNOWLEDGEMENTS

Special Thanks

To Caroline Sinclair, my parents, Tom Seabrook, Nigel Osborne, Mike Barnes, Howard Monk, Co de Kloet, Alessio Franchini, Fred Zollo, Dan Algrant, Steve Monas, Jay Dougherty, Richard Porton, Steve Hendel, Annarita Mancini, Phil Mango, and anyone I might have possibly overlooked here.

Picture credits

The majority of the photographs used in this book come from the author's own archives. Every effort has been made to contact the original photographers, but if you feel there has been a mistaken attribution, please contact the publishers. **Jacket** Jack Vartoogian/Front Row Photos **2** Marco Ugolini **6** Beefheart Glenn Kolotkin **7** David Gahr **8** left photo by David Michael Kennedy, design by Steve Bryam right photo by Ebet Roberts, design by Steve Bryam **9** Marco Ugolini **10** St Ann's Jack Vartoogian/Front Row Photos Tramps Charlie Spear **11** Jack Vartoogian/Front Row Photos **12** Video Stills Andre Grossman **13** St Luke's Audrey Tsui at home Michele Taylor **14** Jeff Patti Ouderkirk/Wirelmage/Getty Images Diana unknown photographer **15** Haydée unknown photographer **16** Alessio Francesca Sera Cauli Paris David Grove.

Song credits

'Grace' and 'Mojo Pin' written by Jeff Buckley and Gary Lucas; published by El Viejito Music/Sony Music Publishing and Gary Lucas Music/Songs of Universal. 'Bluebird Blues', 'No One Must Find You Here,' 'Cruel,' 'Song To No One,' 'She Is Free,' and 'Distortion' written by Jeff Buckley and Gary Lucas; published by El Viejito Music/Sony Music Publishing and Gary Lucas Music/ Music Sales Group. 'Hymne A L'Amour' written by Edith Gassion and Marguerite Monot; published by France Music Corp. 'Sefronia The King's Chain' written by Tim Buckley and Larry Beckett; published by Third Story/Fifth Floor. 'I Never Asked To Be Your Mountain' and 'Once I Was' written by Tim Buckley; published by Third Story Music.

MILLION DOLLAR
BASH: BOB DYLAN,
THE BAND, AND THE
BASEMENT TAPES
by Sid Griffin

ISBN 978-1-906002-05-3

HOT BURRITOS:
THH TRUE STORY OF
THE FLYING BURRITO
BROTHERS
by John Einarson with
Chris Hillman

ISBN 978-1-906002-16-9

BOWIE IN BERLIN:
A NEW CAREER IN A
NEW TOWN
by Thomas Jerome
Seabrook

ISBN 978-1-906002-08-4

TO LIVE IS TO DIE:
THE LIFE AND DEATH
OF METALLICA'S
CLIFF BURTON
by Joel McIver

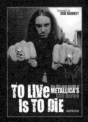

ISBN 978-1-906002-24-4

MILLION DOLLAR
LES PAUL: IN SEARCH
OF THE MOST
VALUABLE GUITAR IN
THE WORLD
by Tony Bacon

ISBN 978-1-906002-14-5

THE IMPOSSIBLE
DREAM: THE STORY
OF SCOTT WALKER
AND THE WALKER
BROTHERS
by Anthony Reynolds

ISBN 978-1-906002-25-1

JACK BRUCE:
COMPOSING
HIMSELF: THE
AUTHORISED
BIOGRAPHY
by Harry Shapiro

ISBN 978-1-906002-26-8

FOREVER CHANGES:
ARTHUR LEE AND THE
BOOK OF LOVE
by John Einarson

ISBN 978-1-906002-31-2

RETURN OF THE
KING: ELVIS PRESLEY'S
GREAT COMEBACK
by Gillian G. Gaar

ISBN 978-1-906002-28-2

A WIZARD, A TRUE
STAR: TODD
RUNDGREN IN THE
STUDIO
by Paul Myers

ISBN 978-1-906002-33-6

SEASONS THEY
CHANGE: THE STORY
OF ACID AND
PSYCHEDELIC FOLK
by Jeanette Leech

ISBN 978-1-906002-32-9

WON'T GET FOOLED
AGAIN: THE WHO
FROM LIFEHOUSE TO
QUADROPHENIA
by Richie Unterberger

ISBN 978-1-906002-35-0

THE
RESURRECTION OF
JOHNNY CASH:
HURT, REDEMPTION,
AND AMERICAN
RECORDINGS
by Graeme Thomson

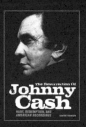

ISBN 978-1-906002-36-7

CRAZY TRAIN: THE
HIGH LIFE AND
TRAGIC DEATH OF
RANDY RHOADS
by Joel McIver

ISBN 978-1-906002-37-4

JUST CAN'T GET
ENOUGH:
THE MAKING OF
DEPECHE MODE
by Simon Spence

ISBN 978-1-906002-56-5

GLENN HUGHES:
FROM DEEP PURPLE
TO BLACK COUNTRY
COMMUNION
by Glenn Hughes

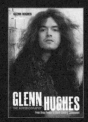

ISBN 978-1-906002-92-3

ENTERTAIN US:
THE RISE OF NIRVANA
by Gillian G. Gaar

ISBN 978-1-906002-89-3

MIKE SCOTT:
ADVENTURES OF A
WATERBOY
by Mike Scott

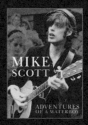

ISBN 978-1-908279-24-8

SHE BOP: THE
DEFINITIVE HISTORY
OF WOMEN IN
POPULAR MUSIC
by Lucy O'Brien
Revised Third Edition

ISBN 978-1-908279-27-9

SOLID
FOUNDATION: AN
ORAL HISTORY OF
REGGAE
by David Katz
Revised and Expanded
Edition

ISBN 978-1-908279-30-9

READ & BURN:
A BOOK ABOUT WIRE
by Wilson Neate

ISBN 978-1-908279-33-0

BIG STAR: THE STORY
OF ROCK'S
FORGOTTEN BAND
by Rob Jovanovic
Revised & Updated
Edition

ISBN 978-1-908279-36-1

RECOMBO DNA: THE
STORY OF DEVO: OR
HOW THE 60s BECAME
THE 80s
by Kevin C. Smith

ISBN 978-1-908279-39-2

NEIL SEDAKA:
ROCK 'N' ROLL
SURVIVOR: THE INSIDE
STORY OF HIS
INCREDIBLE COMEBACK
by Rich Podolsky

ISBN 978-1-908279-42-2